COMMENTS ON "PLUNDER" AND DANNY SCHECHTER

"You've been riding the bucking bronco of the symptoms – credit card debt, development-run-rampant, foreclosures, rising prices, stock market chaos. You have your suspicions, but you don't really know what's going on. Read *Plunder*. Weep. Then get active."

– Chellis Glendinning, author of *Off the Map: An Expedition Deep into Empire and the Global Economy*

"Social critic and journalist provocateur – Danny Schechter, a.k.a. the News Dissector – deserves our appreciation for identifying yet another crucially important issue that has been blissfully ignored by the mainstream media and our national leaders – the consumer debt time bomb."

– Professor Robert D. Manning, author of *Credit Card Nation*

"This man is doing God's work. His very impressive biography at Globalvision doesn't even include his latest works, notably the films *Weapons of Mass Deception: Media Complicity and the Iraq War* and *In Debt We Trust,* the latter on a subject – U.S. debt – upon which Schecter was painfully ahead of the curve and upon which his daily blog/newsletter remains about the most comprehensive and honest source around."

– Blogger Michael Horan, who lists Danny Schechter as one of the Ten Essential Journalists

"*Plunder,* like Schechter's *In Debt We Trust,* speaks truth to power about the infectious greed and malfeasance of the financial services sector that hoodwinked our nation and pushed millions of American families into foreclosure and catastrophe. Schechter speaks with an informed and fearless voice and tells a clear and compelling story of how the subprime crisis has occurred and impacted our nation. A must read."

– John Taylor, President & CEO, National Community Reinvestment Coalition

"Danny Schechter is both a masterly investigative journalist and a proficient political economist. He shines a merciless light on a murky labyrinth of financial deceit and heartless knavery. A gripping account, lively written, strongly informative – a solid hit on behalf of democracy."

– **Michael Parenti, author of *Contrary Notions: The Michael Parenti Reader,* and *Democracy for the Few* (8th edition)**

"No one does it better than Danny Schechter. His spot-on analysis of the financial crisis in his new book *Plunder* reads more like a Tom Clancy thriller than a meticulous investigation of the biggest ripoff in U.S. history. This is a real page-turner. Schechter walks us through the jungle of odd-named derivatives and financial products that were used to dupe gullible investors out of their life savings. He's done his homework, too, and understands how Wall Street really works: the "dark pool" trading, the off-balance sheets operations, and the Enron-like accounting. It's a moral swamp. *Plunder* casts a spotlight on the market's back alleys where all the biggest rats are hiding. Bravo, Danny. You've done it again!"

– **Mike Whitney, writer for many websites on current economic issues**

"The long time human rights activist, filmmaker Danny Schechter was among the first to warn of the foreclosure crisis and the "sub-crime" threat to our economy. Now that the markets are melting down, it's essential to share his timely investigation of the causes of this debacle. *Plunder* is an important book that we all wish didn't have to be written."

– **Reverend Jesse Louis Jackson, President, Rainbow-Push Coalition**

"This is a really good book, Danny. You've put the pieces together and shown the big picture of the massive debt fraud, and convicted the perps with their own words."

– **Michael Hudson, formerly with Chase Bank, economist, professor, author, advisor to the Kucinich Campaign on economic issues**

"Daniel Schechter has done in *Plunder* what countless media outlets and watchdogs agencies failed to do. His work offers an exciting user friendly guide to how 'it' broke, where 'it' broke and why. The 'it' *Plunder* addresses is the fair playing field of opportunity and upward mobility required for a vital and equitable America."

– Max Fraad Wolff, economist, market analyst, and teacher at The New School, New York.

"Not unlike his fabulous documentary *In Debt We Trust*, Danny takes us into the depths of the unregulated greed and blatant fraud that have created not only a bursting housing bubble, but will ultimately result in financial catastrophe for everyone in America except the very wealthy. *Plunder* lets us know how we arrived where we are and offers options for constructing on of the ashes of that economic Armageddon, a system of exchange that will serve the human species and the earth community.

– Carolyn Baker, Ph.D., owner and manager of Truth To Power at www.carolynbaker.net and the author of *U.S. History Uncensored: What Your High School Textbook Didn't Tell You*

Other Comments about Danny Schechter ·

"In the era of the incredibly shrinking sound bite, Producer Danny Schechter stands apart." **– The Associated Press**

"As News Dissector on Boston Radio, Danny Schechter literally educated a generation." **– Noam Chomsky**

"We need 50, 100, 1000 Danny Schechters. And we need everyone to take his words to heart." **– Robert W. McChesney, Media Historian**

PLUNDER

Investigating Our Economic Calamity and the Subprime Scandal

By Danny Schechter
Investigative Journalist
Director of the film IN DEBT WE TRUST

COSIMO

Plunder

Investigating Our Economic Calamity
and the Subprime Scandal

For information, address:
P.O. Box 416, Old Chelsea Station
New York, NY 10011

or visit our website at:
www.cosimobooks.com

Ordering Information:
Cosimo publications are available at online bookstores. They may also be purchased for educational, business or promotional use:
- Bulk orders: special discounts are available on bulk orders for reading groups, organizations, businesses, and others. For details contact Cosimo Special Sales at the address above or at info@cosimobooks.com.
- Custom-label orders: we can prepare selected books with your cover or logo of choice. For more information, please contact Cosimo at info@cosimobooks.com.

Cover Design by Tony Sutton, www.coldtype.net
Cover photo: iStockPhoto.com/782249/DaveL5957

ISBN: 978-1-60520-315-7

CONTENTS

AUTHOR'S NOTE

WHEN A TRADITIONAL PUBLISHER FAILED TO SNAP UP THIS BOOK, despite its timeliness and my track record as an author/reporter, Cosimo Publishing recognized its importance and stepped up to the plate. It is a successor to the e-book *Squeezed*, updated and rewritten. My patient and committed agent Victoria Skurnick gave more than a good old college try to place it with a major publisher.

Yet, the denial and distraction I encountered in trying to distribute my film *In Debt We Trust* seems also operative in the book publishing world. There, "business" books must conform to certain templates and story telling trumps analysis: tips on how to make millions sell; polemics on how we are all losing don't. People who are in the industry or comment on it – often TV "names" – have whole libraries of their books in circulation even though they have little to say. Just look at how much attention former Fed Chairman Alan Greenspan's book received with nary a mention of his role in stimulating the subprime boom. (I even met this God-like svengali on his book tour and he kindly signed a dollar bill for me!) Less well known "News Dissectors" and independents are not considered part of the cognoscenti.

In a world dominated by markets, marketing makes the difference. One publisher I spoke to came right out with it: he didn't think this volume would pass muster with the book buyer at Barnes & Noble.

This is a book about the economic bubbles that burst. What I have encountered in trying to place it are cultural bubbles that haven't.

I have friends who papered their walls with publishing company rejection letters after their books became best sellers. One author I know was "passed" on 32 times before his book received prominent display on many a bookstore shelf. It was on the prized *New York Times* best seller list for 83 weeks.

That happens to some, rarely to me.

When my film came out, the *San Francisco Chronicle* reviewer dismissed it as "alarmist," though he was intrigued that it was among the first to expose subprime loans and forecast the financial crisis we are now experiencing. He wrote:

"The most fascinating possibility in the movie is the looming Depression-like collapse that could happen when America's collective bills come due. Schechter imagines a financial collapse that will turn us into modern-day serfs."

The *Chronicle* wouldn't publish my reasoning or the Op-ed I submitted to respond. This air-headed critic trashed my "imagination." Now I can, on my own nickel, try to spell it out here.

I have a sense of urgency about these issues.

So, I move forward, in the spirit of A.J. Liebling's historic insight, "Freedom of the press belongs to those who own one." Although I don't own one, I an thankful for living in an era that has embraced new forms of publishing.

As a believer in the notion that in the long run we are all dead, I opted to get this book out now, in the short run, as the debate about the issues it explores heats up and before my own frustration about this analysis being ignored gets the best of me.

I may be too angry, passionate, and bull-headed for the sedate world of the printed word, but I believe in the argument presented in these pages and hope you will be persuaded too.

It will be up to the reader to decide if this effort was worth it.

Your comments always welcome:
write dissector@mediachannel.org

New York, June 27, 2008

For a future free of debt and a world
where markets serve the public interest

GRATITUDE

SPECIAL THANKS AND SPEEDY RECOVERY TO MY EXECUTIVE PRODUCER and mentor on real estate issues, Steven Green, who made and lost several fortunes in the business. He knows first hand about sleazy practices in his own industry and had the guts to expose some of them.

My gratitude to our brilliant editorial advisor Dr. Robert D. Manning and to my collaborator Sharon Kayser. Thanks too to blogger-editor Marta Steele for supreme editorial assistance. And to Dawn Reger for distribution help. I also appreciate Nisha Naidoo's input in our outreach strategy.

To our distribution strategists for the film *In Debt We Trust*, Adam Chapnick and Ilan Mandel and everyone who appears in, worked on, or contributed time and talent to the making of the film and our educational outreach campaign, a special thanks.

This book aspires to delve more deeply into this explosive subject.

Extra special thanks to Tony Sutton and ColdType.net for publishing an earlier version of this book, initially called *Squeezed*, first in electronic form, and then being willing to do it all over with this rewritten, updated and newly-named edition – a new book really.

And my appreciation also to my first economics professor at Cornell University, Doug Dowd, who introduced me to the "dismal science" and raised the right questions about who benefits and who loses.

Gratitude to Mediachannel.org and other websites for being there and posting my blogs and articles on this crisis. When we needed an image of Wall Street for the cover, a great people's photograher Stefano Giovannini hopped on his bike and took one for us. Grazie.

Finally, for a debtless future to my daughter Sarah Debs Schechter, and, as always, for my dad and our patriarch Jerry Schechter who spent a lifetime struggling for economic justice.

PREFACE

By Robert D Manning, author of "Credit Card Nation"

OVER THE LAST DECADE, U.S. INDUSTRIAL EMPLOYMENT HAS BEEN RAVAGED by neoliberal "free trade" policies and corporate outsourcing while workers have struggled to retain the basic vestiges of the American Dream. Sadly, as the post-industrial society has eroded the industrial heartland of middle-class America, the mall has replaced the factory as the engine of the U.S. economy. Indeed, one of the distinguishing features of the "new economy" is that it is more profitable to finance consumption than production. And, as real wages have declined and basic living expenses have soared, American families have become increasingly dependent upon consumer credit and debt to maintain their lifestyle and, too often, simply to survive.

Social critic and journalist provocateur – Danny Schechter a.k.a. the "News Dissector" – deserves our appreciation for identifying yet another crucially important issue that has been blissfully ignored by the mainstream media and our national leaders – the consumer debt time bomb. While business pundits and media cheerleaders have deflected attention from the lack of a national economic policy, Schechter has focused his filmmaking and journalistic talents on the seductive and calamitous consequences of banking deregulation. Indeed, through his powerful and entertaining documentary, *In Debt We Trust*, Schechter takes us behind the scenes where the profits and power of the financial services industry are protected by federal regulators, elected officials, and even the U.S. Supreme Court.

Through his movie and the compilation of his most perceptive articles in *Squeezed*, Schechter exposes the corporate forces that are corrupting our fundamental democratic institutions of governance through a symbiotic financial-industrial complex: FINANCIALIZATION. Already U.S. Congressman Bob Ney (R-Ohio), past chairman of the powerful House Financial Services Committee, has resigned over his influence peddling schemes and is currently serving a prison sentence. Many others have left to become million dollar lobbyists for the industry that they were once responsible for regulating. Others, like past Secretary of Treasury Robert Rubin of the Clinton Administration have become executives of financial services companies with multi-million dollar compensation packages; Rubin was recently elevated from Senior Vice-President to Chairman of beleaguered Citigroup as it grapples with its massive subprime mortgage losses.

The problem with the deregulation of the U.S. financial services industry is who CAN or has the fortitude to save the new Gilded Age Executives from a corporate ethos that exhorts: "Greed is Good"? From Sandy Weil who "earned" a billion dollars during his decade at the helm of Citigroup (which coincided with billions of dollars in consumer class-action settlements for questionable business practices) to Stan O'Neal, the past CEO of Merrill Lynch whose gamble on subprime loans cost him his job and the company over 11 billion in losses, yet "earned" him a $160 million severance/retirement package.

Like the ENRON debacle that was perpetrated by the financial complicity of Wall Streets' largest banks, Schechter has led the clarion call for demanding corporate accountability for those whose "creative" genius produced Collateralized Debt Obligations (CDOs) and other "securitarized" or asset backed securities that precipitated hundreds of billions of dollars of losses, potentially over a million foreclosed homes, and the destabilization of the U.S. financial system. Indeed, like Enron's "mark-to-market" imaginary wealth, the manipulation of the mortgage securities and residential housing markets with low "teaser," adjustable rate (ARMs), no interest, no money down, and "liar" loans, presaged the fictitious housing "bubble" and penultimate collapse of the real estate/consumer-driven economy.

As Schechter perceptively explains, "Debt is Profitable" in a deregulated economy where "Democratization of Credit" means the best consumer is someone who will never escape the vise of debt servitude.

With the rise of "Financialization," Schechter not only illuminates the causes and invariable collapse of the U.S. housing market – primarily because the Titans of Wall Street "could" rather than "should." –

but seeks to challenge the mainstream media to investigate the truth rather than seek the platitudes of the "Smartest Guys in the Room." Indeed, with the top ten credit card companies, along with the two major credit card marketing associations (VISA and MASTERCARD) spending over $20 billion per year on various forms of advertising, it is not surprising that editorial media "guidance" tends toward corporate compliance rather than muckraking exposes.

As the subprime mortgage "crisis" subsides and business leaders plead for public bail-outs, Schechter is to be commended for leading the investigative fervor over the emergence of America's consumer debt "squeeze" and culpability of banking execs in the dramatic decline of U.S. economic security.

Indeed, Schechter was among the first to organize a national "Stop the Squeeze" – stopthesqueeze.org – campaign that is intended to help secure financial relief for America's increasingly indebted majority.

As Americans ponder the future of $100-$200 barrels of oil and strategic alliances with authoritarian petroleum producing countries, the reality is that our national dependence on cheap foreign energy resources could soon be dwarfed by our dependence on cheap foreign loans. Indeed, as public discussion shifts from the costs of military unilateralism to the global reliance on potential foreign policy adversaries, Capitalist America's economic security is becoming perilously dependent on Communist China for the cheap consumer mortgage loans that have financed the U.S. housing bubble and concomitant consumer-driven economic expansion. How ironic that the "Democratization" of consumer credit in the U.S. has become inextricably linked to human rights abuses abroad. It is these types of issues that the mainstream media has consciously avoided that makes Schechter's work all the more important in a society whose new mantra is *"In Debt We Trust."*

Robert D. Manning, PhD, Research Professor and Director, Center for Consumer Financial Services, E. Philip Saunders College of Business Rochester Institute of Technology, Rochester, New York

PROLOGUE

MONEY MAKES THE WORLD GO ROUND, AND THE LACK OF IT CAN make your world go down as it has for so many people around the world. The law of gravity is as relevant in this sphere as any other: what goes up comes down. And right now, in the United States and in many countries worldwide, some markets are going down as a full-blown credit/debt crisis brings economic issues into focus.

Suddenly, stories that were buried in the back of the newspaper are up front as a new wave of economic pain ricochets from Wall Street to Main Street and back again. Waves of layoffs are rolling through the housing and finance sector while bankruptcy filings and foreclosures multiply. Suddenly reports of a kind that we have been accustomed to read about in the news, of poverty and downward mobility overseas, are coming home to roost.

At the same time, a friend asks, "Is this book needed... Isn't this story all over the press and well known by now?" As an investigative reporter who doubles as a media critic, I would have to say "no." The sad truth is that most people are not market players, not financially literate, and not well informed about financial issues or decision-making. In fact, as I have shown in the pages that follow, media coverage has often obscured and distorted the truth of how this "mess" occurred and what can be done about it.

Much of the reporting has also been deadening. Leave it to satire to get at the truth. The satirical *Onion* put the financial press in its place with a story "reporting" how the reporting has been largely undecipherable:

JP Morgan Chase Acquires Bear Stearns In Tedious-To-Read News Article

The paper that calls itself "America's Finest News Source" skewered most of the reporting on Bear Stearns because it was written in "obscure legal jargon that can only be described in the most mind-numbingly dense and unreadable way" by readers who "saw its value depreciate almost as quickly as readers' interest in this story." They blasted the coverage for "bogging down the news for anyone who might be remotely interested in grasping what the fuck is going on."

FEAR AND PANIC

There's fear, uncertainty, and even panic in the world of finance. In an interconnected and deeply intangled system, when one sector implodes, others follow. We are now hearing about what's been called the "subprime crisis" as if only one small corner of the economy is in peril. It is like a serious infection which, when untreated, spreads into the whole body, damaging not only its well-being but also the confidence others have in it. An infection is devouring our financial markets.

This is a subject that, alas, daily journalism has tried to minimize, and that many of the most prominent politicians sought to ignore. Its implications reach into every corner of American life and indict many of our institutions and best-known financial companies.

Pick a decade, any decade, and you will find a defining financial scandal, the story of a "rogue" financier or corrupt company. You will read about scammers, crooks, and corporate conspiracies, ponzi schemes and predators. You will also find references to financial crises, even crashes, that reformers tried to repair even as their lessons are forgotten.

In their book on the Enron debacle, *What Went Wrong at Enron*, Peter C. Fusaro and Ross. M. Miller, two financial "experts" write: "While a certain amount of crime and punishment can be built into an economic system, there is a growing school of thought that markets can function effectively only in societies where most people are honest....The true lesson of Enron is that one who lives by the market can also die by the market."

In the year, 2007, five years after this "guide to the largest bankruptcy in American history" was published, an even larger economic disaster is underway, indicating not only a continuing lack of honesty in the markets but also that the market itself is deeply corrupted. An entire industry of white shoe investment firms and dark-suited big-brand bankers congealed, if not conspired, to promote what, in shorthand, was first called the subprime scandal. This swindle would end up rocking the global financial system to the tune of trillions of dollars lost, with, as I write, more to come. The president of Germany now calls the global market a "monster" that needs to be tamed.

The perpetrators, considered predatory lenders by their victims, operated in this instance legally if deliberately, in the shadow of rules and disinterested regulators. They built a huge infrastructure of collaborators, henchmen, and "financial services professionals," demonstrating that a scam, which is said to have created a bubble destined to burst, may have been engineered in public and hidden in broad daylight.

Writing in the *Financial Times* about the difficulties of regulating the financial sector, Martin Wolf refers to a "number of agents" and a "wealth of information asymmetries" behind the crisis. Then he lists all the players needed to securitize the billions of dollars in inflated subprime mortgages that passed through Wall Street on their way to being sliced and diced and sold to investors worldwide through structured investment vehicles or SIVs. Writes Wolf:

> In between the ultimate borrowers and the risk takers, were loan originators, designers and packagers of securitized assets, ratings agencies, sales staff, managers of banks and SIV's, and managers of pension and other funds.

Add in mortgage brokers, advertising agencies with hundreds of millions to promote these shady loans with seductive spiels, and the TV, Radio, and websites that carried the deceptive ads and you have a sleazy army of sizable proportions. We are talking about institutions here, not just individuals. Fronting for these institutions was a powerful lobby called the American Securitization Forum. Its last annual conference held in Las Vegas in February 2008, was called a "predators' ball" by the *New York Times*. It drew a formidable force of 6,500 financial professionals eager to find ways to minimize their loses, or STILL profit from the mortgage mess they had helped to create.

Among the key players who flew in by private jet was Hedge Fund Manager John Devaney, CEO of United Capital Markets, and best known for calling consumers "idiots" for taking on the loans that he and his colleagues were pedaling. Even as the losses from this crisis have approximated, $7.4 TRILLLION, he was still defending his subprime products to CNN as "one of our best performing investments." He was one of the many who profited obscenely on the boom but is now being forced to sell off his yachts and vacation homes.

As Peter Morici explains in the *Globalist*, "Sub prime mortgages are hardly the whole credit market, but the meltdown of their bonds cast a spotlight on the decaying integrity of investment banks and bond rating agencies... Over the last several weeks, creditors have increasingly sensed they cannot trust banks or bond rating agencies, and they have fled to short-term Treasury securities. This was much worse than the collapse of mortgage companies that originated housing loans, because it caused all segments of the credit market to collapse."

It's been called a Ponzi scheme – a manipulated and criminal enterprise. Writes Rodrigue Tremblay: "Like all Ponzi schemes, such pyramidings of debts with no liquid assets behind them are bound to implode sooner or later. And that is what we are witnessing today, i.e. the implosion of unfunded credit derivative-based Ponzi schemes." One consequence of this collapse, reports the *Wall Street Journal*, is that the "wave of corporate takeovers seems to be waning. Homebuyers with poor credit are having problems borrowing. Institutional investors from Milwaukee to Düsseldorf to Sydney are reporting losses. Banks are stuck with corporate debt that investors won't buy. Stocks are on a roller coaster..."

What we have, Bill Gross, manager of the world's largest bond mutual fund, said is a "Frankensteinian levered body of shadow banks promoting a chain letter, pyramid scheme of leverage."

When market players see the problems in such stark terms, why are the rest of us so ignorant? Is it just that most of us don't like bad news? Part of the fault may lie with an asleep at the switch media, and part of it may involve the shrewd efforts to conceal what was really going on. Complex but fraudulent offerings were presented as "financial innovation."

Explains Richard Sylla, professor of economics and financial history at NYU's Stern School of Business: "A lot of financial innovation is designed to get around regulation... "The goal is to make more money, and you can make more money if you don't have to keep capital to back up your investments."

Even six months after the housing crunch that triggered the deeper problem, government officials were admitting that worse was still to come. On January 31, 2007, Diana Olick reported on CNBC that Sheila C. Bair, the chairperson of the agency that insures bank deposits, the FDIC, told a Senate Banking Committee panel that the mortgage crisis has only just begun.

Sheila Bair says: "foreclosures continue at an unacceptably high level while true loan modifications are lagging", but that's just the tip of the iceberg. She also warns that in 2009, $600 billion worth"of prime borrowers will see their 'non-traditional" mortgages reset, and many won't be able to find the cash.

Bair has been calling for a systematic, rather than individual, approach to loan modifications, but by warning about prime borrowers, it feels like she's now bringing in the big guns.

Think of the all the money involved – hundreds and hundreds of billions in this sector alone – and you get a sense of the scale of what is going on. It is a systemic problem now, not just a small blister on an otherwise well-performing machine.

Can the market "correct" itself? Will its "contagion" be contained? Can this immediate problem be "fixed"? Will the market bounce back? All four "fixes" are possible – who wants a total system collapse? – but, many experts agree, a longer-term instability posed by the credit squeeze will continue to haunt us.

This is a major "infection" – a kind of financial flu – threatening the system in a way we haven't seen in years, and American media outlets and commentators across the political spectrum are finally paying attention and sounding the alarm. While most of the media focuses on the problems confronting very wealthy bankers and financial institutions who are likely to have the means to weather this storm, far more cataclysmic challenges face more than three million families who may be losing their homes while others go jobless. Many Americans are just beginning to feel more economic pain as inflation and recession intensify.

So far the debate in the business press has been about interest rates and "default exposure," going way over the heads of most readers and viewers. At the same time, a few voices of a more critical kind who put this problem in a different context are finally being heard.

There's the populist agitator Jim Hightower, who says: "At its core, this is a classically simple story of banker greed and outright sleaze. And the astonishing part is that nearly all of the rank injustice perpetrated by today's money changers is considered legal and is practiced by supposedly reputable financial firms."

The writer Barbara Ehrenreich, a brilliant chronicler of economic problems suffered by the working poor, sees a potential upside – the fall of capitalism itself. She now believes that only capitalists can destroy capitalism. And they had a lot of help from their customers: "The American poor, who are usually tactful enough to remain invisible to the multi-millionaire class, suddenly leaped onto the scene and started smashing the global financial system," she writes in an essay about those seduced into taking on a so-called NINJA loan based on "no income, no job or assets."

As borrowers default on mortgages and other bills, the reverberations cascade. "Incredibly enough," she argues, "this may be the first case in history in which the downtrodden manage to bring down an unfair economic system without going to the trouble of a revolution." It's fascinating that what may have seemed to be alarmist criticism on the left has moved into mainstream journalism, especially overseas.

All of these news outlets say this scandal is not going away any time soon. Many are looking for a silver lining. Paul Krugman commented in the *New York Times*, "Maybe the subprime disaster will be enough to remind us why financial regulation was introduced in the first place."

It is significant that he – a Princeton economist as well as an op-ed columnist – also calls this crisis a "disaster." The writer Lewis H. Lapham sees a parallel between the collapse of the U.S. housing bubble and the war in Iraq that has eluded most commentators. Writing in *Harper's Magazine*, he notes, "I was struck by the resemblances between the speculation floated on the guarantee of easy money on Wall Street and the one puffed up in the preview of an easy victory in Iraq."

These tensions are now or soon will impact on everyone, possibly even bringing on a global recession or worse. We are in what seems to be another boom and bust cycle with global implications.

Writes economist Max Wolff: "So many shares, bonds, vehicles and funds are bloated with leverage that fall-out will be significant. The harder central banks, politicians and pundits fight, the longer and more volatile the adjustment. Continued large central bank cash infusions and rate cuts are in the offing. Hundreds of billions have already been infused."

With billions of dollars at stake, with millions of Americans affected, with tens of thousands of businesses at risk, this is an issue that demands our attention.

It also demands to be reframed because it is not just about finances or the market or the businesspeople who are coping with their losses. It's about a calculated crime, a deliberate strategy to take advantage of a subprime lending initiative intended to help people with poor credit own their homes and turn it, with the active complicity of leading financial institutions driven by greed, into a way to defraud them – and, in the ultimate irony, destroy many of their own companies and financial markets.

Their corrupt practices have put the global economy itself at risk.

• This book chronicles what happened, and what is happening in the arcane world of international finance, reflecting my search for deeper causes and larger meaning. One reviewer of an earlier draft called it a "diary of the upcoming depression."

• It is intended as a wake-up call to political progressives who have ignored economic issues in their war with the Bush Administration.

• It is a call for more concern for the victims of predatory lending practices and the need for the same debt relief that we have supported in other parts of the world.

• It is offered as a challenge to my colleagues in the media who missed the story and could have warned us when there was still time to act.

• And it is a lesson for all of us that democracy must have an economic underpinning and a commitment to fairness.

This book tells three stories and offers some remedies.

• It discusses how debt has restructured our economy and put our people under a burden that many will never crawl out of. It shows how access to credit has, for many, gone, in Steven Green's phrase "from a luxury to a necessity to a noose." (An interesting use of words as the image of the "noose" has been back in the news again, as a symbol of hate and lynching.)

• It identifies some of the shameless profiteers and calls for an investigation and the prosecution of those behind this shrewdly engineered ponzi scheme. It describes how a pernicious form of "Financialization" – rule by a credit and loan complex – has been running our economy and in many ways running it into the ground.

• It offers a critique of press coverage from a media critic who has monitored flawed and superficial reporting on the subject and who is trying to challenge the news media to improve its coverage of the crisis.

• It advocates a debt-relief movement in America and argues that such a movement would have tremendous resonance across the spectrum of political life.

• It urges citizens to get involved and politicians to respond. This book draws on articles, blogs, and essays written by a journalist and filmmaker who is simultaneously learning about these problems and alerting others to them.

It is also a call to action.

"It is shocking to me that intelligent people, educated people, have not taken time to think about this. We cannot sustain over an extended period of time these high levels of debt . . . particularly at high rates of interest. Because . . . what will happen is that whenever it comes to an end . . . and there is an end to the amount of credit . . . in other words, when it gets so leveraged, it will create an economic crisis so deep that it will threaten us as a nation . . . And so we have . . . this real threat to the way we are as a people. And nobody seems to be concerned about it."

– Roy Barnes, former governor of Georgia, in 2006, a year before the crisis broke. He outraged real estate interests by passing a tough law against predatory lending. When he was defeated for reelection with support from the real estate and banking industry, the law was speedily repealed.

INTRODUCTION

"IT'S THE ECONOMY, STUPID"

MAYBE BILL CLINTON WAS RIGHT IN HIS FIRST CAMPAIGN FOR THE presidency when he promoted a slogan that pushed economic issues to the top of his agenda. Since then, they have been eclipsed and, for years, the fallout from 911, the debate over the Iraq war, and the focus on the impact of the Bush presidency have dominated our attention. But now, economic issues are back with the intensity of a hurricane. They cannot be ignored. And speaking of hurricanes, Senator Chris Dodd has called the subprime scandal "a 50-state Katrina."

In the epicenter of this storm are two words that have tended to be buried: credit and debt.

Usually, when we hear about economic distress, it takes place in someone else's country; often in Africa or some place you have never visited, conjuring up images of desperation and sadness. The same is true when you hear about debt. When rock stars like Bono or Bob Geldof crusade for debt relief, they are doing so, however successfully – and there is a big debate about that – around conditions in what we used to call the Third World and what others refer to as "Developing" Countries, even when they aren't.

What is more rarely discussed is economic deprivation and exploitation in our own country and what we think of as "the West." We may hear stories about individuals with problems, but we rarely hear about deeper economic forces and the institutions that create and perpetuate the problems. Discussions of how our own economy has been transformed in a way that accelerates deep economic inequality and all the suffering that flows from it have been minimal.

Beyond that, there had been an assumption, almost a subtext, in much of the reporting on our economy, that its market system somehow reflected the national order of the universe, the human species' greatest contribution to stability and prosperity. This ideological overlay, sometimes explicit, often just implied, colored our understanding and contributed to a sense of confidence, or should I say false confidence?

In just the short period, three years, in which I began investigating these issues, from 2005 to early 2008, there has been a tectonic shift with the financial system melting down. This has produced convulsive strains in an interconnected, or as the analysts say, "entangled", system, as well as losses in the trillions, and continuing uncertainty on whether or not we can avoid disaster.

In Europe, statements were circulated to challenge financialization. There was even a petition published in leading European newspapers. It reads in part:

> Freedom for finance is destroying society. Every day, in both North and South, shareholders silently pressure firms and workers to extract higher and higher returns. The situation becomes dramatically visible when major crises display the excesses of speculative greed and its backlash on growth and employment. Lay-offs, precarious work, deepening inequalities: workers and the poor suffer most from both the speculation and the toxic effects of subsequent financial collapse.

A petition by outsiders is unlikely to do much, but it also reflects anxieties felt by many in in the financial world.

The usually calm and staid *Economist* magazine in mid March 2008 was near apocalyptic in its assessment of an intervention by the Federal Reserve Bank in saving an insolvent investment bank. "The marvelous edifice of modern finance took years to build," wrote its editors about the crisis on Wall Street. "The world had a weekend to save it from collapsing."

Business cycles have been with us forever, but this potential system-destroying swing from boom to gloom over the course of a weekend was extraordinary, suggesting why the subject deserves independent scrutiny from someone who is neither a player nor has fish to fry in this game.

As a journalist, blogger, and filmmaker, I am no stranger to economic issues. I grew up in a working-class home in a family of unionized workers who spoke of the importance of solidarity with people fighting for their rights and economic security. When I became active in civil rights and human rights movements, I saw firsthand how economic forces were driving the mistreatment of minorities and workers in other countries.

When I joined the media, I sought to integrate my understanding of these issues into my own work. I quickly realized that the lack of media attention to labor and the impact of economic policies kept important issues in the dark. When I was producing for ABC's 20/20 news magazine, I worked on stories on the outsourcing of jobs and was among the first to investigate the Savings and Loan scandal of the 1980s.

As the mainstream media itself moved away from in-depth reporting and toward a more superficial focus, distortion and deception assured audience distraction.

I spent many years writing about the need for media reform and the decline in investigative reporting on economic power and the special interests that often stack the deck against consumers. As a reporter myself, for years, I focused on human rights and then media issues, but now I have come back to seeing how directly the economic system imposes itself, for good and, yes, evil, on every corner of our lives. It wasn't hard to realize that, in recent years, our economy has changed from one built around production to one centered on consumption. The mall has now replaced the factory as our dominant economic icon. Debt has been key to restructuring our economy and has kept it flourishing.

As a result, explains Stephen Pizzo, "America and Americans have switched from being net creditors (money lenders) to net debtors (credit junkies). And not just American Yuppies hooked on credit cards and home equity loans. No siree. Corporate America, the folks who got Americans hooked on living beyond their own means fell for their own line and started doing so themselves."

Driving this change is, as I argued, a growing concentration of power in the financial and banking sector. That, in turn, unleashed a process called FINANCIALIZATION, with the economy dominated by a vast CREDIT AND LOAN COMPLEX every bit as insidious as the Military-Industrial Complex. Most Americans have no idea that this even exists.

This "complex" is even more shadowy and even more omnipresent, hidden to all except those who work with it. It is active in funding our politicians and lobbying for laws that benefit their businesses. At the same time, it is hidden from view to most of us. It operates through a covert, decentralized network of shady lobbyists – interconnected institutions working through highly legalized and poorly understood systems. Rules, laws, and procedures underpin the market system, and high-speed computers move money and buy/sell orders around the world in seconds.

It is often difficult for outsiders, including most consumers, to penetrate the dense language that defines the rules of the games financiers play. The outline of the whole system only comes into view when there is a crisis. Recently, Jeremy Grantham, a leading investor, compared the finance system to a large BRIDGE with interlocking pieces:

> Thousands of bolts hold it together. Today a few of them have fractures and one or two seem to have failed completely. The bridge, however, with typical redundancy built in (unlike the Minnesota one that collapsed), can (easily) take a few failed bolts, perhaps quite a few.... What is worrisome is whether or when we reach a "broad-based level of financial metal fatigue" causing simultaneous multiple bolt failures "with ultimately disastrous consequences.

Stephen Lendman adds: "What's also scary is the global financial structure is heavily 'faith based, held together by unprecedented amounts of animal spirits' moving in the same positive direction. If the faith wanes, it's then 'every man for himself' and look out below...'"

Before I travel deeper into this world, let me assure you that I may be considered totally unqualified to tell you any more. I am a journalist but not an economic specialist. I am not an insider. I went to the London School of Economics but studied politics, not economics. I have never worked on Wall Street and am even pretty hopeless in managing my own money, much less "OPM" – other people's money. I did a stint at NBC's Business Channel CNBC but on a talk show, not in the newsroom monitoring market shifts.

I may not know a derivative from a tranche, but I think I do know how to ask questions that the so-called "Masters of the Universe" avoid. The experts in this field are as divided as in any other. They usually do not agree with each other and are often experts at keeping the public confused.

In many ways, moneymaking is as much an art as a science. And despite all the rules that govern the markets or regulations designed to assure transparency and accountability, crooks, swindlers, and even gangsters are commonplace. Corrupt practices are pervasive; regulation is not. When professionals in the field were asked how they define criminal conduct, the majority surveyed said crimes only occur when you are caught. There is also extensive posturing in the industry to mask the often-fuzzy line between risk and uncertainty. In many instances, major decisions are made on the basis of fragmentary knowledge, even ignorance, despite professions of careful reviews and "due diligence."

The *Financial Times* cites a market economist at Lehman who said: "We are in a minefield. No one knows where the mines are planted and we are just trying to stumble through it." Another market participant put it this way: "It is not the corpses at the surface that are scary; it is the unknown corpses below the surface that may pop up unexpectedly."

So if the people in the know admit they don't know, why shouldn't I opine and report on these issues? Many of the "experts" whom I read or see on TV seem clueless, full of hot air. Many of their predictions turn out wrong, even when they seem so self-assured and well informed in making them. Jim Hightower warns against believing them, writing:

> Don't be deterred by the finance industry's jargon (which is intended to numb your brain and keep regular folks from even trying to figure out what's going on)."

A folksinger, Ethan Miller, even sings about the way some of the always all-knowing media pundits have turned their prognostications into a form of entertainment — call it finance-tainment. His song is called "The Market Game." One lyric:

> *Does it seem like we've given up our power*
> *To an entity that we can't even see?*
> *Oh, this is not the first time that it's happened?*
> *You can learn about the others on TV.*

How does one make sense of what is going on? You have to burrow in the business pages and read articles from the bottom because the most revealing facts are often buried. You have to break dependence on mainstream media and check out specialized websites, blogs, and alternative sources.

After the NY Stock Market took a 340-point drop only to quickly recover, I went to the business pages of the *New York Times*. I figured that they would explain it. But THEY DIDN'T KNOW the reason for it either, reporting "Emotion and psychology, not financial fundamentals were mostly at work." They quoted the chief U.S. equity strategist for Citibank: "I don't think anybody can make sense of it."

Part of the problem here is that the traders and brokers have come up with all sorts of highly esoteric and complex financial instruments — ways of securitizing debt and raising capital — that outsiders, even experienced financial journalists, have a hard time understanding, much less explaining. Ditto for regulators (and the laws they theoretically enforce), who are hard pressed to keep up with the pace of change. Market traditionalists are also lost.

Even some bankers like Jean-Pierre Roth, president of the Swiss National Bank, who believes the market turmoil is far from over because tremors from the sub-prime debacle will continue to rock the world, is confounded. "Something unbelievable happened," he said, in the *Telegraph* of London. "People who had neither income nor capital got credit with very attractive conditions. Now reality is striking back."

Of course he does not mention that the subprime loan was a well thought out marketing scheme designed to seduce borrowers with poor credit ratings who would pay more in fees and interest. Everyone complains that the system has gotten too complicated even for players who try to define their own reality. Writes Andrew Leonard on Salon.com:

> The truth of what is really going on is far more complex. So complex that no one has a good handle on exactly what will happen if things go awry. Not regulators, not traders, not even pessimistic journalists. Try reading an SEC filing from a New York investment bank — it is one of the most difficult-to-comprehend documents ever created by the human mind...It is not, in a word, transparent. It serves the opposite purpose: It is an instrument of obfuscation.

No wonder the media coverage is so confusing. Perhaps that's why so much money is now being invested in upgrading and disseminating business news. The market for financial and business news is big and getting bigger as well just to keep up with this information overload. There is a reason that Rupert Murdoch was willing to pay $5 BILLION for the *Wall Street Journal* and Dow Jones.

He spent even more in creating, staffing, launching, and marketing a new global Fox Business channel. His maneuver came on the heels of Thomson acquiring Reuters, while Bloomberg and the *Financial*

Times announced plans to expand and compete. True to form, Murdoch baits his main competitor, the General Electric NBC-owned CNBC channel, as anti-business.

Bear in mind that little of this is being done only to inform the public. Much of it is aimed at the industry itself and high-income consumers. News organizations that specialize in business news often also make money from the information they don't make public but offer in specialized newsletters or other "products" sold for big bucks to elite customers. Finance is itself an information business and the one most striking complaint heard among insiders during a period of market volatility was that their panic was feeding on a lack of knowledge about how much "bad debt" was in their system. It seems to be a mystery, even to them.

For me, mysteries make challenging stories. I gravitated toward trying to understand, investigate, and then popularize some of these fascinating issues because of the massive impact they are having – and because I felt many in our media were doing such an uneven job in explaining and tracking them.

THE UNITED STATES OF DEBT

Total number of Americans 300,000,000

Total consumer debt of Americans $3,000,000,000,000

Average debt per U.S. household $30,000

Number of households not paying off their credit card
balances each month .... 6 in 10

Average length of time, in months, spent paying off
credit card debt 43

Consumer bankruptcies in 1980 287,463

Consumer bankruptcies in 2004 1,500,000

Consumer bankruptcies in 2005 2,000,000

Percent increase in bankruptcies 422

Amount the average college student owes in loans at
graduation $30,000

Amount that same student owes in additional
consumer debt $20,000

Amount $1 invested in stocks in 1963 would have
compounded to today $12.36

Amount $1 invested in real estate in 1963 would
have compounded to today $1.79

Total in 2005 and 2006 lenders wrote in
new home mortgages $3,200,000,000,000

Net profit percentage annually by the major
credit card companies 54

Years it took for America to move from a society
based on production to a nation driven by consumption 25

Date when the first baby boomer was eligible
for early retirement 1/1/2008

THE WARNING

"The combined threat of subprime loan defaults and excessive indebtedness has supplanted terrorism and the Middle East as the biggest short-term threat to the U.S. economy."

The National Association for Business Ethics

CHAPTER 1

THE ORIGINS OF THE SCANDAL

IF THERE'S A WORD THAT IS UNIVERSALLY INVOKED IN THE WORLD OF finance, it's "transparency." The word comes to us from the 16th century with the connotation of "shining through," The idea is simple. Transparency is about being able to see what is going on and to have key practices disclosed. Without that, it is believed, financial markets can't function because of a lack of trust and clear rules that all the players adhere to. It is a market fundamental, a primary rule of principle.

Or so you would think.

When it began, subprime lending was even not a term that most people outside the financial markets understood. (By 2007, the American Dialect Society would call it the most used term of the year.) The Wikipedia would describe it this way:

> Subprime lending, also called B-paper, near-prime, or second chance lending, is the practice of making loans to borrowers who do not qualify for the best market interest rates because of their deficient credit history. The phrase also refers to paper taken on property that cannot be sold on the primary market, including loans on certain types of investment properties and certain types of self-employed individuals. Subprime lending is risky for both lenders and borrowers due to the combination of high interest rates, poor credit history, and adverse financial

situations usually associated with subprime applicants.

In early February 2008, almost a decade after the birth of what would become the subprime industry, the Securities and Exchange Commission, the nominal regulators of financial markets, found the courage to admit that they didn't really know what was going on in their multi-billion-dollar securities market.

They announced an investigation.

One of their "enforcers" explained: "The big question is, who knew what when, and what did they disclose to the marketplace?" These were the words of Cheryl Scarboro, an associate director in the SEC's enforcement division in charge of the subprime working group. This working group, composed of one hundred lawyers, which seems to have only begun working after the scandal erupted, is investigating how banks, credit rating firms, and lenders valued and disclosed complex mortgage-backed securities.

Reuters reported they were looking into three areas: "the securitization process, the origination process and the retail area. Insider trading, which is one of the SEC's highest priorities, is also a key area."

Bear in mind that they are not operating in the interests of borrowers who were victimized by deceptive loans, but inquiring whether shareholders – i.e., investors – were kept in the dark through inadequate disclosures.

Their scope is narrow: "We do have to work very hard at bringing the right cases," says SEC enforcement division chief Linda Chatman Thomsen. "We work on the most 'impactful' cases. ... At the end of the day we have to be about deterrence."

Deterrence? That was a concept born in the nuclear age to prevent/deter war. How it's relevant *after* the collapse of the industry itself was not addressed. What is there now to deter?

This SEC group was reportedly "talking with" but not coordinating with oversight bodies like the Federal Reserve, Federal Deposit Insurance Corporation, Office of the Comptroller of the Currency, and Office of Thrift Supervision. Is it significant that the FBI, which also announced its own investigation into criminal conduct by mortgage firms, is not on this list!

If the regulators who should be in the know about these practices are not, it's not surprising that most of the media and the public share this plight.

The whole area is murky. Even George Miller, the Executive Director of the industry's own trade association and lobby group the American Securitization Forum, told CNBC as this investigation was announced that one of the reforms his organization was advocating was "taking steps to enhance where necessary the transparency in the marketplace." Note the qualifying phrase "where necessary."

While reporting from the Forum's meeting in Las Vegas, CNBC's correspondent joked they had "gambled away our economy." Ha, ha. The Forum has not always been a joke. When the Treasury Department announced, with great fanfare, a program to help distressed homeowners in December 2007, it was widely reported that this industry group had actually written it. The plan offered no help to families facing foreclosure.

They also played a very powerful role in holding off government scrutiny. They were the influential behind-the-scenes player rationalizing the industry and its exotic derivative financial instruments. Their website, which lists their impressive membership list of big banks and funds, describes its work this way: "The American Securitization Forum (ASF) is a broadly-based professional forum through which participants in the U.S. securitization market can advocate their common interests on important legal, regulatory and market practice issues."

According to the *New York Times*, the Forum's Las Vegas Meeting could be considered a "predator's ball." The newspaper did not remind readers that 16 years earlier this same phraseology was used widely about an earlier scandal on Wall Street. This account was published on August 15, 1991:

> They call it the Creditors' Ball: a hundred or so bankruptcy lawyers, bankers and investors, sipping cocktails and feasting on shrimp in the Hamptons in an unabashed celebration of the impoverished 1990's.

> This party of the well-paid, the well-connected, and the well-coiffed is quickly becoming the social event of the bankruptcy set, just as the Predators' Ball was a highlight of Wall Street's social calendar. That Beverly Hills extravaganza, sponsored by Drexel Burnham Lambert Inc., ended with the brokerage's downfall in 1990.

> So much for lessons being learned.

THE IMPORTANCE OF DISCLOSURE

At least now, the industry's public face and the regulators have come around to agreeing with a growing army of critics that inadequate disclosure was at the root of the problem, i.e., a lack of transparency.

And not only in the housing industry!

Well-known banks had also been admitting a little, while hiding a lot. When the finance ministers from the Group of the 7 top industrialized countries met in Tokyo on February 9, 2008, they issued a call to banks to fully disclose their losses from the subprime meltdown. The German Minister Peer Steinbruck said that these write-offs could reach a whopping $400 billion, four times previous estimates.

It must be noted that just a month earlier, in late December, Wall Street firms paid out more record bonuses to the bankers who had made them a vast fortune.

Why the secrecy, why the lack of disclosure?

A top-level corporate reputation consultant, who asked to remain anonymous but who has worked on the issue, summed it up for me in one word: greed. "They were making so much money that they didn't have time for due diligence or transparency. It was just pouring in."

Yet, oddly enough, one of the industry's big traders was still not remorseful. "We need to step back and take a breather," John Devaney told the *New York Times*. "I don't think there is anything fundamentally wrong."

No one asked him about the findings of the Senate's Joint Economic Committee:

• Approximately $71 billion in housing wealth will be directly destroyed through the process of foreclosures.

• More than $32 billion in housing wealth will be indirectly destroyed by the spillover effect of foreclosures, which reduce the value of neighboring properties.

• States and local governments will lose more than $917 million in property tax revenue as a result of the destruction of housing wealth caused by subprime foreclosures.

No one thought about that at the beginning of the subprime boom either.

HOW IT STARTED

According to a Senate report, the starting point of this crisis was in 1997, during the reign of the Clinton Administration. It was then that a period of housing price appreciation began – increasing by nearly 85% until 2006. Home prices jumped by 124%. This was unusual, having occurred only once before in American history, right after World War II.

Soon the housing sector was driving the American economy. Within the next few years, seven million families bought homes with subprime loans.

Homeowners who may have been cash poor, became house rich, by dipping into inflating home equity either by refinancing or taking out low-cost equity loans. As this business boomed, underwriting standards began to "deteriorate." The banks and other lenders had found a new way to make money – and fast. These loans helped homeowners stave off foreclosures.

They were made possible by deregulation lobbied for by financial institutions, credit card companies, and homebuilders, the industries most likely to benefit.

As John Atlas and Peter Dreier explain in the *American Prospect*, they won support from the Democrats and Republicans under the cover of the "Reagan Revolution" to undercut reforms made in the 1970s.

In the 1970s, when community groups discovered that lenders and the FHA were engaged in systematic racial discrimination against minority consumers and neighborhoods – a practice called "redlining" – they mobilized and got Congress, led by Wisconsin Senator William Proxmire, to adopt the Community Reinvestment Act and the Home Mortgage Disclosure Act, which together have significantly reduced racial disparities in lending. But by the early 1980s, the lending industry used its political clout to push back against government regulation.

This was also the period of major bank consolidation through mergers and the S&L crisis, which saw the closures of scores of banks and major losses because of illegal practices including mortgage lending.

A few bankers were prosecuted but most were bailed out by the Congress. As a blog named the Last Hurrah explained: "Without understanding cause, or the reason for these plain Jane savings organizations in sustaining middle and working class home ownership – Congress just bailed out the lenders who had the wit to reorganize, and let it go at that. Essentially they financed the next bump in housing inflation, whether it be in inflated prices for existing homes, speculation in lots for tear-downs in good areas, or McMansion housing far from jobs and culture in the exurbs, that requires vast investment in infrastructure on the part of existing home owners and the states."

Interest rate ceilings imposed by state usury laws dating from "reforms" in the 1980s were then rolled back. The lenders understood that these changes meant that now they could target a large potential market who wanted home ownership but could not qualify. And they could charge them high fees and interest.

The subprime loan was crafted for this community and promoted as a reform, a positive way for minorities to become part of the American Dream of homeownership for all. In this period, the Bush administration was hyping the promise of the "ownership society."

(Now, given the foreclosure rate, ownership may actually decline under his "watch.")

Most subprime borrowers were sold loans called "2/28" and "3/27" hybrid adjustable rate mortgages (ARMs). These loans typically had a low fixed interest rate – called a "teaser rate "by the industry – but only applicable during the first two-year period. After two years, the rate is reset every six months based on an interest-rate benchmark. In many cases, payments rose 30%, which made them unaffordable to people whose wages and income were barely rising. By 2004, 90 percent of the subprime loans had these ARMs.

Bear in mind also that the most vulnerable and hence "higher risk" subprime borrowers – many with low FICO credit scores and poor credit histories – were charged substantially higher interest rates and fees than other borrowers. They were more likely to be subject to pre-payment penalties, which make it costly to refinance loans. It was known in the industry that these are the borrowers who are most likely to default or become delinquent in payments and face foreclosure.

No one can fully explain why housing prices went up so quickly either, leaving the door open to explanations based on deceptive and fraudulent practices such as inflated appraisals.

Quickly, so-called "intermediaries," unregulated and often unscrupulous mortgage brokers, hustled their way into the housing market and quickly dominated, taking a vast market share by a variety of tactics ranging from deceptive advertising to block-by-block solicitations to get people to buy and sell, always promising more than they can deliver.

These efforts were buttressed by large-scale advertising campaigns for firms like DiTech — which used an actor/comedian known for his appearances on *Saturday Night Live* — to hype the mortgages being backed by the General Motors Acceptance Corporation. (For a while the car company was making more on loans than selling automobiles.) Online lenders then joined the carnival of competition with more ads. Media companies raked in several billion from this advertising, which provided little incentive to expose these practices.

Speculators fielded street teams known as "birddogs," rewarded for hunting down and signing up prospects. Abusive, illegal, and predatory practices were common. They enticed. They seduced, and in some cases, they threatened. I was told by a mortgage professional in the know that muscle was used, and that people were murdered in property battles.

According to the *Joint Economic Report*, "For 2006, Inside Mortgage Finance estimates that 63.3 percent of all subprime originations came through brokers, with 19.4 percent coming through retail channels, and the remaining 17.4 percent through correspondent lenders. Their data show the broker share increasing from 2003 through 2006."

These companies were not regulated and did not come under safety and soundness regulations. The percentage of subprime mortgage securitized rose rapidly after 2001, reaching a peak value of more than 81 percent in 2005.

Underscore that: 81%!

As housing sales boomed, lenders just dumped their traditional criteria for originating loans. The Senate later found: "The share of loans originated for borrowers unable to verify information about employment, income or other credit-related information ('low-documentation' or 'no documentation' loans) jumped from more than 28 percent to more than 50 percent. The share of ARM originations on which borrowers paid interest only, with nothing going to repay principal, increased from zero to more than 22 percent. Over this period the share of subprime ARMs multiplied dramatically that were originated."

ENTER WALL STREET

Another more powerful and seductive force soon entered this arena and effectively took charge of this feverish home-selling activity by imposing its own needs on the process. It also gave brokers a new income stream. Now they could make fees originating loans and then

8

even more money selling the paper into Wall Street's secondary market, where mortgages could be securitized (i.e., turned into securities) and sold again for even more money as investments.

The Finmanac financial blog explained the origins of what quickly became a scam:

> The man behind securitization was an Investment Banker of 'Salomon Brothers' – Lewis S. Raineri. In 1980s Salomon launched Mortgage-Based Securities (MBS) – bonds with bundles of mortgages, bought from bank lenders, as collateral. For this, Salomon used a special purpose vehicle known as Collateralized Mortgage Obligation (CMO). Monthly installment was used to pay the interest on these bonds.

This should not be intended: Raineri was not the only pioneer. There were many others. The *North Country Times* reported:

> The origins of the subprime mortgage crisis can be found in Orange County, where an investment banker pioneered the idea of selling bonds backed by home loans in 1990... William Komperda, a former Orange County investment banker now living in Connecticut, tapped into a funding bonanza when he was able to persuade insurers and bond rating firms to give his newfangled security their stamp of approval....

> Through his client, Long Beach Savings FSB, Komperda was able to float a $70 million bond issue backed by home loans. The success of the offering helped Long Beach Savings pull in cash and spawn Orange-based Ameriquest Mortgage Corp., once the biggest originator of home loans to people with less-than-sterling credit.

> "We thought it was just a niche market," Komperda told the *Orange County Register.* "It grew beyond what we imagined." Komperda, who runs Greenwich Capital, said other investment bankers and rating firms did not have a good understanding of the product, but the bonds were snapped up anyway.

(Ameriquest would become well known nationally when it bought ads on the Superbowl. The firm would later crash and burn and was bought for a song by CitiBank.)

The secondary market was born as a marriage between what were thought of as the most reputable financial institutions and the sleaziest grass-roots operators. As is often the case, the sleaze moved upwards.

Finmanac's analyst adds: "Securitization had some negative implications on the mortgage standards. Since anyone can originate a loan and sell it to the Investments Banks, which package them and sell them as MBS, it lead to originators writing risky loans as they need not worry about the payback of loan. This problem was dealt by slicing MBS into tranches on the basis of the risk profile. These tranches which may have different maturity period were given ratings by credit rating agencies like S&P and Fitch. The most risky tranches were difficult to sell except for the hedge funds and some pension funds. These hedge funds were so eager to buy these securities that they didn't care about the huge impending risk associated with these tranches and continued to invest in them."

This became a big business with brokers reporting they were getting "suction" (i.e., pressure) from Wall Street to sell more and more of these loans. One broker called it a "rat race." The *American Prospect* reported:

> Large mortgage finance companies and banks made big bucks on sub-prime loans. Last year, 10 lenders – Countywide, New Century, Option One, Fremont, Washington Mutual, First Franklin, RFC, Lehman Brothers, WMC Mortgage, and Ameriquest – accounted for 59 percent of all sub-prime loans, totaling $284 billion.

> Wall Street investment firms set up special investment units, bought the sub-prime mortgages from the lenders, bundled them into "mortgage-backed securities," and for a fat fee sold them to wealthy investors around the world.

BUBBLES TO FIGHT BUBBLES

This was also a period in which most of the financial world was distracted by the tech or dot.com boom, a bubble that would begin to burst in 2000. Investors were looking for other ways to invest. In some respects the housing bubble began as a response to the high tech bubble's failure. One bubble replaced another with the blessings of the Federal Reserve Bank's chairman Alan Greenspan, who ignored warnings from a colleague on his own board.

Federal Reserve Bank board member Edward M. Gramlich began warning back in 2000 that predatory lending and subprime mortgages were inherently unstable. He wanted the Bank to increase its oversight. Gramlich couched his warnings in the polite language of bankers and was barely heard.

In 2004, he said:

> While the basic developments in the subprime mortgage market
> seem positive, the relatively high delinquency rates in the
> subprime market do raise issues. ... For mortgage lenders the real
> challenge is to figure out how far to go. ... If lenders do make new
> loans, can conditions be designed to prevent new delinquencies
> and foreclosures?

It would be a mistake to lionize him as a populist critic or outspoken advocate of the victims. (After his death, the Fed honored his bravery and the *New York Times* profiled him as a voice of reason and whistleblower.) While being critical, he was often even-handed, also stressing the positives of a process that would later topple the financial system:

> The obvious advantage of the expansion of subprime mortgage
> credit is the rise in credit opportunities and homeownership.
> Because of innovations in the prime and subprime mortgage
> market, nearly 9 million new homeowners are now able to live in
> their own homes, improve their neighborhoods, and use their
> homes to build wealth.

Meanwhile his chairman, Alan Greenspan, was being lionized by the mass media as a genius – "the Maestro" – even as most of his pronouncements were barely decipherable. Greenspan ignored Gramlich as a nuisance. The Fed looked the other way. He also ignored housing advocates who met with him to tell him what was happening in poor communities, where hundreds of billions of dollars in home value were at risk.

UPI reported in December 2007: "Leaders of a housing advocacy group in California, meeting with Greenspan in 2004, warned that deception was increasing and unscrupulous practices were spreading."

John Gamboa and Robert Gnaizda of the Greenlining Institute implored Greenspan to use his bully pulpit to press for a voluntary code of conduct.

"He never gave us a good reason, but he didn't want to do it," Gnaizda said. "He just wasn't interested."

As housing values went up in the late 90s, Chairman Greenspan was confronting a recession and dot-com crash. The economy had fallen precipitously; corporate profits were in a recession. Many of the booming tech stocks so celebrated by investors and the media were in free fall.

In a curious way, when the terrorists struck on 911, they shifted attention from the sleazy practices that led to a market bubble and faulty projections on Wall Street. Now the financial community could blame all their problems on Al Qaeda, and a traumatized country bought it.

Greenspan also blamed globalization for market problems and in late 2001 began to recognize the greater economic potential of mortgage rates, seeing in "the extraction of home equity" a boom for an economy on the skids.

Appearing before Congress in early 2002, he praised "new financial products" that would later cripple the economy. He specifically and explicitly cited and praised "derivatives, asset backed securities, collateralized loan obligations and collateralized mortgage obligations," arguing that "lenders have the opportunity to be considerably more diversified and borrowers far less dependent on institutions for funds."

He contended that all the equity now available to mortgage owners would stimulate the economy and thus end the crisis already underway and made worse by 9/11. He acknowledged the danger of a bubble but dismissed it as unlikely for a host of reasons about rising real estate prices. And he was right – in the short term.

As he cut interest rates, money sloshed into the business world. The economy rallied until, of course, equity began to run out, leaving homeowners trapped with debts they could not afford. He never spoke to the fraudulent practices. Later, in April 2008, he would tell CNN there was extensive criminal fraud at work. He never blew the whistle on it when it could be stopped.

This official endorsement of dubious practices in testimony to the House Financial Services Committee on March 27, 2002, and the interest rate cuts by the Fed that followed in quick order, sanctioned the instruments and practices that gave us the subprime crisis five years later. This revelation appeared in a new book by financial blogger William A Fleckenstein (with Frederick Sheehan) called *Greenspan's Bubbles*. (It adds more evidence to support the view that the current crisis was actually encouraged!)

Economist Anna Schwartz, author of the seminal book on the Great Depression and dubbed "the High Priestess of U.S. Monetarism" by the *Sunday Telegraph* in London and who, at age 92, still works at National Bureau of Economic Research, says the central bank is itself the chief cause of the credit bubble, and is now stunned as the consequences of its own actions engulf the financial system.

"The new group at the Fed is not equal to the problem that faces it. They need to speak frankly to the market and acknowledge how bad the problems are, and acknowledge their own failures in letting this happen. This is what is needed to restore confidence," she told The *Sunday Telegraph*. "There never would have been a sub-prime mortgage crisis if the Fed had been alert. This is something Alan Greenspan must answer for."

THE REGULATORS COLLUDED

The Treasury Department was aware of the problems and also didn't act. Reported the *New York Times*: "In 2001, a senior Treasury official, Sheila Bair, tried to persuade subprime lenders to adopt a code of 'best practices' and to let outside monitors verify their compliance. None of the lenders would agree to the monitors, and many rejected the code itself. "Even those who did adopt those practices," Bair recalled recently, "soon let them slip... An examination of regulatory decisions shows that the Federal Reserve and other agencies waited until it was too late before trying to tame the industry's excesses."

Much of this boom was based on a foundation of fraud, of over-looked lending standards and ill-advised underwriting practices. Community organizations and professional groups like the National Center For Responsible Lending began documenting illegal and discriminatory practices. Many lobbied Congress and media organizations who did almost nothing to expose or legislate against the practices.

In fact, federal agencies acted to block regulation at the state level.

When many states began to hear complaints about deceptive advertising, and predatory practices, they tried to outlaw them. What happened? The banks lobbied the Federal government to stop the states from protecting their citizens, as Harvard law student Nicholas Bagley explained in the *Washington Post*:

> Some of the biggest players in the secondary mortgage market are national banks, and the states' efforts to curb predatory lending clashed with banks' fervent desire to keep the market rolling. So the banks turned to the Treasury Department's Office of the Comptroller of the Currency.
>
> The primary regulatory responsibility of the OCC is ensuring the safety and soundness of the national bank system, but almost its entire budget comes from fees it imposes on banks, which have the

option of incorporating them under state law. Put another way, the agency's funding depends on keeping the banks happy.

Little surprise, then, that the OCC acted when the national banks asked it to pre-empt subprime-mortgage laws such as Georgia's, arguing that they conflicted with federal banking law.

This speaks to the way the Bush administration used government agencies to block protections for homeowners and contributed to the crisis. In Congress, Republicans like Bob Ney of Ohio (later indicted and convicted in a lobbying scandal) introduced laws to pre-empt state regulations on credit card practices. Bipartisan support helped enact a bankruptcy "reform" bill that makes it harder for debtors to pursue debt relief.

This short, incomplete history, mostly based on secondary sources, is nonetheless the missing narrative that other journalists could have stitched together but largely missed. It describes an unholy trinity of private players, Wall Street firms, and non-regulating regulators who pounced on the potential to revive their own failing portfolios through shady and, as we are likely to see when the court cases and prosecutors make their findings public, a criminal conspiracy.

It was the largest robbery in history – not a bank heist but a heist by banks. Its target was the American people – and it enriched a few while leaving whole neighborhoods devastated.

Will the full scope of the rip-off ever be told, assessed, and punished?

CHAPTER 2

THE REAL CAPITOL OF AMERICA (AND THE WORLD)

THERE WAS ONCE A WALL ON WHAT IS NOW WALL STREET. WALL STREET is now the real capitol of our not-always-united States and, arguably, the world. It was once just a wall on a fort, actually a stockade built for the West India Company by the legendary Peter Stuyvesant, after whom one of New York's leading high schools is named. He used African slaves to build it first for the Dutch to defend their colony from the British. And then, over the years, they fortified the wall, expanding it to 12 feet by 4 feet to defend against Indian tribes, who may have been tricked into selling Manhattan Island for a pittance. (The Indian tribes believed that no one could own land because it belongs to Mother Earth, and so many at first thought they were scamming stupid colonists.) For many years, the area belonged quite literally to pigs, thousands of them, binging on garbage. Picture that landscape.

It wasn't until 1792 that the New York Stock Exchange was built on the site of the stockade. The first location of the NYSE was in a $200 a month room at 40 Wall. In 1832, the exchange was consumed by what's become known as the Great Fire of New York.

Nearly 700 buildings were turned into cinders. The Marines were called in and they blew up 17 city blocks to try to stop the fire's spread. They failed in that intervention as they would in the many foreign adventures to come. Wall Street has had a history of causing disasters from its earliest days.

The official history of the City of New York offered this description of the carnage:

Many of the stores were new, with iron shutters and doors and copper roofs, and in burning presented the appearance of immense iron furnaces in full blast. The heat at times melted the copper roofing, and the liquid ran off in great drops. The gale blew towards the East River. Wall after wall was heard tumbling like an avalanche. Fiery tongues of flame leaped from roof and windows along whole streets, and seemed to be making angry dashes at each other. The water of the bay looked like a vast sea of blood. The bells rang for a while and then ceased. Both sides of Pearl Street and Hanover Square were at the same instant in the jaws of the hungry monster.

These images, resonating with references to the imperialism of an earlier era – slavery, pigs, suppression of native peoples, military over-reaction, apocalyptic fire, and the "jaws of a hungry monster" – could easily be reconjured up all these years later to try to make sense of a growing financial crisis identified with modern Wall Street, even though many of its key players have dispersed uptown and around the world, linked by a ganglia of globalized electronic webs and networks.

The investigation of that great fire never identified who was to blame, just as so much of the journalism reporting on the massive market meltdown today, linked to what's been called a "credit storm" or "financial tsunami," avoids deeper analysis or, heaven forbid, assessing blame.

Today, Wall Street is walled off in another way. It's becoming a domestic replica of Baghdad's highly fortified Green Zone, with a small army of well-armed private security guards supplemented by platoons of New York Police. Hundreds of millions are being spent on new security cameras on top of the millions it took to get the markets up and running physically in the aftermath of the 9/11 attacks. New York is now emulating London in a plan to install more surveillance cameras in the financial district. Already, according to the *Wall Street Journal*, "there are at least 500,000 cameras in The City (London's financial district) and one study showed that in a single day a person could expect to be filmed 300 times."

These cameras are pointed outward when they should be turned around to document and monitor the inner world of the unelected deal-making elite who guide the allocation of resources in the world economy. Their choices or lack of them frame the debates of our politi-cians and structure our economy and economies worldwide.

The irony is that this obsession with security has made us more insecure, and in some cases contributes to the insecurity of others. For example, Wall Street firms are tapping the profit potential of a global boom in surveillance technology, even working with Communist China's feared Pubic Security Bureau, as the *New York Times* reports:

Wall Street analysts now follow the growth of companies that install surveillance systems providing Chinese police stations with 24-hour video feeds from nearby Internet cafes. Hedge fund money from the United States has paid for the development of not just better video cameras, but face-recognition software and even newer behavior-recognition software designed to spot the beginnings of a street protest and notify police.

Most of this filming is documenting citizens – not markets. It is spying on the streets – not on the boardrooms, where more transparency is clearly needed. It is there that major financial institutions make secret decisions that ultimately affect all of us. Most citizens don't really understand how the markets work or in whose interest. We know the names of ball players, not those of financial players. So, in a metaphoric sense, Wall Street has walled itself off from effective external monitoring.

A website called Cryptome.org looked closely at this security obsession:

Seven security barriers create a security zone for the New York Stock Exchange. In addition to the barriers and full-time police there are dozens of surveillance cameras. As with most security around the globe, these measures appear to be as much for show as for protection. Greeders with their global telecom network who exploit the Stock Exchange's prowess at fleecing gullible investors are hidden in palatial penthouse and country estate bunkers far away from the touristically inviting bull eye. Telling the truth: except for the 20 feet gated on the tourist sides of the Exchange, the security zone is a squalid and filthy dump.

On the inside, of course, the big banks and investment houses have expensively designed and well-furnished boardrooms and spare no expense when it comes to executive compensation. There are gourmet kitchens and dining rooms served by waiters in black tie. The walls are lined with pricey art and photographs or paintings of their managing directors. I saw such a gallery of the high and the mighty on the wall in the inner sanctum at Goldman Sachs, and thought immediately of other images once displayed on the walls of better post offices. They showcased Most Wanted posters.

These accoutrements reek of privilege and reflect a culture of entitlement that aims as much at personal capital accumulation as the well being of the firm. It is aggressive in its ambitions but gentile seeming in its behavior. There may be moments of bedlam on the trading floors or sales boiler rooms, but in the suites there is a quiet environment of verbal persuasion on telephones and in tele-conferences. Its arrogance is low-key and projected as self-confidence. These are not the kind of people ordinarily associated with white-collar crime.

Author Tom Wolfe went back, twenty years later in 2007, to the scene of the corporate crimes he vivisected in his stunning book, *The Bonfire of the Vanities*. It was there he coined the term "masters of the universe" to refer to the big-footing Wall Street players. Writing in the magazine *Portfolio*, he updated the story with a profile of the new generation of wheelers and dealers who thrive in the financial culture that spawned the subprime crisis.

...Most of these people are in their late thirties and early to mid forties. For men making, in many cases, tens of millions and up per year, they qualify as young. They talk about business in young-warrior metaphors: "pulling the trigger" (making huge risky bets on the market); "mowing them all down" (overpowering companies that try to block your strategies); "This is war!" (Get out of my way – or else I'll make you suffer); "Surrender your booty!" (I'm a corporate raider poised to take over your company); "We don't eat what we don't kill" (if you, the investor, don't make a profit, then we in the hedge fund's management don't take a profit ourselves, something oddly true in spirit although, as we shall soon see, not in fact).

These people tend to be bright and well-educated, many at Harvard, Princeton, and other top-ranked colleges. They come from well-educated families. They still enjoy the virgin animal health of youth. They are flush with optimism and confidence, as well as money. With all that going for them, what inna namegod is their problem?"

Well, a lack of ethics, for one thing. It is a world where getting away with it is acceptable and regulation weak or non-existent. It is a world that rewards clever and devious strategies.

Critics of the way these institutions work are often reduced to making indictments of the "system" in generic terms – an often-vague allusion to larger forces that rarely have names or rap sheets. This type of explanation is also distancing in that it leads to a "you can't fight City Hall attitude" and a passive acceptance of outrageous practices.

Rarely do journalists or so-called TV "money honeys" explain the inner workings of the wheeling and dealing in our financial system, a hard-charging business where investment banks and hedge funds call the shots by orchestrating a money machine with little oversight and less candor. The vice chancellor of Germany called hedge funds "swarms of locusts" in 2005.

Frank Keenan, author of *Ignorance Is Risk*, notes: "Almost all of the information you receive about the stock markets comes from people who are profiting by the decisions they are directing you to make. The stock analyst, the mutual fund manager, the economist that you see on television or whose column you read in the newspaper is typically not the unbiased and objective expert you believe him or her to be."

This is part of the reason why there were so few media warnings of the crisis that the subprime debacle touched off. What was initially suspected as a problem confined to the housing sector, spread quickly into the bloodstream of the financial system worldwide. According to the *New Europe* newspaper:

"The OECD estimates that the cost to American banks from bad credits could reach U.S.D 300 billion, and this is not the total cost to the U.S. economy, which could go as high as U.S.D two trillion, which is more than half the annual GDP."

Another European think-tank, LEAP2020, warned of this danger in December 2006, but was largely ignored when its assessment of where the growing debt load of Americans would lead:

"The U.S. consumer, i.e. the U.S. middle class, basically becomes insolvent, victim of overwhelming debt, a negative rate of saving, the bursting of the real estate bubble, the rise of interest rates and the collapse of U.S. growth. All these elements are dependent, and mutually reinforcing, to plunge the United States, starting from the end 2006, into an economic, social and political crisis without precedent."

This situation is leading to sleepless nights for those in the know. AP quotes a financial insider:

We haven't faced a downturn like this since the Depression," said Bill Gross, chief investment officer of PIMCO, the world's biggest bond fund. He's not suggesting anything like those terrible times – but, as an expert on the global credit crisis, he speaks with authority.

"Its effect on consumption, its effect on future lending attitudes, could bring us close to the zero line in terms of economic growth," he said. "It does keep me up at night."

According to Satyajit Das, a renowned derivatives expert, there is no quick fix in sight.

I think this crisis has a long way to run. It is an extra-innings baseball game and the national anthem still hasn't finished playing. So we really don't know what the worst is.

The worst may be yet to come, but for many the situation is quickly already going from bad to worst. Writes Andy Sutton on a financial website:

Despite a reported GDP growth of 3.9% annualized for the third quarter, it is becoming more and more obvious that we are already in a recession or at least on the verge of one. Housing has continued to be a boat anchor, the banking sector is being hit with massive write downs for mortgages gone bad, and fuel prices across the board have remained stubbornly high, forcing consumers to make the choice between cutting back on other areas or taking on even more debt.

Couple all of this with the tab on our national credit card (now well over $9 TRILLION), and it is hard to imagine a scenario in which we pay off this massive accumulated debt honestly through overproduction and underconsumption. In my view, the fundamentals have been and will continue to be a drag on our economic performance, our economic standing in the world, and the American standard of living.

It sounds bleak, doesn't it? Still to be examined is how a lack of regulation, fiscal policies, and the greed of major financial institutions enabled this situation and permitted the spread of scams that defrauded investors and borrowers alike.

Few media outlets, for example, investigated how the predatory lenders operated by deliberately and intentionally sucking people into loans they could not afford.

It would be months before journalists like Gretchen Morgenson at the *New York Times*, explained that these loans were carefully engineered. She is a very savvy financial journalist and noted in late November 2007 that it "is becoming obvious that these loans were designed to fail. True to their design, they were."

IS THIS INTELLIGENT DESIGN OR CRIMINAL DESIGN?

Similar questions might be raised about policies that seem to be promoting a recession as a way of bringing down trade balances. The dropping dollar and even the Federal Reserve Bank's interest rate cuts can be seen as part of a strategy.

When a friend in Geneva suggested that the Bush Administration planned this, I scoffed. Why would they wreck their own economy? Then I read this: "Yes, America needs a recession. Bernanke and Paulson won't admit it. And investors hate them. We're all trapped in outdated 1990s wishful thinking about a 'new economy' and 'perpetual growth.'

"But the truth is, not only is a recession coming, America needs a recession. So think positive."

That was Paul Farrell explaining to the Marketwatch.com website that the goal is to redress global trade imbalances. If true, this means that while most of us were expecting a war on Iran, it was an economic war they were readying.

Eric Janzsen of the iTulip website says that this strategy will not work:

> The Fed, Treasury, and Congress have been fighting the recession we forecast last fall as due to start in Q4 2007, led by the housing market correction. Throwing the dollar under the bus to briefly boost exports and bring plane loads of tourists into the U.S. has helped avert a far more blatant recession from occurring than the subtle one we're already in.
>
> With inflation rising as quickly as the U.S. economy is slowing, picking the exact month or quarter when the real (inflation-adjusted) GDP growth recession starts – or started – will not be possible until after the inevitably revised GDP and inflation figures come in. We expect to see confirmation June 2008 at the earliest.
>
> As for an economic contraction that "cleanses the system" with debt defaults, bankruptcies, and high unemployment – well, that's coming, too. Sort of. But it won't lead to the hoped for economic and political structural reforms outlined in Farrell's romanticized vision of recession.

This debate is missing in most media outlets, which see a recession primarily as a response just to the housing crisis. It may be more than that. The Federal Reserve Bank, like the markets themselves, has yin-yanged back and forth. At first, they saw no problem. Then they "injected" billions into the financial system worldwide. When that didn't calm the waters, they cut interest rates in the fall of 2007, first by half a point and then by a quarter. When that didn't work, the Fed Chairman expressed confidence in the "resilience" of the American economy and said they do not expect a recession.

The next day, they issued $8 billion in low-interest loans to banks to "ease credit concerns." Meanwhile, former chairman Alan Greenspan denied that his policies had any impact on the fall of the market on the same day that German banker Klaus-Peter Muller said the trouble in Wall Street is far from over.

Yet, the street lives on the hope and faith that the government will fix it, with still more interest-rate cuts and government bailouts for families facing foreclosures. When the market rallied in late November 2007, the brokers and investors were talking up a faith-based "silver lining."

Said Robert Barbera, chief economist at the brokerage and advisory firm ITG. "The bad news gives you the blessing of lower interest rates."

Peter Goodman was more skeptical on the front page of the *New York Times*, the story's placement indicating the importance this up-and-down drama is now receiving, even as upbeat stories like Barbera's have been common.

But even as investors took heart in palpable signs that the government was preparing to dole out more medicine for the ailing economy, a number of economists cautioned that the pain itself was still unfolding, with its ultimate magnitude far from known" (December 1, 2007).

On the same day, the *Wall Street Journal* reported that there was still no consensus on what to do, or how to do it. "The government-led plan to freeze interest rates on troubled subprime loans drew criticism from Wall Street, which thinks it will prolong the pain, while others said it was the right move. The success of the plan, whose details are still under discussion, may hang on the many investors in securities backed by mortgages."

Other news accounts made clear that only a small minority of homeowners are at risk of foreclosure. The most vulnerable were the people who took no documentation loans and borrowed more than they could afford to pay back. It won't help homeowners who borrowed more than their homes were worth. Many of these people were advised that their property values went up. Instead, house values dropped – all thanks to the predatory loans that victimized them. And now they could be victimized again by being excluded from government-backed relief measures.

A WHITE-COLLAR CRIME WAVE?

When the "subprime" problem first surfaced, very few in our media or on The Street suspected that there might have been more to it than market "mistakes." Only a handful of writers and analysts saw it for what is: a crime in progress, a white-collar crime wave. Yes, we are told, errors were made. Interest rates may have been cut too much. There were poor assessments of risk, and even some greed. But the system was working so well.

Was it keeping the world economy afloat or sinking it? This question became pertinent when bank after bank wrote down billions in liens with no real assets backing them. This may have been the biggest and most deceptive financial scandal in history in terms of the total amount of money stolen and then lost. We are talking about trillions here.

There are two views of this crisis, one benign – reflecting the widely embraced "screw-up theory of history." That argues that most of the industry wanted to do the right thing by families who couldn't afford homes, but standards grew too lax, the lending process was sloppy, and things got out of hand. It may have been wrong in part, but, in this view, understandable and forgivable.

Alternatively, the other view reflects a more conspiratorial analysis. Michael Blomquist, a California millionaire, who says unscrupulous real estate financiers bilked him out his assets, argues:

> Our current credit and housing crisis was not created from low interest rates or "laxed" guidelines. This crisis was created by unconscionable greed, breaches of fiduciary duties, lack of regulation, embezzlement and fraud.

He is suing and demanding a full-scale investigation. He wants to blow the whistle on what he sees as a web of deceit and theft. For the most part, the industry was silent about any crimes that may have been committed. Few journalists investigated this angle and few editorial writers demanded a full probe.

This began to change as the crisis became more severe. In mid-February 2007, Basil Williams, chief executive officer of Concordia Advisors, a hedge fund, wrote an op-ed for the Bergen *Record*, his hometown paper, calling for "a safety net for the innocent and a drag-net for the guilty." He outlined ways the government might provide relief and argued that those responsible for the crisis should be made to pay for their misdeeds.

Writing in the Bergen N.J. *Record*, he urged "going after those who profited handsomely and unfairly from the multitude of transactions that touched the industry, including:

• Mortgage brokers who originated loans to those who didn't understand the conditions, couldn't afford them and should not have qualified.

• Appraisers who overvalued homes, knowing that the higher the value they gave a property, the more business they would reap from a dishonest broker.

• Banks and brokerage firms that purchased, packaged and resold the mortgages for huge fees.

In many cases, these players had relationships with the mortgage brokers. Both had a hand in issuing lax or even fabricated loan documents in order to fulfill the demand for collateral to feed subprime asset-backed securities they were pumping into markets. The bankers took home million-plus pay packages based on the transactional fees they generated regardless of how the security performed for the investor or whether the homeowner lost his piece of the block.

Williams outlines a chain of responsibility that shows how extensive the complicity was, including the role played by ratings agencies that certified worthless paper as AAA "asset-backed."

Most business journalists distrust connecting the dots this way. Many call it conspiracy thinking even as they cover organized crime trials prosecuted under RICO anti-conspiracy laws and occasionally investigate systematic abuses in some industries while giving the benefit of the doubt to others. Often these journalists don't read their own newspaper archives or any history books.

The hunger for land, real estate, and wealth – often thought of as the same thing – motivated the discovery, colonization, settlement, and expansion of the United States. Men of property installed a property-oriented system. Big landowners ran slave plantations while robber barons bought and built and plundered. This was always a nation of a small number of winners and a large number of the people who served them. And throughout the centuries, land scams and questionable real estate deals drove economic "progress." Bruce Springsteen did not come up with the concept of "mansions of glory."

Wrote Montaigne: "No man profiteth but by the loss of others." Scratch the story of the development of many cities and towns and you will find stories of corruption, pay-offs and government subsidies leading to the rise of real estate fortunes and modern day icons like Donald Trump. "Those with the gold make the rules," said real estate mogul Samuel J. Lefrak. Explained Winston Churchill, "Land is not the only monopoly, but is by far the greatest of all monopolies – it is a perpetual monopoly, and it is the mother of all forms of monopoly."

So a collapse in the world of land and real estate can easily lead to the mother of all financial crises. Five years before I sat down to write this book, Scott Paltrow, a staff reporter for the *Wall Street Journal*, asked and answered a key question:

Why do Wall Street scandals recur with the grim regularity of earthquakes and forest fires? The obvious answer, of course, is that Wall Street is where the money is. Beyond the inevitable appeal of billions of dollars changing hands daily, however, lie more peculiar reasons why knavery on a grand scale periodically racks the securities industry....

While scandals are nothing new, the pain they cause is being felt more deeply.... Indeed, the language Wall Street traders and brokers use sometimes betrays disdain toward individual investors. Nasdaq market makers commonly refer to buy and sell orders from individuals as 'dumb order flow,' meaning their orders are almost certain to be profitable for the market makers because small investors typically trade without any hard information that could give them an advantage over these dealers.

The economist Paul Krugman, who writes a newspaper column for the *New York Times*, indicated that the lust for lucre and monomaniacal fever on Wall Street that drove continued investments in questionable securities even after the scandal broke.

...even as the danger signs multiplied, Wall Street piled into bonds backed by dubious home mortgages. Most of the bad investments now shaking the financial world seem to have been made in the final frenzy of the housing bubble, or even after the bubble began to deflate.

In fact, according to *Fortune*, Merrill Lynch made its biggest purchases of bad debt in the first half of this year – after the subprime crisis had already become public knowledge.

Now the bill is coming due, and almost everyone – that is, almost everyone except the people responsible – is having to pay.

"GREED IS GOOD"

I have never been a market watcher or an investor. I don't know that much either about the inner workings of an industry known mostly for its avarice. I saw the movie *Wall Street* with its invocation of that mantra of our times, "greed is good," and was, like many, disgusted. As a journalist, I have been in the inner sanctum of Goldman Sachs and partied with the delegates of "Davos In New York" on the floor of the New York Stock Exchange. I was meeting with an investment banker during the crash of 1987 and heard the moaning and anguish coming up from the trading floor as fortunes vanished with the click of a computer. I have spoken with more moguls than I want to admit.

They are a seductive group, so smart, so charming and at the same time so controlled. It's hard not to be impressed with the obvious success of the often lampooned but also widely envied "masters of the universe" who know how to make fortunes by shrewdly assessing the comers and ignoring the losers. These are well- schooled and often well-dressed men and women who understand the inner dynamics of industries and business strategy. They seem so analytical and skilled at what they do.

It's not surprising that so many students are in business schools going for their MBAs and an opportunity to serve in a machine which seems, on the outside, to be so rational, calculating, and even wise. It makes a certain kind of sense. After all, the entire average wage in the financial sector was $8,280 a WEEK! Not bad. And it went up $3,000 in the last three years. Who doesn't want to be a winner?

Yet a closer look, usually in times of crisis, offers a window into another kind of financial world, a world of panic and fear, where irrationality is the order of the day, an irrationality that goes by the name of "Market Psychology."

One financial author, Troy Dunn, blames "amateurs" for these problems on the Street. He contends the stock market was intended for logical, levelheaded professional investors, saying: "The decision process for deciding where to invest and when to pull out is supposed to be a brain decision! But too many amateurs are making their investment decisions with their HEART! This current economy, especially the current housing market is proof that emotions can kill any market- including the stock market. Cooler heads must prevail."

I disagree. The subprime schemes that triggered the crisis were not emotional. They were well thought through and systemic. They were made by hardened pros, not foolish amateurs. Forget the bulls or the bears...this is a world of sharks deeply in need of shrinks. When things go well, the wizards of Wall Street are anointed by the media as geniuses. When they don't, you get *Time Magazine's* condescending putdown of "Wall Street's mad scientists blowing up the lab again."

This kind of humor seems out-of-place when we are talking about what many fear can lead to the collapse or at least a severe wounding of the global economy. Over two million families are expected to lose their homes along with as many renters. (This figure has fluctuated. In Spring 2008, that number jumped to three million!) The Banks have written off hundreds of billions and the total bill has been estimated at two trillion – with the crisis still at an early stage.

WHO KNEW?

When I started poking around on the fringes of this story late in 2005, I was motivated by a much smaller problem – how to understand my own dependence on credit cards, and why my savings account was shrinking away. As a journalist and filmmaker, I assumed this situation was not just mine and would interest a lot of people. I had no idea that a story that had often been covered as a consumer issue, usually focused on people who got in over their heads or were the victims, and of identity fraud was actually the tip of a very large and insidious iceberg.

The experience of making the film *In Debt We Trust* has led me to understand how many ways policies and practices are tied to a growing national debt burden that have an impact on all of our personal finances.

Even as a former network journalist and long-time investigative reporter, I was shocked and outraged when I started examining the roots of these issues. This is a problem involving millions of people and billions of dollars, yet it was downplayed and rarely discussed in all of its disastrous dimensions.

It's about a growing inequality that some experts fear will lead to a new 21st century serfdom. It's about the transfer of wealth from working people into the vaults and accounts of a relatively small number of financial institutions and real estate interests. The lenders are not only profiting by charging usurious rates but doing so legally, in part because they have mastered the art and science of marketing financial products and then manipulating our media, politicians, and political institutions to allow them to do whatever they want. Lobbying and political pay-offs (i.e. campaign contributions) are just a cost of doing business, part of the greater game.)

Most often, credit card abuses are examined in terms of individuals and consumer scams like identity theft. My film started with that approach but evolved into a much deeper look at what's been called "financialization." This is an institutional problem involving a growing debt and credit complex that threatens the very fabric of our nation, not just in terms of a possible financial crash in the future but how it is impinging upon our lives and livelihoods right now.

Over the course of my career, I have made 20 doumentaries and won many awards and some recognition. Many have been shown at top festivals and aired on TV. I am attached to all of them but *In Debt We Trust* is different because it doesn't just document suffering, it warns of the implications of consequences that will affect all of us. Perhaps that's why this issue cuts across party and partisan lines in a way that can potentially unite a nation. Perhaps that's why mostly everyone I tell about the film tells me about how they too became personally ensnared in the debt trap.

At first my hope was that this film would spark a national response – a demand for economic fairness and justice, regulation in the public interest, along with a heightened sense of personal responsibility by consumers seduced by the false promise of "free money." That didn't happen. It was tough to get distribution, to have it seen in theaters, or to get reviewers to take it seriously. Some considered it as "alarmist,"

I knew things were bad but I had no idea how much worse they could become. Slowly this issue moved into the mainstream as the subprime loans that I pointed to in the film, along with the role played by Wall Street, imploded in our lives and consciousness.

I then started reading and pouring over financial reports that I used to ignore. First I had had to translate them into language I could understand before I could make sense of them for others. Financial language can be dense and technical, but I persevered, warning anyone who would listen that this crisis was on the edge of exploding. Not too many people did listen at first.

The media largely consigned the story to the back of the paper, to business news sections. Their language was obtuse, too. I really don't think that initially many journalists or political leaders understood how serious and crazy this problem was. They had no idea that in a few months the markets would be melting down and the central banks like our own Federal Reserve Bank would be "injecting" billions of dollars to bolster confidence and avoid a serious downturn.

In the past we have had booms and busts and even stock market crashes. We have had inflation and recessions. Everyone in the finance industries and many pundits speak endlessly about the "resilience" of the system. But what if it comes up against a problem of its own making that cannot easily be contained? What if there is a proverbial tipping point from which there is no return?

This book chronicles the events of this tumultuous year, a period of time in which a debt bomb went off in America and was a sound heard round the world. Like a contagion, it corrupted many financial institutions and we are still assessing the full impact.

During the summer of 2007, as the subprime mortgage mess moved from the business pages to the front pages, it was clear that the press and the financial industry had failed to anticipate the problem. The people trying to call attention to the crisis were ignored.

The *New York Times* actually admitted this in a business section article, although not in the kind of editorial mea culpa it ran in admitting its flawed journalistic practices in the run up to the Iraq War. This revealing admission appeared at the end of the summer of 2007.

As far back as 2001, advocates for low-income homeowners had argued that mortgage providers were making loans to borrowers without regard to their ability to repay. Many could not even scrape together the money for a down payment and were being approved with little or no documentation of their income or assets.

In December [2006], the first subprime lenders started failing as more borrowers began falling behind on payments, often shortly after they received the loans. And in February, HSBC, the large British bank, set aside $1.76 billion because of problems in its American subprime lending business.

Over the last two weeks, this slowly building wave became a tsunami in the global financial markets.

I had been writing on this issue, even using the term tsunami, for weeks before the *Times* woke up. The signs were there, but many eyes were closed because they were looking elsewhere – mostly, at all the money they were making.

To its credit, the *Times* story acknowledged the greed factor without calling it that:

The cast of characters who missed signals like the rise of delinquencies and foreclosures is becoming easier to identify. They include investment banks happy to sell risky but lucrative mortgage debt to hedge funds hungry for high interest payments, bond rating agencies willing to hope for the best in the housing market and provide sterling credit appraisals to debt issuers, and subprime mortgage brokers addicted to high sales volumes.

What is more, some of these players now find themselves in a dual role as both enabler and victim, like the legions of individual borrowers who were convinced that their homes could only keep rising in value and were confident that they could afford to stretch for the biggest mortgage possible.

One of the challenges we all face is learning how to connect the dots – to understand the relationship between private industry and policy makers – and the role well-funded lobbies play in weakening restraints on powerful but irresponsible profiteers.

We have to recognize how many of us are kept in the dark about finances and encouraged not to learn about them or seek out alternatives. Few schools offer financial literacy education. Few TV programs offer information about financial responsibility in part because it is perceived as boring and not in the interests of companies who prefer us to be uninformed. Remember, we are all seduced and influenced by marketing and advertising ploys in structuring our choices as consumers and encouraging us to spend now and pay later.

We also need to challenge our media and political leaders to protect an uneducated and gullible public from itself and the seductive but false claims of credit and loan companies.

This is a big story – one of the biggest. What lessons can we learn from it, and how can we respond as consumers and citizens?

CHAPTER 3

THE UNSPOKEN CONTEXT

THE CRIMES OF WALL STREET

WERE CRIMES COMMITTED BY THE MORTGAGE INDUSTRY IN COLLUSION with some of the top banks, investment managers, and securitization specialists in the world? Did regulators, and even the Federal Reserve Bank ignore evidence of systematic wrongdoing or collude in it? Why has NBC's TV show "Catch the Predators" not been focusing on these corporate crimes?

In early February 2008, the FBI announced it was investigating 14 unnamed mortgage companies. FBI director Robert Mueller said the crimes committed were "substantial" and in every state in the union.

Clearly large numbers of borrowers were ripped off, lied to, suckered, and knowingly persuaded to take on far more debt than they could afford. Many were scammed and some scammed the scammers by misrepresenting their incomes and their ability to pay loans back. It's been estimated that ten million subprime loans were made worldwide.

There have been many reports of companies deliberately, with malice and forethought, steering customers to more expensive loans, often in a discriminatory manner, and not disclosing all payments and fees. In some cases these fees were jacked up unfairly to extract even more money from those least able to afford the payments and usury.

These predatory practices had been going on for years before they attracted attention. When the revenues were going up, no one noticed. When the system ran into troubles, the hand-wringing began. Housing advocates have been warning about sleazy and unregulated practices for years.

In the summer of 2000, a year before the *New York Times* even acknowledged learning about massive fraud in the mortgage market, Shelterforce, a coalition of organization concerned about housing denounced predatory practices. It cited government studies tracking back to 1994 – 13 years before this crisis exploded, so there was nothing secret going on:

> Predatory lending is becoming more of a problem as the home mortgage market undergoes rapid change. Banks – the sector of financial services that control the lower interest "prime" market – are issuing a declining share of home mortgages, and the subprime market is booming.

The line between consumer finance – including credit cards and small home improvement loans – and home mortgages is blurring as homeowners borrow against their houses to consolidate their debt. Mortgage brokers and loan "originators" on the staffs of banks or mortgage companies are often paid incentive commissions for placing borrowers into rates higher than the risk-based price that the underwriting guidelines call for.

Those most hurt by the growing subprime market are black and Hispanic borrowers. A September 1999 study by HUD shows that since 1994, conventional, prime lending to black and Hispanic borrowers has dropped, and that black borrowers are increasingly being turned down for prime rate loans in numbers that far outstrip whites.

The same study shows that lending by subprime companies to minorities is on the rise. Not all subprime lending is predatory; higher credit risks are normally charged higher interest on loans. But the growth in subprime lending to minorities, when coupled with the decrease in prime lending, leads to concerns that minority borrowers with good credit are being shut out of conventional markets and channeled instead into more expensive, subprime loans.

A Spring 2008 study confirmed these practices with more specifics. Reuters reported on the study, conducted by Inner City Press/Fair Finance Watch, which found that

... banks such as JPMorgan Chase, Citigroup, Bank of America, and Countrywide issued subprime loans to minorities more than twice as often as whites. At some institutions, the number of subprime loans issued increased, even amid a growing credit liquidity crisis.

"One of our most surprising findings was that the largest players just continued making subprime loans in a disparate way even as the industry collapsed around them. To us, this means that they intend to continue this gouging of customers just with fewer competitors in the future," said Matthew Lee, executive director of the Bronx, New York-based group.

Good subprime lending to borrowers with risky credit can be profitable without any predatory practices. However, reports by Freddie Mac and Standard & Poor's indicate that 63 percent of subprime borrowers would have qualified for conventional "A" or "A-" quality loans.

Their report called mortgage brokers "the wild, wild west of Capitalism," noting that fully seven years before this book was written, they were originating 50 percent of all subprime loans. And it was a profitable enterprise: "The higher the fees and interest rates a mortgage broker packs into a loan, the greater their compensation."

These shadowy operators also had operatives aggressively marketing especially in ghetto neighborhoods. They used phone solicitation and door-to-door canvassing. They offered themselves up as debt consolidation experts with home improvement schemes and foreclosure "rescue" services.

Explains Texas economist Dr. Mark Dotzour, chief economist for the Real Estate Center at Texas A&M University in College Station, Texas, in an article posted by the Mortgage Foundation:

Under the terms of a "rescue loan," predatory lenders promise borrowers they can use their loans to catch up on payments. In exchange, the lender takes over the title and promises the borrower they can live in the home and pay rent. The only problem is the "homeowners are neither rescued, nor do they actually receive loans," said Dotzour. In most cases, the predatory lender sells the home and sends an eviction notice.

Some of these homeowners had substantial equity in their homes but not enough money to pay their bills.

In many cases this army of the merchants of sleaze that are targeting the vulnerable in distressed areas were selective in what they told their customer/victims, often hiding the real facts about how these deals would drive families deeper and deeper in debt. Shelterforce compared these widespread practices to "sharecropping, an economic system that is unequal and unfair." It is also discriminatory and as such does violate the law.

Criminal fraud has been pervasive in this business, as the *Washington Independent* reported:

> As loans made to borrowers with decent credit begin to fail at a surprisingly rapid rate, it's becoming clear that widespread fraud helped support the entire mortgage system – from borrowers who lied on their loans, to brokers who encouraged it, to lenders who misled some low income borrowers, to the many lenders, investors and ratings agencies that conveniently and deliberately looked the other way as profits rolled in.

> Despite its widespread role, fraud hasn't yet been at the forefront of proposed rescue plans, which center on refinancing people out of loans now resetting to higher rates.

Why would reputable bankers and respected investment houses engage in these types of activities? The short answer: money, and lots of it.

Sales from Collateralized Debt Obligations jumped from $157 billion in 2004 to $559 billion in 2006, according to a study for the North Star Fund by Kevin Connor. Ten investment banks in all were underwriters for 70% of some $486 billion in securitizations in 2006. The banks had a motto: "It's all about capital."

Subprime-related securities produced large multi-million dollar bonuses for traders and executives as well as high revenues for the firms. Even after these practices came to light, the bonuses continued. Wall Streeters walked away with $31 billion at the end of 2007, only one billion less than the year before. Executives who were fired still walked away with multi-million-dollar payoffs.

None of this was considered shocking or illegal.

Some of these loans were called "liars' loans" in the industry, as when loan orginators colluded with or advised borrowers on how to lie on their applications. It was all done with a wink and a nod, reported the *Washington Independent* ,which interviewed many insiders and experts who contended that

> ... pervasive fraud was, indeed, a problem – on the lender's side. At the peak of the housing boom, they say, the nation's mortgage

system was set up to promote and encourage outright fraud in order to close a loan – and everyone, from brokers to loan officers to Wall Street, looked the other way. Borrowers also were put into products like payment-option arms that were unsuitable - and lenders knew it. "They were pushed like Vioxx, with very little regard for their dangers," said Kathleen Keest, senior policy counsel with the Center for Responsible Lending, a research group that investigates predatory lending.

Patrick Madigan, an Iowa assistant attorney general who has investigated mortgage fraud, said it makes no sense to conclude that lenders are somehow victims. Madigan's office engineered a settlement with Ameriquest over its subprime practices, including high-pressure "boiler room" sales tactics. Regardless, Madigan said, there is a movement to "blame the borrower."

... borrowers were encouraged by brokers to suddenly create businesses in their basements, like day care centers, to boost their incomes. If they questioned it, brokers would say that lenders required it, or not to worry. Still, borrowers signed on the bottom line, some knowing the information was false. Consider this borrower's account in the *San Francisco Chronicle* of a sales conversation with a broker:

"He didn't say anything illegal out loud," she said. "He didn't say 'lie,' he just made a strong suggestion. He said, 'If you made $60,000, we could get you into the lowest interest level of this loan; did you make that much?' I said, 'Um, yes, about that much.' He went clickety clack on his computer and said, 'Are you sure you don't remember any more income, like alimony or consultancies, because if you made $80,000, we could get you into a better loan with a lower interest rate and no prepayment penalty.' It was such a big differential that I felt like I had to lie, I'm lying already so what the heck. I said, 'Come to think of it, you're right, I did have another job that I forgot about.'"

Wall Street was not a passive player because of all the money they made from transactions like this.

"These are the trades that make people famous," said Christopher Ricciardi, a former top-earning executive at Merill Lynch who called himself the "grandfather of CDOs," raking in $8 million annually for his role in the affair.

In the years when business was booming, CEOs at big firms were making $10 to $50 million annually apiece. Collectively, in 2006, a year before their fall, the big banks earned a stunning $130 billion.

In some cases, borrowers paid more for loans with predatory characteristics. Loan originators at the local level – as sleazy as many were – reported that it was the Wall Street firms who dictated the types of loans they wanted and the underwriting criteria. Thus the so-called "Secondary market" was really in charge.

Wall Street pushed and pulled for more predatory practices. The people who had the most were deeply involved in ripping off the people who had the least. What's worse, they had no legal liability in these unscrupulous deals.

While this was happening, it was being justified as a stimulus for the economy even as income inequality deepened. In an interview with Peter Boyle on the Green Left website, economist John Bellamy Foster of the University of Oregon, explains that these payoffs led to even more investments into the financial sector, which is essentially non-productive:

> So all the profits the capitalists can't find investment outlets for are poured into finance. So we have a huge growth of the financial superstructure of the economy, which is now far bigger than the productive base, what the economists call the "real economy of income."
>
> The financial structure dwarfs that. Financialization means a shift in gravity from the real economy (production centered-economy) to financial speculation.
>
> This system has become more and more unwieldy. As it expanded, they have had to take on larger and larger amounts of risk. They've had to develop more and more exotic financial instruments and the system has become opaque, multi-layered, gargantuan and uncontrollable ...
>
> The potential chain reactions were enormous because the system is opaque, which means that nobody knows where the financial toxic waste is buried. Nobody knows because the interconnections are too complex and nobody wants the mortgage-based securities anymore because they are seen as too dangerous.

They call them "nitroglycerine" or "weapons of mass destruction." The whole thing is unstable.

In short, the system they built – a shadow unregulated and unaccountable banking system, was riddled with so many contradictions and driven by so much greed that to no one's real surprise, it collapsed like a deck of cards. And, oddly, while Washington went to war over non-existent WMDs, in Iraq, real ones on Wall Street were undermining our national security.

Some predicted it, but few were ready for it.

How did America's leading business magazine respond after the credit crisis brought Wall Street to its knees? *Fortune* called the credit crisis "both totally shocking and utterly predictable." For them it was shocking not because of the human devastation or the millions of families who were cheated and face foreclosure or because of the rippling effects on our society, but because the "best minds in the business...managed to lose tens of billions."

And "predictable?" Again, not due to the lack of regulation or the enabling of shoddy products by government but "because whether it's junk bonds or tech stocks or emerging-market debt, Wall Street always rides a wave until it crashes."

This is the "what did you expect, anyway" argument, a way of making it all seem so unavoidable, as if this type of disaster is embedded in the DNA of Wall Street. What a contrast to the usual celebratory financial coverage, but also what a cop-out. (*Fortune* had praised Enron, later it exposed its practices.)

Many news outlets then became more concerned about how investors in these bonds, and the other banks which bought them as highly rated securities, were ripped off than what this has meant for the real victims facing foreclosure, who, as of May 2008 have yet to receive real relief.

Were crimes committed? The government agencies that should have been paying attention weren't. But, at last, in that same month of May, government agencies announced they had begun a criminal investigation that went beyond an FBI probe announced earlier into relatively minor local practieces by brokers. Reported the *New York Times*,

> The F.B.I. and the I.R.S. are said to be investigating whether some mortgage lenders turned a blind eye when prospective borrowers used inflated income figures.
>
> The latest inquiry is broader and deeper than a separate F.B.I. investigation of mortgage lenders that is also under way.
>
> While the new task force is focusing on the role of mortgage lenders and brokers in low- or no-documentation loans, it is also examining how the loans were bundled into securities.

"This is a look at the mortgage industry across the board, and it has gotten a lot more momentum in recent weeks because of the banks' earnings shortfalls," the official said.

Countrywide Financial was at the center of the probe, reported the Housing Panic blog:

In March, the Justice Department and the F.B.I. began investigating whether the Countrywide Financial Corporation, the troubled mortgage giant, misrepresented its financial condition and loans in filings with the Securities and Exchange Commission. Countrywide is also under scrutiny by California and Illinois; federal prosecutors in Sacramento; and the United States Trustee, the federal agency that monitors bankruptcy courts. The S.E.C., meanwhile, is examining stock sales by certain Countrywide executives.

And as the investigations continue, the patriarchs of the industry sought to distance themselves from the disgrace. Alan Greenspan now blames criminal fraudsters for engineering the crisis. Veteran investor Henry Kauffman says Greenspan and the Fed are at fault.

And Warren Buffet, perhaps America's most successful investor, is just disgusted:

"Wall Street is going to go where the money is and not worry about consequences," he told a press conference a day after his Berkshire Hathaway Inc.'s annual meeting. "You've got a lot of leeway in running a bank to not tell the truth for quite a while."

"Both the regulators and the accountants have failed the rest of us terribly," said Berkshire's vice chairman. "If this were an Alice in Wonderland fable, you'd say it's too extreme. It wouldn't work as satire. Adults are not going to behave this way."

But adults did – and continue to. So far, they have also been well rewarded.

In England, Roger Bootle, writing for the *Telegraph*, was polite but contemptuous and colorful in excoriating bank executives:

The silence about the corporate behavior which led us to this pretty pass is scandalous. Come off it boys, you were sucked into a bubble of the classic sort. You were persuaded to believe that nothing could go wrong. Yet any study of financial history would have set the alarm bells ringing. But do you ever read any? To his great credit, the Governor of the Bank of England warned explicitly and publicly of the risks. But did you listen? Outside commentators and analysts, and even, in some cases, your own in-house experts, pointed out the over-valuation of property. But did you pay any attention?

We cannot go on like this. There are all sorts of ways in which banks must be restrained and regulated to be better behaved in future, including with regard to their remuneration packages. But the structure and behaviour of boards and banks' procedures for assessing risk should also be an important part of this reform.

He suggested replacing risk assessment specialists with historians.

Homeowners who sued mortgage companies claimed that local courts were bought off or biased against them. Jack Wright of Dallas, Texas, accused the EMC Mortgage Company of stealing his home and wrote about it on one of thousands of websites used by allegedly victimized individuals to advertise their plight:

> In April 1997, I was alleged to be in default on my mortgage and the mortgage company, claiming to be the true party in interest (the owner/holder), was going to foreclose.
>
> I was not in default and had all the documents to prove it. After one year of the mortgage company's refusal to correct their accounting errors, I was forced to file a lawsuit to protect my home from an illegal foreclosure.
>
> For the next seven (7) years (costing me more than $2 million in legal expenses and lost wages), I watched the court[s] repeatedly grant judgments in favor of the mortgage companies. These errant judgments were granted without either mortgage company presenting a scintilla of evidence to support their allegations and in stark contrast to my preponderance of evidence and material facts.

Some of the firms engaged in shady practices got caught. Ameriquest was fined six million dollars by arbitrators for using "boiler room tactics." UPI reported that "the company was accused of fabricating data, fabricating documents and hiding fees... The arbitrator was outraged at the lender's disregard for the borrower's right (1) to be free from physical intrusion into the home and (2) to be represented by counsel." In 2007, Ameriquest, which advertised its services in pricey TV ads, went out of business.

Two mortgage professionals who run the Mortgage Porter website tell of other stories of families who don't know the laws or their rights and act too late:

Believe it or not, when applied correctly, subprime mortgages could mean the difference of someone being able to save their home assuming they were able to be disciplined enough to keep (or get) their finances healthy. This family will not qualify for FHA or FHASecure (they don't have an ARM that's adjusted). What they need is a subprime (now known as "non-prime") mortgage to buy them a little time. Now their time is running out.

Part of their problem began with working with an unsavory loan originator who is now out of the business. The LO brokered their loan to a subprime company I would not work with. (Even though we're approved with around 80 lenders, give or take depending on the day, I tend to select 5 preferred prime lenders and 3-5 a/alt-a... this lender was not on my list of preferred).

Shortly after closing, their lender informed them that they did not have homeowners insurance... they did. They provided documentation showing their insurance to the lender. The lender did not respond and instead, ordered insurance for them at a hefty price...jacking up their payment beyond what they can afford. Now they're sliding down a very slippery slope and the lender is not cooperating. They are behind on their mortgage a couple months. They called out for help too late.

In some cases, higher income families were also victimized. These are people who don't qualify for conventional financing. They fell below the 620-660 credit score threshold generally needed for prime financing and require less-stringent income documentation. Taken together, however, subprime lending for years was the fastest growing market. Realtor associations held industry conferences calling "subprime their hottest segment." (By 2008, some high-priced "McMansions" began going into default.)

"Hot" it was. The fever was contagious, linking Main Street with Wall Street, stretching a financial umbilical chord to connect the demise of the poorest neighborhoods in America to the affluence of the richest. It was as if they the lenders were all making too much money to reflect on the ethics, legality, and sustainability of their operations.

As writer Michael Panzer explained on the Financial Armageddon web site: "No matter where they came from, what language they spoke, or whose money they were looking after, they all had one thing in common: they had lined up to buy products they didn't understand, offering returns that made no sense, from middlemen who couldn't care less about what they were selling."

And of course some of the borrowers were complicit in these frauds, finding ways to get financing and then turn their homes into ATM Machines as residents tapped equity to pay bills or even finding more properties to buy at a low cost and then "flipping" them at a profit only to buy more properties and do it again. Many mortgage services have also been indicted for committing fraud in the way they handled home equity loans.

In some cases, homeowners have sued banks for failures to make legally mandated disclosures. All too often these suits are filed too late and the courts dismiss them without deciding on the bank's culpability. Legal procedural rule seem to take precedence over truth in lending.

Some homeowners spend years financing and refinancing to try to stay in their homes but ultimately fail. There were many stories of this type of abuse in the press but few of them connected them to the practices of Wall Street institutions.

In one such story in 2004, *USA Today* told the sad story of a borrower, Martha Lawler of Brooklyn, New York:

> Martha Lawler stands outside the Brooklyn property she nearly lost after falling behind on her payments and refinancing into a mortgage with an 18.25% rate.
>
> Desperate to hang on to her Brooklyn, N.Y., home, Lawler, 55, took out a new mortgage with a local finance company that carried an 18.25% interest rate, big fees that were rolled into her balance and a "balloon" payoff due in five years. Unable to make the higher monthly payments, Lawler refinanced into what she thought was a more affordable loan.
>
> The pattern continued through six lenders, 10 years and thousands of dollars of dubious charges that eroded her home equity and pushed her mortgage balance from $50,000 to $198,000.
>
> "For 10 years I've been going in a circle, robbing Peter to pay Paul, trying to keep this mortgage up," Lawler said. "No fly clothes. No new car. My mortgage is my life."

The focus of this press report was on unscrupulous brokers, not the legitimate bankers who her loans were sold to. The mortgages themselves were designed to trap owners. The journalists didn't seem aware that the brokers and originators knew they were flawed, and understood the suffering they would cause, as Bruce Marks, the CEO of the Neighborhood Assistance Corporation of American explained to me:

"Never in our history have millions of homeowners been on the verge of foreclosure, not because they lost their jobs, not because of a personal crisis, not because of life circumstances, but because the mortgage is pushing them into foreclosure. Never has it happened before that people have the same income, the same jobs, but are losing their homes."

Few of the victims realize that there was a chain of other players also targeting them, and profiting off them. The *Charleston* (West Virginia) *Observer* investigated how that works in a major series, but only after this process had been underway for years. The newspaper carried a flow chart showing how predators work.

TARGET: Low Income, elderly and minority people, people with bad credit.

Arrow to:

LOAN ORIGNATOR: Contacts targets, tries to persuade them to sign. No special training required but must not have bad credit or criminal record.

Arrow to:

BROKER: Arranges loan between target and lender; receives fees and percentages from loan proceeds for arranging loans. Anyone can open an office but the manager must have two years experience.

Arrow to

APPRAISER: 850 West Virgina licensed appraisers are willing to inflate appraisals, Mortgage attorneys say. It's a problem nationwide, according to the American Society of Appraisers.

Arrow to

LENDER: No experence required. They may "bundle" new loans and sell the bundle to nigger institutions. Nobody is sure how many lenders operate in West Virgins. State cannot regulate many of them.

Arrow to:

WALL STREET AND INTERNATONAL BANKS

Millions of loan bundles are redistributed into pools to back up investments worldwide

Of course, most borrowers have no idea of the existence of this larger interconnected network or how organized and relentless it is.

They didn't know how Wall Street was often sitting on top of it, in the "catbird seat," pressuring brokers to turn over more loans. They didn't know about the "suction" of Wall Street.

The *Wall Street Journal* reported:

Lou Barnes, co-owner of a small Colorado mortgage bank called Boulder West Inc., has been in the mortgage business since the late 1970s. For most of that time, a borrower had to fully document his income. Lenders offered the first no-documentation loans in the mid-1990s, but for no more than 70% of the value of the house being purchased. A few years back, he says, that began to change as Wall Street investment banks and wholesalers demanded ever more mortgages from even the least creditworthy — or 'subprime' — customers.

"All of us felt the suction from Wall Street. One day you would get an email saying, 'We will buy no-doc loans at 95% loan-to-value,' and an old-timer like me had never seen one,' says Mr. Barnes. 'It wasn't long before the no-doc emails said 100%.'"

We never read many media accounts like this of local businessmen blaming Wall Street for orchestrating this scam. Could these practices have been stopped? Of course, if there were real regulators and rules protecting consumers and the public interest.

And, perhaps also, if there was a social movement that championed economic justice. Alen S. Gabor, another citizen-journalist, claims these practices were permitted by the negligence of the Securities and Exchange Commission:

Their negligence has perpetuated the largest Ponzi scheme ever invented by man. It is run by Fannie and Freddie while Washington Mutual, Countrywide and the ten largest banks in the world are all bit players next to the Wall Street underwriters who float bonds backed by fishy mortgage deals originated by even sketchier mortgage brokers."

Taken together, these practices reveal a pattern that was ignored even as they caused enormous harm to our society, as yet another homeowner, Dawn Sears explained on a financial website expressing deep anger and frustration:

This Market was a House Of Cards, that has now collapsed. It is a Real Storm of the Century. It will not be over any time soon either. The rise of foreclosures in the United States is astounding. It is a devastating blow to our People, Economy, and Way of Life.

Our traditions are out the window. Many people are forced to live in such a way that reflects nothing of their personality, or themselves. People of all walks of life are losing their homes; their credit is being destroyed as we speak. Every Business is being affected in Trickle Down patter. People are fearful to spend money, they are trying to refinance and can't. All guidelines have become so strict that the majority of the general public does not qualify for a Home Mortgage.

Some areas have been more hard hit than others. Leslie Schwab wrote on the Helium website:

I live in South Florida, an area which has been especially hard-hit by the sub-prime market... I am seeing more new housing developments with unsold homes. Many sub-prime lenders have gone out of business, and other lenders have made borrowing much more difficult even for those with good credit. The only good news is that sub-prime lenders aren't bothering me any more!

Here's another story by Michael D. Larson of Bankrate.com:

Are predatory lenders really that big of a threat? Helen Ferguson thinks so. After all, the 78-year old widow almost lost her home.

"I thought I could handle things myself," Ferguson says. "I saw these people on the TV and read the newspaper and they were so kind and good, so I thought."

But according to court documents, a mortgage company she dealt with flipped her loan repeatedly over the course of several years, charging more than $30,000 in fees. Because the transactions were done in such a way that Ferguson couldn't possibly make her loan payments, advocates charge, she almost lost the Washington, D.C. home she's lived in since 1965.

"They worked with me pretty good — until things got out of hand," Ferguson says. "Oh, I was almost drowning and I didn't know what to do."

These are just some of the "little people" targeted by predators who "didn't know what to do." Their stories are at last being told. But the people and institutions behind these scams have yet to tell theirs.

Beyond targeting individuals, these firms worked together to securitize and pool mortgage paper with the connivance of ratings agencies to pass this off as valuable "asset backed commercial paper." Some investors, including banks, believed in the integrity of these questionable transactions. Others knowingly became part of these complex financial schemes, without recognizing the risks or understanding the social impact of practices that are a sophisticated form of theft. These practices have imploded in many institutions, sinking their own balance sheets and leading to layoffs. Writes Pam Martens on the ongoing crash of Citibank:

> The saga of how the top minds in Washington and on Wall Street have dealt with the deepening financial crisis in the U.S. would make a great Hollywood screenplay, except for this: it's absurdly unbelievable.
>
> Storyline: The largest bank in the United States (by assets), Citigroup, is discovered to have stashed away over $80 Billion of Byzantine securities off its balance sheet in secretive Cayman Islands vehicles with an impenetrable curtain around them. Citigroup calls this black hole a Structured Investment Vehicle or SIV. Wall Street insiders call it a "sieve" that is linked to the breakdown in trading of debt instruments around the globe and the erosion of wealth in assets as diverse as stock prices to home values. Additionally, tens of billions of dollars in short-term commercial paper backed by these and similar Alice in Wonderland assets are sitting in Mom and Pop money market funds at the largest financial institutions in America, with a AAA rating from our renown credit rating agencies.
>
> Setting: Picture the Titanic shortly after it crashed into the iceberg. Imagine that its officers want to pretend to all its passengers and crew and investors that there is no serious damage because the giant floating Citi did not really hit an iceberg; it just hit a wall of worry.

Should there be an investigation into the forces behind this crisis? Where is the special prosecutor? Where is the Watergate-style Congressional probe?

Where are the prosecutors?

Couldn't indictments be drawn up to prosecute those implicated in this broader disgrace just as Enron and WorldCom executives were finally brought to justice for "their crimes and misdemeanors" that were actually felonies?

Just asking.

TYPICAL PREDATORY PRACTICES

HERE ARE JUST A FEW OF THE PREDATORY LENDING PRACTICES AS documented by a research and advocacy organization in *Alternative Currents*, October 2000:

Pricing and terms, whether interest rates or fees that far exceed the true risk and cost of making the loan.

Targeting persons who are perceived to be less financially sophisticated or otherwise vulnerable to abusive loan practices.

Inadequate disclosure of the true costs and risks of loan transactions.

Loan terms and structures, such as negative amortization, designed to make it more difficult or impossible for borrowers to reduce their indebtedness.

Aggressive marketing tactics that amount to deceptive or coercive conduct.

Padding/Packing – charging customers unearned, concealed, or unwarranted fees.

Flipping – frequent and multiple refinancings, usually of mortgage loans, requiring additional fees that strip equity from the borrower.

Collection of up-front single-premium credit insurance – life, disability, or unemployment, when the consumer does not receive a net tangible financial benefit.

One-way referrals, i.e., a prime lender refers subprime applicants to its subprime subsidiary but the subprime subsidiary does not refer prime applicants to the prime lender.

Significant differences in the proportion of minority or female applicants between a prime lender and its subprime subsidiary.

Significant differences in the proportion of loans made in predominantly minority geographic areas between a prime lender and its subprime subsidiary.

Home Improvement Scams in which the service provided is worth far less than the mortgage taken.

Mandatory Arbitration Clauses that obstruct legal remedies.

Spurious Open End Mortgages that add other financing onto the home mortgage.

Paying Off Low Interest Mortgages with low monthly payment, high interest loans.

Shifting unsecured debt into mortgages.

Making Loans in Excess of 100% Loan to Value (LTV).

Force placed insurance that adds to borrower's cost when insurance lapses.

Source: NEDAP – New York's Community Economic Justice Resource Center

WILL SHOPPING SAVE US?

THE EASY AVAILABILITY OF CREDIT HAS CREATED WHAT ROBERT Manning calls our Credit Card Nation, where we are encouraged to shop until we drop. In the aftermath of the terror attacks of September 11, 2001, President Bush made that point shamelessly when he told the American people that the best way to help in that traumatic period was to go shopping again. He knew, even if most Americans didn't, that it is their non-stop consumption that drives the economy. Without it, I guess, the terrorists could have won.

"In fact," Robert Manning writes in his seminal book on credit cards, "with the ascendance of the post-industrial economy, bank credit cards have become an essential technological and financial tool for commercial transactions as well as an increasingly important macro-economic tool for U.S. policy-makers."

Shopping is our real national pastime, but it comes, as he warns, at a price that is not advertised in the malls:

> The idyllic wonderland of consumer credit too often belies a reality of unknown sacrifices and enduring debt... the credit card industry is playing a crucial role in transforming American consumer attitudes. The promotion of "immediate gratification" ruptures the cognitive connection between earnings/saving and credit/debt that has traditionally shaped consumer behavior. It is this "cognitive disconnect," with its siren song "Buy, buy, buy. It could be free, free, free" that constitutes the cornerstone of the Credit Card Nation.

And so it is not surprising that holidays are used or created as national events to spur consumption. They have become rituals of shopping. None is as important as the first day after Thanksgiving, itself a day set aside for overindulgence at the kitchen table. That day now has a name, Black Friday, so called because it is supposed to be the day when the whole retail sector goes into the black financially. (This may not have been such a wise use of language since the Wall Street crash of 1929, ushering in the Great Depression, started on a "Black Thursday.")

After months of financial volatility, Black Friday of 2007 was seen as a make-or-break event. Would it send a cathartic and upbeat signal that the economy was back? Shoppers had been tasked to launch the Holiday season with a big bang.

On Wall Street, buyers jumped the gun, sending prices higher with their hopes. AP reported, stocks rebounded as investors engaged in a bit of Black Friday bargain hunting and looked for signs of how well retailers might fare during the holiday shopping season. The market was voting its own money.

In the malls, preparations had been made for five months with advertising dollars set aside for promoting sales and deep discounts to lure the shoppers who had almost been boycotting the stores in September and October. Ingenious plans for opening earlier and staging "midnight madness" sales to trigger a stampede were put in place.

The hype machine went into overdrive with TV ads having the expected effect of getting TV News, especially in local markets, actively building anticipation.

I was watching local news stories in Boston, featuring perky local news "correspondents" who were stirring a buying frenzy with upbeat reports on manic consumers waiting feverishly to rush into malls the night before. It was, in the words of Reverend Billy of the Church of Stop Shopping, a "shopopocalyse." His crusade against out-of-control consumption is pictured in the new film *What Would Jesus Buy?*

This highly relevant film was not on TV, of course, because our media is deeply complicit in promoting/encouraging mindless consumerism through newspapers, commercials, and on newscasts.

This is a well-practiced formula mirroring TV's promotion of the war in Iraq, as the line between selling and telling disappears. Media outlets are amply rewarded with endless ad revenues hyping all the discounted goodies you can get, with the *Boston Globe* packing no less than 43 advertising/sales supplements (down from 47 a year ago) into a paper that had wall-to-wall Macy's ads, including some offering $10 coupons to bribe you into the stores. Marketing like this is what the media does best.

The only negative note was the fear among some that toys might be unsafe because of lead or other dangers. Some 26 million toys, most made in China, had been recalled in 2007, a sign that the regulators were asleep on this front in the economic wars as they were on Wall Street.

The real danger may not be lead in the toys but another type of lead – in our heads. It's that "lead" that leads to denial on the part of millions that we can go on with our addictive, well-cultivated crazed consumption habits.

Bill Bowles writes about this on his CNI Blog:

The problem is that many of us have been force-fed with a diet of nothing but passive, uncritical consumptionism, indeed, we are addicted to the stuff; breaking such powerful habits is what this is all about; it's about getting people to think critically again about what's going on and why and what, if anything, we can do about it.

Bowles also ties this cultural affliction, sometimes known as affluenza, back to our dependence on a media system that won't really allow other voices to be heard.

It would be an understatement to say that the world has changed almost beyond recognition in the past two decades, we appear to have re-entered the age of the dinosaur, gigantic creatures stomping across the planet, "guided" by pea-sized brains. So ... we have increasing concentrations of powerful media – media that is actually an entire raft of processes critical to the survival of capitalism – either in the hands of vast corporations or the state (which in any case is now openly in bed with the big corporations)...

Were most media outlets connecting any dots between the annual shopathon and the "severe recession" that many economists are forecasting? Were there any warnings to the public to save their rapidly inflating money for the expected hard times? Was there any explanation of how prices have sharply risen and, thus, the discounts – often "teaser" rates just like the ones offered loan victims – are really not all they are cracked up to be?

No way.

What about the larger trends? Yes, there has been reporting on how bad things are – but this reality was largely NOT depicted in the "shop now, be happy" coverage. This euphoria was deliberate and deceptive. The *Boston Globe* did run a story in the B Section where the business news is buried. At the very end of the AP report (not theirs) you read this:

> Last year, retailers had a good start during the Thanksgiving weekend, but many stores struggled in December and a shopping surge just before and after Christmas wasn't enough to make up for lost sales. This year, analysts expect sales gains to be the weakest in five years. Washington-based National Retail Federation predicted that total holiday sales would be up 4 percent for the combined November and December period, the slowest growth since a 1.3 percent rise in 2002.
>
> Holiday sales rose 4.6 percent in 2006 and growth has averaged 4.8 percent over the last decade.

Where were the stories alerting us to this coming calamity on the front pages? They weren't there. It is not in their interest to carry them, clearly a big No No. It gets worse. MTV pointedly rejected an ad from the Cultural Jammers Network urging a Buy Nothing Day. Commented one blogger, "The station that markets itself as the voice of hip youth has censored the burping pig."

But why? Their advertising standards representative, Elisa Billis, said, "The spot goes further than we are willing to accept on our channels." Too radical for self-styled "hip" MTV, which routinely carries military recruiting ads with no qualms.

The *Boston Globe* did carry a cartoon lampooning local sports mania in a town with winning teams. In its last panel, set in a mortgage office, a fan is being told he will be able to pay off his Red Sox/Celtics/Patriots tickets in just a few decades.

Many of the shoppers this season are charging it even though all the credit card companies have jacked up rates, driving the real cost of shopping higher, and even though credit balances are at an all-time high. The companies are just waiting for them. The day after Christmas, VISA will report on how much business was done. In years past, they called it "disappointing."

And then in January, the returns — consumers bringing back purchases and gifts — will start as the bills come due. Experts — including former Treasury Secretary Larry Summers — are warning that the credit card system itself may be the next to fall.

Writes economist Robert Samuelson:

> "The specter of the subprime debacle is that it's just a start. Huge amounts of auto loans, credit-card debt, commercial mortgages

and equipment leases have also been securitized. If similar problems emerged, it would shake confidence in the securitization model and, by magnifying investors' losses, threaten to turn the credit crunch from a slogan into a reality. A broader crisis, though a long shot, can't be excluded.

Thanksgiving this year fell on the anniversary of the John F. Kennedy assassination. The *New York Times* predictably marked the event with one more op-ed article – one in a long line – assuring us that there was no conspiracy. (Even as 80% of the public continues to believe that Lee Harvey Oswald did not act alone.) In some ways obsessive debt-creating consumption patterns are a form of self-assassination as a nation of shoppers shoots holes in their financial futures.

While they discredit suggestions of a past conspiracy, they seem to be ignoring a current one. That involves the steady decline of our economy, thanks to illegal practices through white-collar predatory lenders backed by our biggest banks and hedge funds, as well as the inability of regulators to regulate, and a complicit media to blow the whistle, which caused a multi-billion dollar economic crime that is still in progress.

So what happened? Was the day the big success we were told it would be by the media's relentles upbeat coverage? In a culture where perception itself is carefully managed, Black Friday didn't appear to be dark at all. On Friday night, after a day of boosterism disguised as journalism, retailers and media promoters were, like President Bush in Iraq, proclaiming victory – "mission accomplished."

Not so fast.

Yes, Black Friday showed better results than expected, but the retail industry afterward said it still expected a weak Christmas. Remember, the stores were open longer than ever and the advertising/hype was more pervasive. Also. the discounting was deeper and the bargains more extensive. We know that the sales were up, but what about the returns and expected credit card defaults?

The *New York Times* sent reporters into the stores and found "desperation rather than celebration." By Monday, Wall Street was glum, according to Fox News: "So much for a 'Black Friday' bounce for Wall Street. Instead, negative market sentiment and another ugly day for financial stocks sent the Dow plunging 237 points lower."

And what about consumer sentiment? Robert Manning did a survey of consumer attitudes, concluding:

The signs of "belt-tightening" are clearly evidenced by the data.... Together with the less than expected level of holiday expenditures by the wealthiest households, the data suggests a generalized sentiment of consumer financial anxiety across all income and wealth groups at the end of 2007.

This portends a moderate decline in winter holiday expenditures as the strained but persistent purchasing expectations of the lower income households are balanced by the more restrained purchasing plans of the highest income households. Clearly, the winter holiday shopping season will need a much more enthusiastic response from higher income households if it is to exceed the modest forecasts of many retailing analysts.

The Associated Press reported that most of the Black Friday shopping was "mission-oriented:"

The signs were encouraging, but stores are now wondering whether bargain hunters will keep up the pace as they face an escalating credit crunch, depreciating home values and rising daily living expenses.

Frederick Crawford, managing director at AlixPartners, a turnaround consulting company, said that amid economic challenges, people are buying fewer gifts. "Clearly, it was mission-based shopping," Crawford said. "People had their list, and they were very specific in what they were looking for."

Lurking in the background — and in the foreground for many shoppers — is anxiety about the deepening economic crisis. (A later study in April 2008 by Robert Manning found four out of ten Americans postponing life decisions because of uncertainty about the economy.)

Explained Manning: "The self-reported delays and expected reduction in U.S. household consumption appears to reflect a perception of deteriorating personal and general economic conditions driven by a negative 'wealth effect' following declining housing prices and the escalating cost of energy supplies. Furthermore, American households' sense of financial well-being is now being influenced by the falling U.S. stock market as financial losses by major banks and investment houses begin to spill-over into personal investment and retirement portfolios."

So even the malls were not immune from the meltdowns in the markets.

THE SECRET LANGUAGE OF FINANCE

THERE IS A SECRET INTERNAL LANGUAGE INVOLVED IN THIS SCANDAL, which most experts and most journalists don't have the tools to comprehend, much less explain. At the risk of contributing to the MEGO (My Eyes Glaze Over) EFFECT that we in TV News were taught to avoid in all our stories, let me cite one such paragraph from Nouriel Roubini's financial blog – RGE Monitor – explaining what was happening on Wall Street one day in August.

> First, you take a bunch of shaky and risky subprime mortgages and repackage them into residential mortgage backed securities (RMBS); then you repackage these RMBS in different (equity, mezzanine, senior) tranches of cash CDOs that receive a misleading investment grade rating by the credit rating agencies; then you create synthetic CDOs out of the same underlying RMBS; then you create CDOs of CDOs (or squared CDOs) out of these CDOs; and then you create CDOs of CDOs of CDOs (or cubed CDOs) out of the same murky securities; then you stuff some of these RMBS and CDO tranches into SIV (structured investment vehicles) or into ABCP (Asset Backed Commercial Paper) or into money market funds. Then no wonder that eventually people panic and run – as they did yesterday – on an apparently "safe" money market fund such as Sentinel. That "toxic waste" of unpriceable and uncertain junk and zombie corpses is now emerging in the most unlikely places in the financial markets.

If you found your mind drifting in reading that, you are not alone. Sometimes words and nicknames are chosen only to be understood by insiders, whether in finance or in the military.

Below are just some of the terms I needed help understanding and found in just two articles I consulted. There are so many more. Is it any wonder that most of the public turns away from this type of dense language and often esoteric references? Only the real players and financial insiders understand these terms.

Perhaps that's why one investment banker was quoted as saying that "playing the market without being a specialist is like a farmer buying a cow at midnight on a dark night." Writer Lewis Lapham drew parallels between some of these acronyms and the language used to obscure the war in Iraq in *Harpers* in November 2007.

Here's an incomplete list of terms that initially puzzled me:

- Repackaged loans
- Subprime loans
- "No-doc" loans
- Adjustable rate mortgage (ARM) loans
- Asset-backed securities
- Mortgage-backed securities
- Closed-end second-lien loans
- Subprime second-lien loans
- Alternative-A mortgage loans
- Piggyback loans
– Asset-backed commercial paper (ABCP)
- CDO – collateralized debt obligations
- Cubed CDOs
- Speculators
- Arbitrage
- Leverage
- The rise in credit derivatives
- Regulatory
- Oversight SEC
- Investor
- Investment Bank
- Investment Broker
- Transparent
- Pension Funds
- CD
- U.S. Treasury bonds
- Financial Instruments
- AAA+ Ratings
- Rating Services
- BBB
- A pool of risky mortgage loans

- Slices
- Culpability
- Tranches
- 25 standard deviation events
- Asset bubbles
- The opacity of financial markets
- Fat tail events
- LTCM debacle
- Hedge Funds
- Delinquencies
- Near prime and prime lenders
- Mis-rating of new instruments
- SIV (structured investment vehicles)
- Residential mortgage-backed securities (RMBS)
- A Minsky Moment

Oh yes, what can all this add up to?

Translation please: Back to a sum-up from economist Nouriel Roubini:

> So combine an opaque and unregulated global financial system where moderate levels of leverage by individual investors pile up into leverage ratios of 100 plus; and add to this toxic mix investments in the most uncertain, obscure, misrated, mispriced, complex, esoteric credit derivatives (CDOs of CDOs of CDOs and the entire other alphabet of credit instruments) that no investor can properly price; then you have created a financial monster that eventually leads to uncertainty, panic, market seizure, liquidity crunch, credit crunch, systemic risk and economic hard landing.

There you have it, a "monster."

HOW DID WE MISS THE SIGNS OF AN IMPENDING CRISIS?

THAT QUESTION. AGAIN? IT WAS ASKED ABOUT 9/11 IN CONNECTION with the U.S. government ignoring warning after warning about likely terrorist attacks. The CIA raised it again about its own ostrich-like behavior in the run-up to the war on Iraq.

Now it's being asked by the *New York Times* about the failure to anticipate and potentially pre-empt the subprime mortgage crisis, which has escalated into a deeper meltdown in global financial markets leading to layoffs and serious fall-off in economic growth.

Did this "just happen," like a hurricane appearing one morning out of blue skies?

Of course not! The signs were there for all who wanted to see them, and warnings were plentiful even as they were ignored. It's odd how on the front page of its widely read Sunday edition, the "newspaper of record" could splash a story on how the media and the markets looked the other way as massive deals were being financed by securities cobbled together from subprime loans backed with no assets. Why were the signs missed, asked the *Times*? Unlike the CIA, the *Times* did not assess its own reporting and its role in all of this. A few days later, the newspaper's business columnist showed that, in fact, many did know and tried to raise the alarm.

This revelation seems to be an example of the front pages not knowing what the business pages had reported. The *Times* columnist reminded readers that Ben Bernanke, Chairman of the Federal Reserve Bank who had just pumped billions of dollars in the markets to keep them liquid and then followed up with a cut in the discount rate, was asked about these issues two years earlier:

> It came in November 2005, toward the end of his all-day Senate confirmation hearing, when Senator Paul Sarbanes brought up the mortgage business.
>
> Mr. Sarbanes, the ranking Democrat on the Banking Committee then, pointed out that the number of people taking out adjustable-rate mortgages soared in 2004. "Are you concerned about the potential for a bubble in the housing market?" the senator asked Mr. Bernanke. "And specifically, does the drastic increase in the use of risky financing schemes, including interest-only and even negative amortization mortgages, concern you?"
>
> Mr. Bernanke replied that the Fed was reviewing its guidelines for

these loans and planned to issue new ones soon. The guidelines, he added, "would have on the margin some beneficial effects in reducing speculative activity in some local markets." At no point, though, did Mr. Bernanke suggest that he was concerned.

And what about the larger media? Where was their concern? Back in the spring of 2006, I published an article in *Nieman Reports*, the journalism review published at Harvard and read by top editors. I specifically lambasted the lack of reporting on the issue. It was titled "Investigating the Nation's Exploding Credit Squeeze."

Its thesis: Questions of and by whom and for whom need more and better investigation, as well as a look at who are the losers and who are the winners.

The article in a magazine widely read by newspaper editors suggested some concrete approaches media outlets could take based on my own experience inside big media organizations:

• Report more regularly on these credit issues; billions of dollars are involved, not to mention millions of lives.

• Identify the key corporate institutions and contrast the compensation of their executives with the financial circumstances of their customers.

• Shine a spotlight on how special interests and lobbyists for financial institutions contribute to members of Congress and other politicians, across party lines, to ensure their desired policies and regulations. Investigate political influence affected by campaign contributions. Some reporting about this took place during the bankruptcy debate, but there has been little follow-up.

• Examine the influence credit card companies have on media companies through their extensive advertising.

• Take a hard look at the predatory practices in poor neighborhoods – and crimes committed against poor and working class people, who are least able to defend themselves. Legal service lawyers tell me that they are overwhelmed by the scale of mortgage scams involving homes whose value have been artificially inflated.

• Focus attention on what consumers can do to fight back. Robert Manning, author of *Credit Card Nation,* explains: "If ten percent of American credit cardholders withheld their monthly payments, it would bring the financial services industry to a standstill. At a larger issue, what we have to do is to get people involved at the state level, get their state attorney generals involved, aggressively filing class action lawsuits and then putting pressure on key legislators to say, 'This is unacceptable that they're not representing and balancing the issues of commerce with consumers. The balance is tilted dramatically against the average American.'

The response was tepid. I followed up by organizing a Media For Democracy online e-mail campaign. (Media For Democracy is an advocacy effort tied to Mediachannel.org, the media issues website I edit.) Media For Democracy members sent tens of thousand of requests to media outlets urging that the issue be given more coverage. This was well before the market meltdown. The appeal read in part:

> We are dismayed by the superficial reporting we have seen on the debt crisis in America. The press has been asleep at the switch in reporting on this story, often showing more compassion for wealthy businessmen than abused consumers.

> We believe that our media outlets have a responsibility to offer more context, background and information about how this debt crisis occurred and what we can do about it.

What was the media's response?

Not much. Most responses came in the form of yada-yada-yada form letters as in "Thank You For Writing to the Today Show." Responding to public concerns and suggestions are not high on the media agenda.

The media has still not given us a reason for burying the story. It's hard not to wonder if their disinterest has something to do with advertising. Mortgage lenders have spent more than $3 billion on TV advertising, radio, and print since 2000. Much of it is deceptive and misleading, say experts – the industry denies it – yet media outlets have not challenged their accuracy.

Is it any surprise that this industry has received so little scrutiny from another industry benefiting by its largesse? Eventually, on the Iraq War, some media outlets admitted they practiced poor journalism even as many of their mea-culpas did not basically change their narratives. Why not on this issue? The only media controversy I saw revolved around whether Jim Cramer of CNBC and TheStreet.com was right to demand that the Federal Reserve Bank cut interest rates. His TV commentary on the issue was a screaming rant, the type of approach he takes on his TV show *Mad Money*. The commentary later had more than a million views on YouTube.com.

When the Fed later did cut its discount rate, Cramer claimed credit but then, later in the same broadcast, had second thoughts, admitting that the Bank did not follow his advice. Cramer has yet to scream about justice for those tricked into signing up for subprime loans. (When the iTulip.com website, which critiques shallow financial journalism, mocked the Cramer commentary, Cramer's TheStreet.com went berserk, demanding that You Tube take it down and threatened to sue. It appears that this TV bully and critic is really very thin-skinned when he is criticized.) To be fair to Cramer, he can be a very astute critic as he is in the pages of *Lapham's Quarterly* where he denounces "the damn bankerman who broke us. No, there won't be a police officer to investigate, and the government, at least this federal government won't save us.... Get ready, many more dollars will soon vanish before you discover you've been robbed."

Other media critics have been scathing about the dereliction of duty that is so obvious here. Dean Starkman of the *Columbia Journalism Review* was contemptuous: "What's wrong? Why ask us? This kind of after-the-fact financial reporting I equate with a National Transportation Safety Board investigation — kicking through smoldering wreckage after the plane has already crashed. There's nothing intrinsically wrong with this kind of reporting. It just feels a little late. Also, I always find it disinguous to talk about napping watchdogs, as in the headline above, when the Journal and the rest of the business press themselves slept on the job and had to scramble to catch up to the corporate scandals earlier in the decade."

The problem with media coverage of business and economics is not just spin or bias. Some of the reporting is quite good. What is often missing are the references to deeper structural problems that lead to economic pain and disparities.

Ongoing reporting gravitates toward offering the most upbeat interpretations of government reports, almost as if they have been spun.

Consider this story carried by the Associated Press and run in the *New York Times* on February 7, 2008:

After years of denial and spin about the financial condition of U.S. households and consumers, you might think the newswires and salesmen on cable would be buzzing with the key findings in Wednesday's Bureau of Labor Statistics report on U.S. hours worked, real compensation, output and productivity. You would be wrong.

Or this story with the headline, "Productivity Growth Slows and the Costs of Labor Rise," ran in the *New York Times* the same day:

Worker productivity, a crucial factor in rising living standards, slowed sharply in the last quarter of 2007 while wage pressure increased.

The Labor Department reported Wednesday that productivity, the amount of output for each hour of work, increased at an annual pace of 1.8 percent from October through December, down from a 6 percent pace in the July-September period. The slowdown reflected an overall weakening in economic activity.

Labor costs rose by 2.1 percent, after having fallen by 1.9 percent in the third quarter and 1.1 percent in the second quarter.

Charles McMillion analyzed this story for the Campaign for America's Future.

This is a very clear example of how the media spin the news every day to hide economic troubles and mislead those who believe they are following economic conditions. All the major media spun this story in almost exactly the same way as the AP, with the key findings either not mentioned at all or they are relegated to an afterthought as space permits.

The key finding in that report is that the total number of hours worked (and paid) in non-farm businesses during the fourth quarter of 2007 fell at an annual rate of 1.5 percent. Indeed, the total number of hours worked in the fourth quarter was less than in the fourth quarter of 2006. The report shows total non-farm jobs also falling at a 0.5 percent annualized rate in Q4 and rising by only 0.4 percent year over year.

Furthermore, after adjusting for the increased costs of gasoline, health care, etc., real average (not median) salary and benefit compensation for all U.S. workers fell at an annualized rate of 0.3 percent in the fourth quarter and by 0.3 percent year over year. Since total hours worked fell even with meager year over year job growth, this means that average real weekly and monthly hours paid per job were reduced along with the decline in real compensation per hour. With lavish soak-the-customers-and-shareholders bonuses on Wall Street lifting average compensation, the median decline in compensation was surely far worse.

Unfortunately this kind of coverage is not an anomaly but part of a pattern.

When the focus is just on the ups and downs of markets, we tend to see a sanitized world of men in ties, computers, and experts. When we go out into the streets, we see something very different.

In an essay on economic trends called "A "Slow Motion Train Wreck" that quoted my own views, writer/economist Stephen Lendman notes that "the problem is deep, structural and aided by stripped away regulatory protections giving predatory lenders and Wall Street schemers free reign to target unsuspecting victims."

He ticks off some of the major trends in our economy that are rarely cited:

- Soaring consumer debt;
- Record high federal budget and current account deficits;
- An off-the-charts national debt, far higher than
  the fictitious reported number;
- A high and rising level of personal bankruptcies and
  mortgage loan delinquencies and defaults;
- An enormous government debt service obligation
  we're taxed to pay for;
- The systematic loss of manufacturing and other
  high-paying jobs to low-wage countries;
- A secular declining economy, 84% service-based, and mostly
  composed of low-wage, low or no-benefit, non-unionized
  jobs;
- An unprecedented wealth gap disparity;
- Growing rates of poverty in the richest country in the world;
- A decline of essential social services.

Now parts of this story are being covered but it is often the wrong story. The reporting tends to focus far more on panicky markets than on victims of predatory lending. Some years back, a hamburger chain challenged its competitors with commercials asking, "where's the beef?"

My questions to media colleagues, including the progressive blogosphere to which I contribute, is not just where's the pick-up, where's the follow-up, but where's the outrage?

AS THE PROBLEM BECOMES AN ISSUE, RESISTANCE EMERGES

WE KNOW NOW THAT THE MEDIA MISSED THE RUN-UP TO WHAT'S being called the subprime crisis. We know that the regulators seem to have been looking the other way. But what about the people most affected at the grassroots? Where were advocacy groups and their many activists and protesters?

Where were they?

I raise the question because of a belief that until there is noise on these issues, and bottom-up pressure, the foreclosure problem and the financial crimes that caused it will never turn into an issue that the society has to confront. That's the case with all social problems that powerful interests have no self-interest in addressing.

This view is not based on an abstract political ideology but my own on and off activism over the years on civil rights, apartheid, and several wars. My own understanding of how issues get on the agenda for debate and political response goes back to my days as a civil rights worker and community organizer working in several cities and movements – often on housing issues.

I was an organizer of rent strikes in Harlem and housing-project tenants in Syracuse in a war on poverty project involving Saul Alinsky, a theoretician and practitioner of social activism. All of this grassroots outreach echoed the understanding articulated earlier in American history by the anti-abolitionist Frederick Douglas who understood that "power concedes nothing without a demand."

As it turns out, many groups, often small in number and large in policy proposals, were raising holy hell on these issues but often with little publicity or media attention. The *New York Times* admitted that they first heard about the injustices in the predatory lending issue from community advocates in 2001, a year when certain bigger news was all we read about.

In Boston, the Neighborhood Assistance Corporation of America (NACA) has mounted campaigns against predatory lenders for 20 years, battling banks and embarrassing them with protests, even campaigns exposing the complicity of executives to their own children as a way of forcing them to change their practices.

This approach grew out of the labor movement and uses trade-union type organizing methods. It began in 1988 in Boston as the Union Neighborhood Assistance Corporation (UNAC). Its roots are with the Hotel Workers Union – Local 26, an activist union that won and established the country's first housing trust fund for union members.

According to their official history, NACA employed the union's activist tactics to confront lenders that were redlining communities by denying credit to minority neighborhoods and exploiting low- and moderate-income homeowners.

I met their articulate leader Bruce Marks, a tough-talking organizer who insists he does not want to be an insider. He has been waging a guerilla war against predatory lenders using abrasive tactics, media publicity, and lobbying. According a short bio on the NACA.com website, "Under his leadership, NACA has defeated many of the most powerful bankers and lenders in the country. He is well respected, feared by some, but to all he has become a force to be reckoned with."

When former Senator Phil Gramm of Texas called NACA leader Marks a "terrorist" on the Senate floor for harassing Boston's Fleet Bank on its predatory lending, NACA responded by taking out ads on radio stations in Texas congressional districts chastising Graham and Fleet. The bank soon capitulated and cooperated with NACA, funding affordable mortgages for its members. (Gramm was later a lobbyist for the finance industry, and at this writing is an advisor to Republican John McCain's presidential campaign.)

NACA, a well-organized and businesslike not-for-profit corporation, has grown into a national organization with 500,000 members. Nevertheless, its base is in Boston, and not in a media capitol like New York or Washington, and its work with homeowners whose concerns are perceived as parochial may be responsible for its relative obscurity. As a larger economic justice movement grows, NACA may move into a position of leadership.

NACA's strength – in addition to protests, it says – provides "the best homeownership program in America." NACA members are required to participate in five actions of their own, choosing one every year to qualify for their low-cost mortgages. They sign a participation pledge along with their mortgages and NACA membership.

While making my film, I sought out other advocates. They were not always easily accessible or media savvy. The community-based but very decentralized organization ACORN has been holding protests and lobbying in Congress. When I finally did reach them, I found frustration. Their chief lobbyist described how tough it was for them to even raise the issue:

> When we have committee hearings, they'll have one panel for us ... one panel for the banking and industry and the brokers and so forth, then they'll have another panel for consumers. ... We'll fly someone in from Minnesota or somewhere, a person who has been victimized by predatory lending who could tell their story. I mean, this is heart wrenching, look, by then the bankers are gone, the brokers are gone, members of congress, some of those have filtered out, it might be after lunch, maybe they don't give a darn, really, it's all about money.

Travis Plunkett of the Consumer Federation of America, a veteran advocate, told me that the laws are made with heavy input from lobbyists behind the scenes. "A lot of the discussion, a lot of the wheeling and dealing isn't done on the floor of the Senate or the floor of the House, it's done in these office buildings or in restaurants nearby. And the major decisions regarding whether legislation is green lighted or red lighted, that's all done behind the scenes."

He seemed practically resigned to getting nothing done on the hill or at least as long as it was controlled by Republicans and free market ideologues.

But he also stressed that the probem was not just on the Republican side. Many Democrats took money and support from industry lobbyists, he explained. Many voted, for example, for the so-called Bankruptcy reform law.

He seemed very diasappointed when he admitted this to me in the lobby of the Hart Senate Office Building:

> "The people who listen to the credit card companies, ignore consumer organizations, and women's groups, and civil rights groups, and unions, and pass a very harsh bankruptcy law, came from both parties. Both Republican and Democrat. So it is not a partisan issue.

The National Center for Responsible Lending has been effective in issuing excellent research reports and creating model laws in their home state of North Carolina. But they too, more ofen then not, struck out in Washington. One of their lobbyists, Josh Nassar, told me: "For every time that I'm able to to meet with a member of Congress, most times that member of Congress has met with tons of industry people already."

We took a stroll on Capitol Hill past the Capitol Hill Club and the National Republican Club. He said that's where the real business gets done, where the industry lobbyists get one-on-one time with Congress members, often leaving behind donations of $500 to $1000.

Here's the reaction when I passed this information on to a roomful of black community activists at ACORN's offfices in Washington DC, not far from the Capitol.

"You are up against powerful forces, a big industry, big budgets, big lobbyists," I said. "They go to meetings.... A guy was telling me, he goes to a meeting with guys giving out checks with thousands of dollars."

They responded by smiling knowingly. Here's some of what they said:

ACORN LOBBYIST: It's not about race and so forth anymore. It's more of a class separation in this country, and the very very wealthy continue to thrive and survive. The rest of us are just trying to scratch and make it.

ACORN WOMAN: When you go to the best communities, the gas prices are the lowest. When you go to the poorest communities, the gas prices are the highest. You see it outside because its posted outside of the gas stations, but the same pricing policies apply to our stores, apply to our clothes, apply to our furniture, applies to our loans.

ACORN WOMAN: Somebody's always calling me up, sending me a letter, trying to get me to refinance my home, because they can do it cheaper... you know... they can do it cheaper.

ACORN HOMEOWNER: We need to have someone in our neighborhood and actually educate us so we could be aware of the – how should I say that nicely? – of the unkind folks coming in and trying to take over our homes after we've been in them 50 or 60 years.

ACORN LOBBYIST: Then they come in with a loan to lower your monthly payments, consolidate your debt, give you a new credit card and so forth, and people go for that, but they fail to tell people that the insurance and taxes and principal, all that is not included in this new monthly payment that they come up with. And there is no way that people on fixed income can afford it. It's designed for you to lose your home.

I also visited a neighborhood activist group in Brooklyn's Bushwick neighborhood, then in the midst of a large-scale gentrification. As I waited to interview organizer Rick Echeverria, I saw staff members comforting an older Hispanic woman who was crying uncontrollably. She had been served with eviction notices and said she and her husband planned to kill themselves if they were thrown into the street. It was a dramatic moment that drove home to me that ultimately this problem is about people's lives that are on the line.

One of their organizers explained her plight. "She has to move out by next month. She says she was thinking of suicide because she comes from a family that has suicide history so she's thinking of suicide for herself and her husband because she can't find any housing. But we told her to hold on, we're gonna try to help her."

Echeverria then asked: "How do you go to someone like the mayor and say, 'You know, we have a bank lending problem that's really driving your homelessness problem.' "

A neighborhood priest, Monseignor John Powers, told me that city policies and bank loans were funding and supporting gentrification:

The powers to be don't really want to look at it too hard. They don't want to see it. But they fail to realize that these are good, hard working families that are being destroyed by being put out of their apartments.

Echeverria explained, "Debt is profitable. One of the questions that we're often asked is, 'Well, Rick, uh, how is it that a bank would lend $600,000 or $800,000 on a property that's only worth three or $400,000? I mean, what are they goin' to do if the mortgage borrower doesn't pay the mortgage?' And I explain to them the first lender is selling the debt and being completely reimbursed. So there's no risk for them.

A Legal Aid lawyer in Brooklyn who runs a foreclosure hotline confirmed this view. Josh Zinner told me:

They're selling these mortgages into the secondary market through Wall Street. So what they're doing is they're having these mortgages basically selling hundreds of millions of dollars' worth of these mortgages into these securitization trusts.

I sat in a living room near the JFK airport in Queens with a woman, Michel Fayez-Olabi, who was tricked into giving up her house deed to an unscrupulous broker. She and her family of five were evicted by marshalls on ten minutes notice while her kids were having lunch. She asked the District Attorney's office to investigate. It didn't. The courts were unympathetic. She told me: "We wanted to keep our house as an inheritance for our children. It's not something wrong. And we weren't well educated as to how swift and conniving these people are."

It was heartbreaking.

Hofstra University Law Professor Ronald Silverman is a nationally known expert on real estate law and predatory lending. When I told him about the people I had met in the neighborhoods, he quantified the issue so boldly that it sounded unbelievable.

"The severity of a problem of home mortgage lending in a predatory way may be quantified in the following terms; you are talking in recent years, of a problem that every year transfers hundreds of billions of dollars ..."

Hundreds of billions?

"Hundreds of billions of dollars."

You said billions?

"I said billions, not millions, from the pockets of the poor to people who are in a far better position than their so called victims."

As people began to lose their homes, as their economic pain deepens and anguish escalates, I wondered why there was so much passivity nationwide in other social movements, including those in minority communities.

Part of the reason is that the war in Iraq was getting all the attention from the activist camp. Economic issues seemed secondary when compared to the bodycounts and casualties in Iraq and Afganistan. When the Democrats began to focus on what to do to get out of the quagmire, that became the debate. There seemed to be almost no interest in other issues, especially complicated financial ones.

In May 2007, I challenged this approach in a widely placed op-ed:

The mainstream AND indy media focus on every tick and burp in Washington assume that the politicians are the real power – and often ignore the big money and corporate clout stage-managing the process.

Too many bloggers focus on the smoke and mirrors of politics, as if it is a recreational sport or parlor game, taking polls too seriously and economic trends not seriously enough. There's still more of an obsession over the scandal of the day than over the interests in the wings – the people who are financing the politicians and orchestrating their maneuvers.

The political crisis engages the bashing brigade of message-point polemicists on the right and left who both tend to ignore corporate interests. They are the forces that are devastating the lives of so many Americans, who have lost their jobs, can't pay their bills, and are victimized by the growing inequality in our nation, which does not seem to have become a political issue yet.

No one's marching on the banks or Wall Street to demand economic justice.

In June I went to Washington to attend the Take Back America Conference, organized by Progressive Democrats. There was no space on the agenda for me to show my film on debt. (The organizers did help with a congressional screening later.) Their focus was on who the Democratic candidate should be, not the economy. They did support one march by trade unions fighting for laws to protect themselves.

I felt as if I was on my own planet, peddling concerns that did not resonate with the activist base of the Democratic Party. I approached leaders of MoveOn.Org and asked them to help get the word out. I was told that debt and the issues I was raising were not on their agenda.

I even spoke with Reverend Al Sharpton. In a conversation on his radio show, he offered to screen my film and raise the issue. Afterward, I couldn't get anyone in his organization to follow up, despite frequent calls and letters on my part.

About a month later, I was at the New York hotel hosting Bill Clinton's Global initiative. When I was walking out, Jesse Jackson was walking in. I know him from my days at ABC News when I covered a trip he took to Southern Africa to publicize South Africa's attacks on it neighbors and the ravage of apartheid. We had stayed in touch.

I asked the Reverend for a few minutes to tell him about my film and the threat of the coming mass foreclosures. I asked where black leadership was on the issue and why the politicians, including black leaders, were so silent.

He listened and agreed. I mentioned the idea of a march on Wall Street. He heard me and then soon translated the idea into a Jesse Jackson-sized initiative. I think the first time Jesse Jackson and I marched together was on Washington in 1963. That was the march made famous by Dr. King's "I have A Dream" speech. Most people don't remember that that march had an economic demand. It was for jobs and justice, and led by trade union leader A. Phillip Randolph. There seems to be historical amnesia about its demands for economic justice as well as an end to racial segregation. Its "dream" was not just about racial equality.

On November 27, Jesse Jackson's Rainbow Coalition issued a press release and made the announcement at New York's City Hall, backed by leading members of the City Council. The release read in part:

> Rev. Jackson will host rallies across the nation and on Wall Street in New York City on December 10, 2007, to put pressure on the corporate community to address the needs of Americans who have been devastated by the foreclosure crisis.
>
> "Two million homes nationwide will be at risk of foreclosure by 2008," Rev. Jackson said. "We need restructure to avoid these foreclosures. Without it, the country is bound to go into recession."
>
> Rev. Jackson appeals to Wall Street leaders to create long-term restructured mortgage repayment plans for squeezed homeowners. He has toured Michigan, Georgia, and California in recent months to investigate victimization of homeowners by "schemes and unfair practices that have gouged many hard-working Americans."
>
> Rev. Jackson also met with Federal Reserve Chairman Ben Bernanke and leaders from Congress to discuss proposals to help homeowners struggling with mortgages they can't afford, and to press for relief for homeowners via consumer-oriented legislation and policies.
>
> "This is not about literacy, not about ignorance," he says. "Most foreclosures result from shady products that have been offered by subprime lenders ultimately financed by Wall Street."

I attended his small press conference. In it he lashed out at the Democratic candidates for not raising this issue in their debates. He said it must be included in the campaign. Clearly, Jesse saw the vacuum on the issue and stepped in to provide leadership.

WALL STREET PROTEST MADNESS UPDATE

ODDLY, UNKNOWN TO US, WHILE WE WERE AT CITY HALL WHERE HE was picking up endorsements from local politicians, a small group of activists from the Bronx were not waiting to respond to Jesse's call. They were already marching outside the investment bank of Goldman Sachs.

The story was first reported, almost as a joke, by a reader of the tabloid website Gawker.Com.

From the mailbag: "There's a protest outside of the Goldman Sachs building on Broad Street... They are chanting and waving signs around... They apparently have a theme song too, they are all singing it. The Goldman security guards came out to shoo them off and are now standing around nervously. The revolution is at hand, America! Sacco and Vanzetti must not die!"

The protesters are apparently from the Northwest Bronx Community and Clergy Coalition and the New York City Anti-Predatory Lending Task Force and they're walking up and down Wall Street protesting everyone else now. They are singing a song, to the tune of Jingle Bells. The words to the song are unclear. Our source reports: "There's only about 20 of them. They have tiny signs! Tiny signs of justice!"

Soon Gawker readers were posting inane comments:

"Goldman paid them to protest there so that their employees could feel the smug sense of NOT being protesters and then swipe another couple mill from unsuspecting retirees with added fervor."

"Image of Ha Ha Sound BY HA HA SOUND AT 12:25 PM"

"It's actually investment bankers who are protesting. They were informed via inter-company memo that eating puppies for breakfast is illegal."

"I'm going on a hunger strike until this is resolved."

"I got a close look. They're all investment bankers wives, very blonde, skinny with gorgeous bags chanting 'No more cheating' to the theme of Jingle Bells."

Soon Wall Street's own tabloid website, Dealbreaker.com, read by many workers in the financial district, was on the story. John Carney wrote: "The best part of all this, of course, is the cause: the protesters are protesting predatory lending. Of course, since Goldman doesn't originate residential mortgages and made money last quarter shorting mortgages, it's a bit odd to protest them for predatory lending. If anything, they engaged in predatory anti-lending. Details!"

What is remarkable is the response from their readers, much of it nasty and condescending, written up in the suites about people down in the streets. One commented: "I'm still lost at the irony of people claiming these (former) mortgage originators were predatory lending. I mean, if someone is unable to afford a big screen TV, it isn't the sales-man's job to make them buy a smaller one; it's the purchaser's respon-sibility. They were predatory borrowers: taking advantage of the investors who they are now chastising. Also, this should (but won't) teach the government to stay out of markets for moralistic reasons."

Not all of the comments were putdowns:

"... it was not the individuals that leveraged up capital on the backs of these bad loans. Blaming the individual is one thing but it is entirely different when the bank margins itself into insolvency because it is in a race to compete with the Goldmans of the world."

Another reader wrote:

"Please remember that GS securitized billions in subprime mortgages over the last few years. I'd guess overall revenue on this was 4%-can't say what the profit margin was. Thus Paulson and Steel at Treasury got some pretty big bonuses on the backs of poor borrowers who are now getting foreclosed."

And another:

"Let's face it, Wall Street showed it only cared about the current year bonus to the detriment of the subprime idiots, the companies they worked for and the confidence of the entire financial system."

And yet another:

"Predatory brokers and banks who originated mortgages illegally should be punished. However, perpetually blaming someone else for one's own stupid mistakes is pointless."

Unfortunately, this online debate did not take place in the main-stream media that had largely ignored the story and poorer residents for years. It is revealing because it represents the language of financial pros and reflects their inner culture. Some realize and criticize the role their own institutions played, but many remain as insensitive and self-ish in their outlook today as they were when they schemed up the financial instruments that led to the crisis.

As anger mounts among the victims of subprime loans, some are trashing their homes. Explained Scott Thill on Alternet:

As housing markets tank, "trash-outs" are on the rise, leaving owners, lenders and banks fighting over who should pay the clean-up bill....

Professionals in the insurance and lending industry are bracing themselves for all manner of similar situations, as homeowners either trash or simply leave their trash lying around their houses, often taking off without even claiming their furniture. This is already a dirty problem in the housing business, with owners, lenders, and banks having to figure out a way to stick each other with the check when tenants destroy their property on their way out the door. Woe is the person left behind to clean up the chaos.

Are actions like this a surprise?

This gap in comprehension seems to also reflect the class differences that have led to so much inequality. It also underscores why an economic justice movement is so vital.

In a subsequent chapter, I describe another protest by NACA members who invaded the lobby of the Bear Stearns building in New York to protest the bank's bailout by the Fed and JP Morgan.

CHAPTER 4

CHRONICLING THE IMPLOSION, 2007

The crisis began to come to a head during the summer of 2007. What began with a few incidents turned into a nonstop drama of economic convulsion, fear turning into panic, and calls for intervention. Slowly, like an apple being peeled, the truth got more apparent the closer you got to the core. Suddenly, a crisis that many had warned about or feared was beginning to erupt exploded.

I tracked the evolution of the crisis week by week in blogs, newsletters, and articles. This is a story that is still evolving about an economy that is, as I write, still unraveling. It is instructive to see how it unfolded.

This is the chronicle I kept.

JULY 18: TWO STREETS EXPLODE

THERE WAS PANIC IN THE STREETS OF NEW YORK AFTER A STEAM PIPE exploded in mid-Manhattan. One person died, another is in coma, but the real fear is that asbestos belched into the air could eventually have a deadly effect on many more people like it did at the World Trade Center in the aftermath of 911. In that event, city officials like Rudy Giuliani did not insist on protective clothing and safety rules. Thousands of rescue workers are still dying.

This time the city responded more swiftly with clean up crews in space suits. The cause of the explosion was determined to be buried beneath the surface in an aging infrastructure which only gets tended to AFTER highly visible accidents occur, rarely before. The public, initially worried about the presence of terrorists, appears to have relaxed when the culprit was identified as an old pipe. New Yorkers are a hearty lot and the saying "shit happens" is commonplace.

Yet the real danger may not be explosions in the center of town, but "implosions" on Wall Street. The former can be covered easily because they are localized; the latter spread globally and seem harder to track.

The press was all over the mayhem in midtown right on their doorstep, but down the island, in the downtown financial district, another shit storm is building steam although this one is hard for most people to decode. That is, unless they follow the business news closely and understand arcane terms like "securitization." That describes a financial instrument in which mortgage money, often borrowed by poor people in subprime loans, is recycled by Wall Street firms and turned into leverage used to finance all of these buyouts we have been hearing about.

Armies of too-clever-by-a-half money managers had been making a fortune on all of this with practices that are now being characterized as "outright fraud" by none other than President Bush's Chairman of the Federal Reserve. Most of their wheeling and dealing flew under the radar of public scrutiny with the press bolstering the rise of the stock market without examining the precarious "infrastructure" under that street, also known as "THE STREET."

A week earlier, Credit Suisse predicted a big stock market fall in 6 months because securities are overvalued. The Fed warned of $100 billion in credit losses. The *Guardian* reported, "Some analysts said they feared a broader credit crunch if a collapse in confidence in the US mortgage market rippled out to other parts of the debt markets." A *New York Post* article suggested that over two TRILLION dollars is at risk. Of course, all of this is speculative, but as they say, when there is smoke in high places, fire can't be far behind.

Last Saturday, the *New York Times* reported, "Anxiety over securities backed by risky mortgage and rising interest rates has roiled the credit market for several moths. Now the CONTAGION [caps mine] from those troubles seems to be spreading into other parts of the marketplace."

Terms like "roiled" and "contagion" are insider words for a spreading panic. Writing on Money And Markets.com, Mike Larson declares

"ITS ALL HITTING THE FAN." He reports that two Bear Sterns funds simply "VAPORIZED" explaining,

In plain English, here's what happened:

These funds invested in complicated mortgage securities ...

They used extensive leverage, or borrowed money, to improve returns ...

Then, delinquencies and foreclosures started surging, and the value of the underlying loans and bonds tied to them began sinking fast.

Now private equity firms, which have been making monster deals built on debt, are being squeezed. Much of the debt is being seen as junk. We have also learned that the agencies' rating credit and debt offerings had their heads in their rear ends. They have lost credibility, putting the market at more risk.

The excellent website Ml-explode.com reports that since late 2006 100 major U.S. lenders have collapsed or "imploded." The editor sums up the reasons this way: "Thank you greed; thank you delusion; thank you anti-regulation – we couldn't have done it without you!"

The press is beginning to wake up and realize how important this is. They have been talking about the rise of the stock market as if that tells the whole story. Yes, some corporate profits are up but what's happening down below is alarming. Note: the market fell nearly 150 points after last week's high of 14000.

Business Week reports that the subprime crisis is spreading to other kinds of debt, and far more serious than it was initially thought to be, writing that it is "only a surprise to those who listened exclusively to sound bite-based talking-heads belaboring 'subprime' as an isolated implosion. Around here, long ago we were forwarding along data and analysis showing sharp rises in delinquencies in virtually all classes of consumer debt."

MORE CONTAGION

We are finally beginning to talk about real money and a real danger of the kind that terrifies bankers and the elite. They may not care about the poor, but they do about themselves!

As Mike Larson suggests: "Ultimately, losses on subprime mortgage bonds alone may total as much as $90 billion, according to one estimate. Losses on collateralized debt obligations (CDOs), investment vehicles created from slices of various mortgage-backed securities and asset-backed securities, may total billions more."

In an interdependent interlaced economy, a problem in one sector quickly ripples elsewhere just like the South East Asian financial crisis ten years ago. Its like cancer, not easily checked.

I went to a dinner party last week and met a credit expert who works at one of Wall Street's top investment firms. He acknowledged to me that the people shoveling out those subprime loans KNEW many of the borrowers couldn't afford to pay back.

I asked: "So what happened to due diligence?" It's one of the "market disciplines" that these bankers are always preaching.

He shrugged, indicating that there was so much to be made that normal safeguards and standards were pushed to the side or forgotten. He says there are many investigations underway right now.

Can we allow them to investigate themselves?

AUGUST 1: PLUNGE

IN LATE JULY, THE STOCK MARKET WAS UP, UP AND AWAY, HITTING A record 14,000. The American economy was riding high and my fears about the debt bubble seemed to many to be exaggerated if not misplaced. But then, as if in accord with some law of gravity, what went up started coming down.

NEW YORK (AP) — Wall Street suffered one of its worst losses of 2007 Thursday, leading a global stock market plunge as investors succumbed to months of worry about the mortgage and corporate lending markets. The Dow Jones industrials closed down more than 310 points after earlier skidding nearly 450. Investors who had been able for months to largely shrug off discomfort about subprime mortgage problems and a more difficult environment for corporate borrowing finally decided it was time to sell after the Commerce Department issued another disappointing home sales report.

When I started investigating the debt crisis for my film *In Debt We Trust*, I thought I was just making a film about consumer credit issues. I didn't really understand how those issues relate to much larger forces, if not the whole global economy.

I didn't appreciate how abuses that impacted one group, and of course benefited others, could mushroom into a crisis that would rock the whole system.

I wanted to focus on the pain of Americans because so many activists had defined the debt problem as something that only impacted Africans and the Third World. For years, the World Bank and IMF have been targeted (correctly in my view) for taking advantage of poor people.

But then I saw our own financial institutions, some regulated, many not, targeting poor and working people who wanted to better their lives and buy new homes. They wanted to be part of what President Bush was touting as the "ownership society."

So along came the subprime loans, which appeared at first as a reform, a way for people without credit to pay a little more and get a mortgage.

Appearances, however, are deceptive. Soon, small companies and then humongous banks saw an opportunity to get even richer and started shoving out money and then selling paper into so-called securitization trusts or CDOs. These instruments were then used to finance all kinds of business transactions.

The middle men were making a fortune but it was all based on what was once called JUNK... and the bad credit funded bad deals and bang – the quicksand became more visible. And now, unheard warnings have turned into a full-fledged crisis.

In the following weeks the market went beserk. The press called it "volatile."

AUGUST 9: THE PRESIDENTIAL PRESS CONFERENCE

QUESTION: Mr. President, I want to get your thoughts about the volatility in the financial markets, but specifically, a series of questions. Do you think that housing prices will continue to fall? Do you think that the inability of people to borrow money the way they used to is going to spill over into [the] economy generally? And what are you prepared to do about it? And, specifically, are you considering some kind of government bailout for people who might lose their homes?

THE PRESIDENT: David, I'm wise enough to remind you that I'm not an economist, and that I would ask you [to] direct predictions and forecasts about economic matters to those who make a living making forecasts and predictions. I suspect you'll find on the one hand, on the other hand, in how they predict. (Laughter.)

Now, what I focus on are the fundamentals of our economy. My belief is that people will make rational decision based upon facts. And the fundamentals of our economy are strong. I mentioned some of them before. Job creation is strong. Real after-tax wages are on the rise. Inflation is low. Interestingly enough, the global economy is strong, which has enabled us to gain more exports, which helped the second quarter growth numbers to be robust, at 3.4 percent.

Another factor one has got to look at is the amount of liquidity in the system. In other words, is there enough liquidity to enable markets to be able to correct? And I am told there is enough liquidity in the system to enable markets to correct. One area where we can help consumer[s] — and obviously anybody who loses their home is somebody with whom we must show enormous empathy.

The word "bailout," I'm not exactly sure what you mean. If you mean direct grants to homeowners, the answer would be no, I don't support that. If you mean making sure that financial institutions like the FHA have got flexibility to help these folks refinance their homes, the answer is yes, I support that.

One thing is for certain, is that there needs to be more transparency in financial documents. In other words, a lot of people sign up to something they're not exactly sure what they're signing up for. More financial literacy, I guess, is the best way to put it. We've had a lot of really hardworking Americans sign up for loans, and the truth of the matter is they probably didn't fully understand what they were signing up for. And therefore, I do believe it's a proper role for government to enhance financial education initiatives, and we're doing that, we've got money in the budget to do that.

AUGUST 9: THE WATERS ARE NOT CALMED

THE PRESIDENT BLAMED BORROWERS FOR NOT UNDERSTANDING THE documents they signed. If you have ever tried to read the documents banks prepare for mortgage closings, you will know that they are written by risk-minimizing lawyers and are too long and too dense to be understood. (Later in the day, the stock market reacted to Mr. Bush's upbeat assessment by plunging once again.)

The financial insiders who watched were more than skeptical. Here are some quotes from a discussion on the Ml-implode website. One of the discussants calls our fearless leader, "President Pumkinhead."

Why'd president pumpkinhead have a news conference in the morning? Probably hoping no one would see it and he wouldn't have to lie to as many people.

Another described what he was watching with more than disbelief:

He's being hit with a lot of questions on mortgages, credit crisis, and the economy ... and of course the economy is "in for a soft landing," he's been assured by the treasury that "there is plenty of liquidity," yadda-yadda-yadda.

But he is stumbling over his words more than usual, not making eye contact, not finishing his sentences ... and when he wanders a bit, he quickly goes back on script. It is very odd to watch, to say the least.

Odd? Not for him, but, of course, there's more than one man to hold accountable. This is a deeper structural problem that implicates a whole industry and the "financialization" it promotes. This crisis is an example of what goes around comes around as the companies that suspended their usual "standards" and "rules" and self-styled "due diligence" knowingly sucked money out of people with poor credit records and who now find their own companies imploding and collapsing worldwide.

Government jawboning and even the "injection of funds" by central banks didn't have much impact because it was becoming clear that this was NOT just a subprime problem but far more structural, serious and global. You began reading articles like one by Greg Ip and John Hilsenrath: "Credit problems once seen as isolated to a few mortgage-mortgage lenders are beginning to propagate across markets and borders in unpredicted ways and degrees. A system designed to distribute and absorb risk might, instead, have bred it, by making it so easy for investors to buy complex securities they didn't fully understand. And the interconnectedness of markets could mean that a sudden change in sentiment by investors in all sorts of markets could destabilize the financial system and hurt economic growth."

Historian Carolyn Baker was one of the few bloggers I read arguing that we all must become more engaged with these issues; she is "profoundly aware of the role of economic issues – perhaps more than militarism, healthcare, education, politics, or any other institution, in the dead-ahead demise of empire. I also notice that few in the left-liberal end of the political spectrum have a firm grasp on economic issues which I suspect comes from a fundamental polarization between activism and financial intelligence..." She began stressing the role of fraud, theft, and malicious intent in the American and global financial train wreck which has been exacerbating over recent decades.

We would see that word "train wreck" more in the weeks to come.

AUGUST 18: WILD SWINGS

NOW WE WERE BEING TOLD ABOUT "WILD SWINGS" AND OR "CRAZY ups and downs" on Wall Street with the Federal Reserve Bank rushing in by easing rates for banks, but not for the general public. That maneuver seemed to have worked in that it was a sign that the FED was "doing something."

It's weird that these super-rational financial wonks act as emotionally as they do. The Federal Reserve Board said it was acting to "promote the restoration of orderly conditions in financial markets." In other words, they are in the "perception business" more than the banking business. The *Washington Post* added that The Federal Reserve "...said for the first time that it viewed turmoil in financial markets as a major risk to the U.S. economy." (The day before, the *New York Times* reported that "the Treasury Secretary didn't feel he needed to say or do anything.")

Maybe The Fed Chairman saw how ignorant he looked?

The *New York Times*'s take on the issue added a class spin suggesting that the Fed acted NOT because poor and working class people were losing their homes but because rich people were now having trouble getting mortgages.

> The Fed, while not yet cutting a rate that wields more influence over the economy, moved to stimulate lending in part because it recognized that even well-to-do families with good credit ratings were having difficulty getting mortgages.

Underscore those words: "even well-to-do families."

How will this symbolic measure likely impact on the rest of us? The answer is NOT encouraging."

"Markets should not be calmed by this tactic," wrote Carl Weinberg, chief economist for High Frequency Economics. "This move is not going to provide any relief to the overall economy." Said another commentator: "The Fed is in a tight box, and anytime they do move the markets react violently one way or the other (or both!). Calm will arrive, but it won't be today."

In the meantime, Wall Street was taking out its begging bowl and asking the Fed to help. Help was soon on the way.

Fortune magazine reported:

Wall Street loves to talk about letting financial markets weed out the weak. But when the Street itself gets in trouble, it sticks out its little tin cup, asking for help. And gets it.

The subprime-mortgage-market meltdown is a classic example of the way small fry get devoured, but the whales of Wall Street get rescued. Here's the deal: People with crummy credit who took out mortgages are being allowed to fail in record numbers. The mortgage companies that made those loans are being allowed to fail.

On the Street itself? It's bailout city. Even before the Fed made a symbolic half-point cut in the discount rate, it and other central banks from Switzerland to Singapore were trying to rescue the Street by injecting hundreds of billions of dollars into the financial markets and announcing they will put up more, if needed.

Hello? If you believe in markets – which I do – this rescue is especially galling, because Wall Street enabled this mess in the first place.

A reader wrote to the *Wall Street Journal* challenging its tendency to emphasize the positive:

Things will get worse before they get better.... This is a house of cards that our leaders are trying to segment. It isn't a subprime problem, it isn't a foreclosure problem, it isn't a mortgage problem, a bond market problem, a hedge fund problem, or a bank problem...This is a full systematic collapse of our economy.... The problems are masked and hidden throughout every layer of our economy...being too slow to react will only compound this problem as it builds momentum...We have no idea how bad this is really going to get.

AUGUST 25: THE INJECTION

The people who weren't listening are paying attention now — because of the whooshing sound of money, large amounts of it, being flushed away as the market drops and central banks start pumping HUNDREDS OF BILLIONS into the financial system worldwide as the subprime – what I call the subCRIME – scandal leads to an alarming loss of confidence in credit markets.

Let's recap. Last week President Bush tried to bolster confidence in the system with a morning press conference. While all may have been well in his mind, the market got the signal and went KABOOM. A 387-point drop in the afternoon and then the big money boys got scared and started pumping money like ballast to keep the ship afloat.

We know that it was more than $100 BILLION from the Fed but other central bankers joined in to try to "CONTAIN the CONTAGION" of more slippage. As far as I know, I was the only one who called for a CRIMINAL INVESTIGATION in a commentary.

The plot is, shall we say, thickening because of concerns that the government's response will aid Wall Street, and bail out the very people who caused the crisis in the first place.

Horrors, what irony – or maybe that is what we have come to expect

"The issue is often referred to as 'moral hazard,' " reports the now shrunk-in-size *New York Times*, meaning that the risk-takers who brought on the panic would feel bailed out and would be more likely to do it again. (A week later, the *Times* would drop criticisms of a federal bailout and justify it as necessary to strengthen markets.)

AUGUST 27: DIG WE MUST

"Dig We Must," was once the slogan of the repair crews of CON-ED, New York's bumbling Electric utility. It is also now a metaphor for what is happening on Wall Street as all the financial heavy-hitters fled their summer mansions in the Hamptons to return to the trading desks to try to help dig their industry out of the hole it has fallen into since the meltdown of the subprime real estate market revealed much vulnerability for the global economy. (Asian markets slumped this week.)

Those who don't travel by helicopter have been burning up the Long Island Express to join bankers burrowing in their bunkers. This scary crisis is shaking up the worlds of the high finance boys who were raking it in until they weren't, as economist Max Wolff writes using the road as a metaphor:

"That is the heady road we traveled. It felt great to insiders speeding down the yield superhighway. That was until the sub-prime tire blew-out. Forced to stop and unable to re-inflate the tire with the usual hot air, folks began to look under the hood. That is where we are now. Peek under the hood and you see a lot of shiny borrowed chrome, a debt fueled engine and a lot of rot!"

There's suddenly been a wake up call for executives and media pundits who seemed so "clueless" in seeing the "rot" or anticipating and trying to defuse a meltdown that has now cost billions with no end in sight.

Comments London-based journalist William Bowles in the *Atlantic Free Press:*

It should be obvious to all and sundry by now that capitalism is in dire straights. Last week's meltdown of the world's major capital markets was only "rescued" by the injection of literally hundreds of billions of dollars from by the European Central Bank, the Bank of Japan and the US Federal Reserve. So much for the magic of the "market" which, we are continuously told, solves all problems. And in fact, last week's injection by the European Central bank of something like $100 billion dollars didn't do the trick! More had to be "injected" in order to stave off a total collapse of the world's stock markets. The "injection" is in reality a bailout of the commercial banks.

Bowles quotes the *Guardian* of August 10, 3007, an article called "Central banks pour in billions – but global slide goes on":

Investors have no idea which institutions own what debt, leaving the markets to be riven by rumor and counter-rumor. "There is great uncertainty as to how far risks are spread within the financial system and exactly where the losses reside," said Paul Niven, at F&C Asset Management. "The market is trading on fear."

Bowles then says: "the real cause of the current panic is financial speculation caused by unrealistically cheap credit and almost no regulation of speculative markets…"

Feeding our ignorance on the origins of this rollercoaster, which some fear could lead to other bubbles bursting and a global recession, or something worse, is a media that mythologizes markets and presents them as neutral self-correcting mechanisms that fairly regulate supply and demand and deserve confidence.

There is nary a word on how these market can be controlled, dominated, monopolized and olgopolized. (Is that a word?) Last week we were warned about "contagion." This week, the calming buzzword is "correction."

Left out in all this is any discussion of the shadowy forces that we don't see who's calling the shots and the many ways in which the game is damaging our society and is even self-destructive to business. (Remember Lenin's warning: "Sell them enough rope and capitalists will hang themselves.")

Well now they seem to be hanging a good part of the capitalist system. It is bizarre.

Steven Lendman writes, "Some astute financial observers now believe current excesses and resulting turmoil were caused by the intentional engineering of the US housing bubble with the Fed in on the scheme." The Federal Reserve Bank, by the way, contrary to appearances, is NOT a government agency but a private body run by big banks.

Lendman continues, "Insiders made loads of easy money in the process and now stand to cash in big troubled assets for a fraction of their value the way they always do in the wake of market meltdowns. It's called 'vulture' investing with shrewd buyers profiting hugely in good and bad times that are all good for them."

He concludes, "The problem is deep, structural and aided by stripped away regulatory protections giving predatory lenders and Wall Street schemers free reign to target unsuspecting victims." In other words, see who benefits.

SEPTEMBER 10: BAD DEBT FINANCING BIG DEALS

SOMETIMES I JUST SIT HERE, PUZZLING ON HOW IS IT POSSIBLE FOR our society and all of us to have become so dependent on debt. All the big deals on Wall Street are being funded in part by debt, some of it from securitized subprime loans. Some of it through other debt-related maneuvers. Example: Sallie Mae goes private and is sold to "avoid scrutiny" in the spreading student loan scandal in which the company is deeply implicated in getting college administrators to steer students to their higher priced loans. The price for the company: $24 BILLION, of which 16.8 BILLION is in debt. (This deal later faltered as the credit squeeze intensified.)The Cablevision company is being sold back to its founding family. Over 10 BILLION in debt is involved.

CEOs are borrowing debt to buy back stock and in the process, just coincidentally I am sure, use some of the money to hike their own salaries to obscenely high levels. It doesn't stop as our mortgages are bought and sold back into the market through so-called securitization trusts. This money then leverages more speculative investment. Meanwhile the money manager who looks after Dick Cheney's finances is warning that the whole world is becoming a bubble that can burst.

And did you know that General Motors is deeply complicit in the subprime lending crisis? I didn't until I found out that what was once the world's biggest automaker saw its profits fall as the subprime loans they were doing on the side imploded. This little item was in the *Financial Times*:

> General Motors' first-quarter earnings shrank almost 90 per cent, with improved automotive operating profits more than offset by heavy subprime mortgage losses at GMAC, the financial services group in which the carmaker has a 49 per cent stake.

Hmmmmm. Meanwhile and not un-coincidentally, the Motor City of Detroit, GM's hometown, has been named the FORECLOSURE CAPITAL OF AMERICA because so many people are losing their homes as their wages drop and their bills climb. (Later in the year, GM would declare a $39 billion loss after making money on car sales, in part because of its GMAC division's irresponsible lending to car buyers and home owners.)

━━━━━━ 1Q: THE FED STEPS IN

sychology lead financial markets to
een exuberant greed and catatonic fear.
unemployment. Times of greed are like-
ıg inflation. — Economist Brad DeLong

. STOCK MARKET RECEIVED A GIFT FROM the form of a half percent interest rate cut, twice the amount most analysts expected. The move followed another week in which the debt crisis rolled over financial institutions worldwide and people's lives like an out-of-control freight train.

Why?

There is panic in high places. They know this crisis is far more serious than most of us realize, and that the interest rate cut will not address the subprime problem or bring relief to the millions facing foreclosures and a tighter economic noose around their necks.

It will, say many financial wizards, lead to higher inflation, which is a way of making our money worth less. The dollar's status as a currency took another whack.

One analyst in the *New York Times* called it "shock therapy," the very term writer Naomi Klein explores in *The Shock Doctrine*, her new book on "disaster" capitalism showing the link between the shock therapy once doled out in mental hospitals, shock and awe bombing, shock interrogation techniques whose aim is to "disorient" prisoners, and shock strategies used in economic policy that has devastated so many countries in which it was tried.

Now shock therapy has come home to the U.S. – the country that has been exporting it overseas. On a recent Democracy Now radio show, Klein explained:

The history of the contemporary free market was written in shocks. Some of the most infamous human rights violations of the past thirty-five years, which have tended to be viewed as sadistic acts carried out by anti-democratic regimes, were in fact either committed with the deliberate intent of terrorizing the public or actively harnessed to prepare the ground for the introduction of radical free-market reforms.

To which Carolyn Baker adds:

The only difference here is that, so far, there have been no serious reforms proposed and the market is anything but free. With its interest cut, the Fed bails out and rewards the very institutions that were profiting on ill gain profits from predatory lending.

In some countries, people are starting to stir. Americans remain too caught up in the primaries and the war on one end, and the new wave of OJ mania on the other, to take action against the looting of their pocket books. We are becoming a shell-shocked nation.

We saw customers at Northern Rock, a credit-starved mortgage bank in London, lining up in the streets to pull their money out, and the Bank of England pumping money in just a day after warning others, in the name of "moral hazard" rules, not to bail out lenders.

The *Times* of London carried a cheer by Libby Purvis for those demanding their money, arguing:

Salute the queuers for their nerve, patience and admirable impermeability to patronizing advice.

For how dare the stuffed suits, financial and political (and indeed journalistic) use expressions like "Don't panic" and "Keep calm." The withdrawers are perfectly entitled to choose who looks after their lavishly pretaxed savings. Some of them actually need money right now — like the chap on the news who wanted to pay his builder — and others just prefer not to rely on an institution that goes begging to the "lender of last resort."

By their presence on the streets, most of it not at all panicky in demeanor, the queuers utter a resounding raspberry to the financial industry and its political masters. It is time someone did.

In recent years, we have seen a dangerous erosion of the rules and principles that have allowed our market to work and our economy to thrive. Instead of thinking about what's good for America or what's good for business, a mentality has crept into certain corners of Washington and the business world that says, "What's good for me is good enough."

The world's top business magazine, *The Economist*, wrote about the crisis spreading to England:

A century ago, the depth of a banking crisis was measured by the length of the queue outside banks. These days, financial panics are more likely to be played out through heavy selling in share, bond or currency markets than old-fashioned bank runs. That makes the sight on the morning of Friday September 14th of a queue of people waiting (patiently in most cases) to take their money out of Northern Rock, a wounded British mortgage bank, all the more extraordinary.

Yes, "extraordinary" has become the word, as this crisis becomes frighteningly global.

The bankers know how bad it is. Here's Jim Glassman of JP Morgan: "The credit-market storm is a far more dangerous thing than anything we've seen in memory." More and more news reports are glum. Here's the *Sydney Morning Herald* in Australia reporting on "How Bad Debt Infected the World": "The foreclosure butterfly flapped its wings in small town USA and the hurricane built and tore through world banking."

Here's the *Independent on Sunday* drawing a parallel with the Great Crash of 1929:

> In his classic work *The Great Crash: 1929*, J K Galbraith put the decline down to the bad distribution of income; the bad corporate structure; the bad banking structure; the dubious state of the foreign balance; and the poor state of economic intelligence. He might have been writing about George W Bush's world rather than that of Herbert Hoover.

Remember: you can't rely on what officials are saying to calm us. One financial website noted: "The time to panic is when officials say, 'don't panic.'"

Remember Andrew Mellon, Hoover's Treasury Secretary, who said famously: "I see nothing in the present situation that is either menacing or warrants pessimism."

The comment was made on 31 December 1929, just after the Wall Street crash and ahead of the Great Depression.

No, I am not expecting or hoping for a depression. Who would? But the parallels are eerie, and I am not the only one making them.

WILL THE INTEREST RATE CUT HELP?

The Federal Reserve Bank cut the interest rate for the first time in four years, seeking, they said, to prevent a housing slump and turbulent markets from triggering recession. *Bloomberg's Financial News* explained the Fed's "dilemma":

> While a quarter-point reduction in the federal funds rate may not be enough to bolster growth and investor confidence, a half-point cut might fan inflation and be perceived as giving in to pressure from Wall Street firms that made bad bets, especially in the market for securities backed by subprime mortgages.

> Bernanke and fellow policy makers "are really caught," said Robert Eisenbeis, a former research director at the Fed's bank in Atlanta who attended meetings of the rate-setting Federal Open Market Committee before retiring early this year. "The Fed needs to avoid the perception of bailing out the markets, lenders or borrowers."

"Needs to avoid?" Huh? No, it doesn't. The Fed is not in the PR business and in the end cared not a whit about image, but at the same time, it *is* all a "perception game." The rate cut was praised because it looks like something good was done. It wasn't.

Look at what the experts were saying before the Fed overacted.

The *Wall Street Journal*: "Too Much Hope May Be Pinned On Rate Cut," E. S, Browning said the rate cut "would offer little immediate help for the fundamental problems weighing on the country's economy and financial markets."

The *Economist*: "In the short term, lower interest rates will not achieve all that much."

So why all the hype?

Perhaps because symbolically this appears like the government is coming to the rescue, even though the Fed is not really the Government, but a private institution with government sanction. The cut will help stock sales, as it already has when the market soared. It will bail out bankers but not the people who are suffering under the burden of debt and foreclosures.

No one is talking about how to create economic equality, lower prices, control gas and food costs, and raise wages for working people. No one.

I wondered why. "Don't be naive," a friend responded. "The Fed is not there to help us. It is run by bankers, for bankers. It's part of the problem, not the solution."

True, but what will we do to help ourselves, or is it already too late?

That is what should be shocking!

OCTOBER 7: A JOBS REPORT IS OFFERED UP AS A SIGN OF HOPE

ON SUNDAY, OCTOBER 6, THE PUBLIC EDITOR OF THE NEW YORK TIMES pointed to all the discrepancies and conflicts in the violence figures coming out of Iraq. He called for more nuanced reporting and increased public skepticism. He noted that the perception of progress there has been bolstered by the release of questionable statistics.

What's true of reporting from Iraq is also true about the job figures that the government releases monthly, gauging the health of the U.S. economy. Can they be trusted? And what about the reporting on them? This is an especially timely issue as Fox News gets ready to launch its own heavily hyped new Business Channel.

For weeks, we have heard all these warnings about the financial crisis sharpening and a possible recession. Reality intruded after a big subprime relief rally sent stocks soaring. Wall Street was quickly back in a swamp, and it looked like the Federal Reserve Bank would have to cut interest rates again to further bail out the markets.

But then, on Friday October 4, the Bush Labor Department announced a new jobs report and much of the coverage turned upbeat. The report offered preliminary data claiming that the economy added 100, 000 jobs in September. Suddenly, lower job figures from July and August were also magically revised upwards.

Wall Street went crazy. The S & P went up and the headlines went positive.

Here are two examples of the spin: The *New York Times:* "JOB GROWTH LOOKS ROSIER, EASING RECESSION FEARS." The *Wall Street Journal,* "U.S. ECONOMY DOWN, NOT OUT."

The new numbers suggested a turaround? Bear in mind, back in the 1990s, in the Clinton years, 200,000 new jobs was what was expected on a monthly basis to assure economic growth. That was the gold standard. Now that number has been cut in half and is suddenly being treated as a Great Leap Forward. How did the job numbers turn around? Or have they?

Reports the *Journal,* "much of the revision was caused by recalibrating seasonal fluctuations in government employment, including teaching."

Mmmmm. "Recalibrations of seasonal fluctuations!" I'd love to let comic Stephen Colbert loose on that phrase. Look more closely, and you will see these recalibrations deal with GOVERNMENT EMPLOYMENT, not jobs in the private sector. There were 71,000 jobs "recalibrated" in local education.

Yet establishment economists are saying these jobs are not what the economy really needs. The *Journal* quotes Nigel Gault, chief economist at Global Insight, to the effect that "private sector jobs are the underlying driver of the economy."

Yes, they are, but these are not them. The biggest jump here is in government jobs. NBC News reported on yet more job cuts in Flint, Michigan, Saturday and that manufacturing jobs are at their lowest point since 1950.

Presumably you would think the disappearance of these jobs

would be upsetting to the wise men of Wall Street. In fact, they are, but their concerns are being buried in stories that fuel the perception that the corner is being turned.

Example: way down in the 19th paragraph of the *Journal* article, the Vice Chairman of the Federal Reserve Bank Donald Kohn says he expected that the nation's "economic performance would be better." He says, "You should view these forecasts even more skeptically than usual."

But the business press, like the market that loves any excuse for a good rally, is not that skeptical. They tend to like positive numbers and downplay negative ones, often without analyzing them.

Back at the *New York Times*, you had to jump from page one in the Business section with its "Job Growth Looks Rosier" headline to page 8. There, at the very bottom of the last page, next to the corporate bond data – a place most readers don't venture – was this paragraph:

> "I don't think we're totally out of the woods yet," said Jan Hatzius, chief United States economist for Goldman Sachs. "There are some real problems at the foundations of the economy. If nothing really bad happens, we can muddle through and unwind some of these problems over a lengthy period of time. And if something bad happens, we go into a recession."

So there it is, that depressing "R word" again but pushed all the way down in the story. In journalism, we used to call this "burying the lead."

Clearly the recession threat hasn't gone away. Not at all! As for "bad things" to fear, that surely includes the expected jump in oil prices and more unemployment. The actual rise reported in unemployment was minimized in most of the press accounts. (On Sunday, London's *Observer* reported: "Tens of thousands of New York bankers are braced for a crippling round of job cuts as the aftershocks of the credit-market collapse reverberate the length and breadth of Wall Street.")

Says Ethan Harris, the chief United States economist at Lehman Brothers in the *New York Times*, "We're likely to go through an extended period of slow economic growth. We're likely to see a further drop in the job market, a further rise in the unemployment rate, and ultimately the fed will come back again and cut interest rates."

So there you have it, expectations of more bad news and hopes for another intervention by the Fed. These experts quoted in the stories actually contradict the upbeat tone of the stories and their headlines. Next month's jobs report will have to factor in the 100,000 plus jobs lost in finance and housing, which have already occurred but are not yet reflected in the statistics.

In other words, these reports, like the coverage that says the surge is working in Iraq, are selective and inflated. They are aimed more at influencing perceptions than providing truth.

My questions: How do they get away with this? Why does the market buy it? Why does the press do it? And what are they leaving out?

Businessman and financial analyst Eric Janszen says our economy is increasingly showing the features of a Banana Republic with low-paid government and service jobs for all. He writes on his website iTulip.com that the private goods producing sector so vital to a sound economy is shrinking. He quotes an AP report:

Construction firms cut 14,000 jobs in September, Factories slashed 18,000. Retailers got rid of just over 5,000 jobs. Financial services companies eliminated 14,000 slots.

However, gains in education and health services, professional services, leisure and hospitality, and in government work more than offset those losses, leading to a net gain in new jobs in September.

Jobs in government now parallel jobs in the goods producing sector, he reports, as the dollar is being depreciated. Jantzen writes:

The magic of a depreciating currency is working. Foreign investors are buying UBRA (United Banana Republic of America) stocks and other assets at fire sale prices. Tourism is up as visitors from Asia, Europe, Canada and all other countries whose currencies have appreciated ... visit the US for a cheap UBRA vacation, driving leisure and hospitality jobs within the service sector where most of the job growth occurred.

And wages? They are not rising as fast as prices. His conclusion:

Suppression of wage increases has been the centerpiece of monetary and government policy to manage inflation in the Production/ Consumption Economy since 1980. Given the difficulty in acquiring legitimate measures of actual inflation rates in the US economy, there is no way of telling whether these wage increases translate into increased purchasing power. Given the rise of oil and other commodity prices, it seems doubtful. In fact, it looks like the

UBRA is going full-bore banana republic, including wage and price inflation to maintain employment going into an election year.

So there you have it: politically influenced numbers, another reason not to trust the mainstream media and search out more thoughtful analysis elsewhere.

As the old saying holds, "Figures lie and liars figure."

UPDATE: DECEMBER 1 – ADMISSION: JOBS ESTIMATE WAS WRONG

IN FOLLOWING THIS CRISIS CLOSELY, I OFTEN FOUND THE PREDICTIONS of many experts, and the conclusions of widely covered reports were wrong. Yet they fed hopes and generate impressions that led to financial actions based on faulty intelligence, very much to what happened with the Iraq War. The big players want to keep us reassured and keep our confidence up while at the same time, they know of the great gap between perceptions and reality. I used to think they were just lying – and many do – I believe now that, sadly, many wouldn't know the truth if it hit them on the head.

They buy their own hype, that is, when they think it serves their interests. This correction appeared buried in the last pages of the *New York Times* business edition on a Saturday, the day when they say the paper is least read. Not surprisingly, many agencies release negative data or "sharp downward revisions" late on Fridays to insure that it will have little impact.

The American economy appears to have created far fewer jobs this spring than has been reported so far, a new government report indicated yesterday. That could provide further impetus for the Federal Reserve to lower interest rates when it meets Dec. 11.

The report included a sharp downward revision of the government's estimate of personal income growth for the second quarter. Because the changes were made as soon as better employment figures were available, the revisions made it seem likely that figures on job creation are also likely to be revised downward in coming months.

The new report concluded that personal income from wages and salaries grew at an annual rate of 1.6 percent in the second quarter, far below the 4.5 percent that had previously been estimated.

OCTOBER 13: IT'S BAD AND THAT AIN'T GOOD

"I could never buy a house. I can't travel. I can't do anything. I feel like a prisoner." – Michigan Attorney Kristin Cole, 30, who owes $150,000 in student loans.

THE SQUEEZE IS GETTING WORSE WITH THE DEBT LOAD GROWING AND more families unable to pay their bills. The dollar may be in a free fall. Hold on to your hats and your homes.

We are now in the third quarter of 2007 with Citibank reporting a 60% plunge – over $5 BILLION – in profits partly because of subprime loan "write downs." UBS reports a $3.4 BILLION hit for the same reason. This proves how deeply complicit big banks were in financing the subprime scam.

The Marketwatch website has a front-page feature titled: "COULD IT – CRASH AGAIN?" They are referring to the market drop of 1987. On Monday, the stock market rallied dramatically in what one observer called "A subprime relief rally." That does not mean the problems have gone away.

In fact, the *New York Times* headline said just that: "Stocks Soar on Hopes Credit Crisis Is Over." In truth, it is not over, not by a long shot.

Reuters reports:

The warning from Citigroup that its quarterly earnings will drop 60% could be a sign of things to come from U.S. banks and brokerages. "I believe there is a systemic debt problem and it will take years to work out – and the Federal Reserve cannot resolve the issues," said Richard Bove, bank analyst at Punk Ziege.

New York Mayor and financial guru Michael Bloomberg also says the causes are deeper. He says the global credit crunch has as much to do with public debt as the U.S. subprime meltdown. The billionaire media and business mogul talked about the "lunacy" of debt levels in the U.S. and the U.K. at the Conservative Party conference in the Britain: "This is not a mortgage crisis," he insists. "It's a crisis in confidence and we're all in it together."

So don't be fooled by the rise in the Dow. Deep debt problems are not going away despite all the rosy optimism. It masks a deeper denial among those who think that if they believe or hope everything is ok, it will be. No sooner did I write that last line than I read on the Housing Panic blog: "The housing market may still be in denial, but it appears that Wall Street and foreign markets are in Denial Squared."

That is lunacy!

OCTOBER 15: THE BANKERS' DEBATE, THE PUBLIC GROWS ANXIOUS

THERE IS A TERM IN FINANCE CALLED "MORAL HAZARD." IT REFERS TO policies and practices that reward wrongdoing by bankers and investors instead of allowing them to suffer their losses in the win-lose environment of the rigged casino that we refer to as markets.

On one level, it suggests that yes, there is some notion of rules and, dare I say, "morality" lurking in the anything-goes-if-I-don't-get-caught financial vampire land responsible for the collapse of credit markets in the aftermath of the disclosure of the subprime ("sub crime") scandal.

The bankers themselves are furiously debating what to do as they post record losses. The Bank of England opposes cutting the cost of credit, something that many expect the U.S. Federal Reserve Bank is about to announce as a "moral hazard." Other bankers overseas are bitterly denouncing their American counterparts. Two banks in Germany had to be rescued.

There seems to be an air of desperation among financiers.

Measures are being taken similar to locking the barn door after the horses are gone. The Securities and Exchange Commission, the nominal regulators, were caught napping. They are only now setting up "Enforcement Groups," including one on subprime abuses. They say they are going to be looking at "everyone involved."

Already big banks and credit rating companies that certified the crooked "securitization packages as kosher" are firing top executives. Hedge Funds are reporting "shock losses." There is a clear "contagion" as losses in one sector spread to others. Only the high price of oil is keeping the market afloat.

The industry and government response may be too little too late. Already the dominoes are falling as these problems move into the real world or "real economy," as Treasury Secretary and ex-Goldman Sachs chief Hank Paulson puts it. Just read the headlines in newspapers such as the *Financial Times*: "Rise Forecast In Company Default Rates."

Company default rates are forecast to rise nearly 300 percent as the credit squeeze hits the wider economy and raises the prospects of a global recession.

So, it's not just homeowners who are defaulting anymore. Companies are. One expert says we are already in a recession even though, technically, the economy has to be "contracting" for two quarters for a recession to be acknowledged.

But those in the know do know it's happening. They just don't want to panic the rest of us. This headline says it all: "The R-Word Surfaces On Wall Street. The White House is predictably complacent but the head of the National Bureau of Economics, Martin Feldstein, says there is a 'very serious risk of a very serious downturn.'"

Part of the reason for this is that the predators who came up with all these securitization and derivative scams were enabled by big Wall Street investment houses with the Bush Administration looking the other way. They figured it would only entrap poor people they didn't care about and so not affect them. How wrong they were.

And can you believe that these geniuses don't know how much of their own investments are contaminated by funny money (i.e., asset-based securities with no real assets backing them)?

The *Financial Times* put this more politely. "Credit Turmoil Shows That Not All Innovation Has Been Beneficial." They lament: No more champagne and "bumper bonuses" for the scammers.

This is the time bomb that may be freaking out the big boys now, but the rest of us will be affected as this crisis "rolls out" with rising unemployment and a credit squeeze. Billions are at stake. Tens of thousands have lost jobs. The housing sector, a core part of the economy, is a mess. People are having their homes stolen. Other speculators, in our country and others, are waiting to pounce and pick up bargains at fire sale prices.

We are seeing more stories on TV such as "I can't afford my life" detailing the economic noose so many families are experiencing but little about why it's happening and who has been profiting off so much misery.

Millions of Americans are affected, so why are so many people sucking their thumbs and looking the other way?

How can we make this a people's issue, not just a financial story? Who has the courage to take this on? Who is ready to act?

OCTOBER 20: WHEN THE POLITICAL IS ALSO PERSONAL

THE DEBT CRUNCH IN AMERICA IS NOT JUST AN ECONOMIC PROBLEM – it is often a personal crisis, affecting how millions of Americans live and what bills we can afford to pay. This was brought home in the *Boston Globe* in a story about a couple calling off their wedding because of fears of future indebtedness.

A young man was quoted as saying: "I want to marry her, but I don't want to marry her debt, and I can't justify spending anything on a wedding when our finances don't make sense at all."

You can just feel his dilemma. In *In Debt We Trust*, the conservative Nashville-based radio host Dave Ramsey explains: "Money problems are a big reason behind divorces. Financial pressures impose on every family and often lead to domestic violence and alcohol or drug dependency. The pressure is often too much."

Some family members don't even tell their loved ones about the debts they are running up. As a result, there can be lying and even stealing when the bills come due. That's happened in my life. I just saw a segment about this conflict on Big Love, the HBO series set in a polygamous marriage.

No one wants to talk about their personal finances unless they have to, but the pressures they are confronting is often the result of economic and political decisions made by others.

When Congress fails to protect consumers, that's one political decision. When big banks and credit card companies are allowed to get away with predatory practices or outrageous interest and fees, that's another one. That's why this whole issue has become one of personal survival and economic justice. Where is the fairness, transparency, and accountability in lending?

Look at what happened involving student loans. The press has been full of stories of conflicts of interests, payoffs, and gifts to schools and colleges to steer students to higher-priced loans, etc. Here's a headline from the *New York Times*: "LAWMAKERS SEE A RESPONSIBILITY FAILURE."

And, for once, the irresponsibility is not being blamed on us, the consumers. Even Margaret Spellings, the Education Secretary in the Bush Administration, admitted in testimony, "The system is redundant, it's Byzantine and it's broken." She said the system is "CRYING OUT for Reform."

Thank you Madam Secretary – finally some truth in high places... but only after the press started exposing the situation, not before. Commenting on one of the documented rip-offs, Representative John Tierney said, "It boggles my mind."

Suddenly, many minds at the top are being "boggled."

OCTOBER 27: THE FAILURE OF LIBERAL ACTIVISM

AS I TRIED TO DISTRIBUTE IN DEBT WE TRUST ARTICLES AND SPEECHES TO activists and spark interest in the issue, I found inertia, disinterest, and occasional lip service from the very activist media outlets and organizations I assumed would engage with the issues I was raising.

The Iraq war remained THE only issue for many radicals, while many liberals had been sucked into the presidential campaign, which had begun a year earlier than usual. One reason may be that most people don't want to talk about money – many feel they haven't or can't manage theirs well. If they are deeply in debt, they are often embarrassed and silent. The economic situation seems beyond any-one's control and for the majority of Americans who lack confidence in the economy, it can be scary to think about.

"Da Nile," as the joke goes, is not just a river in Egypt.

Also, stories of corruption and controversy out of Washington seem lots sexier than complicated economic issues tied to Wall Street with so many terms most of us tune out of.

Many of the people who should care the most have been silent.

Most unions are fighting for their lives and many are selling credit cards, not challenging them. The shift in the economy from production to consumption – driven by credit and debt – did not seem to change the way they do business.

They remained an adjunct to the Democratic Party when it came to activist campaigning and were supportive in theory but silent in practice when it came to tackling them. Not surprisingly, we were to learn later that John Edwards, the one Presidential candidate who was raising economic justice issues, was himself invested in a fund that financed subprime loans.

(He was not the only compromised candidate. Hillary Clinton's campaign manager would be connected to a firm making subprime loans while Barack Obama's finance chairman had the same distinction. John McCain's top advisor, former Senator Phil Gramm lobbied for financial companies when he left office.)

I later saw similar conflicts play out at a national conference in Washington to mobilize the progressive agenda.

The buses were arriving as I was leaving the Take Back America conference to join union members rallying for passage of the Employee Free Choice Act, which was being debated in the Senate.

According to one report: "Defying 97-degree heat, heavy humidity and a planned Republican filibuster, several thousand workers and their allies rallied in Washington Tuesday to demand the Senate pass the Employee Free Choice Act."

The unions were fighting an uphill battle for their survival and the right of workers to join unions. This issue is one of many that is critical to Democrats who want to take the government back because unions have long been main funders and grass roots energizers of the party.

Writing on TomPaine.com, Dmitri Iglitzin reprised labor's challenge and eroding position.

In many ways, the lack of overwhelming support for EFCA is surprising. Under current law, workers who want to form a union must currently undergo a risky, grueling and time-consuming "pre-election" period that culminates, if they're lucky, in an election held under the auspices of the National Labor Relations Board (NLRB). If they're not lucky, the workers are instead fired or otherwise discriminated against. One recent study, conducted by the Center for Economic and Policy Research, found that about one in five union organizers or activists can expect to be fired during the pre-election period.

Should the workers succeed in unionizing, moreover, their chances of ever obtaining a collective bargaining agreement with their employer are grim. According to the Federal Mediation and Conciliation Service, a federal agency, nearly half of newly organized bargaining units fail to negotiate a first contract within two years of a successful organizing drive. The result of these barriers to successful unionizing is manifest in the steady decline of union membership, now 12 percent of the workforce (7.4 percent in the private sector), down from 20 percent in 1983 and 35 percent in the 1950s.

It's not surprising, then, that in a corporate-dominated country, labor has to struggle endlessly for its rights. Leading the fight against the bill are big lobbyists fueled by big money. According to the AFL-CIO, these groups camouflage their special interests by claiming to be champions of democracy in the workplace, and never revealing their economic interests in the issue. Here's what the battle turns on, according to the Center for American Progress:

> Under current law, an employer can insist on a secret-ballot election, even after a majority of employees express their desire to organize. The proposed law "would give employees at a workplace the right to unionize as soon as a majority signed cards saying they wanted to do so.

Suddenly, business interests, which usually line up against extending more democratic rights in the society, insist on it for employees, knowing they can intimidate them to vote against unions. Those well-known guardians of democracy, the Chamber of Commerce, spent a record $72 million on lobbying. VP for labor policy Randall Johnson told the *New York Times*, "We've targeted [The Employee Free Choice Act] as our No. 1 or No. 2 priority to defeat."

But there is something more profound underway here that neither the unions nor the activists that rallied to support them seem to connect with: the fact that our economy has changed fundamentally. It is easy to see workers getting targeted as a group but harder to understand how we as consumers, especially workers, are under a more profound economic attack. As privatization sweeps through the society, there has been a privatization of economic pain.

As jobs are outsourced and unions shrink, there are new and often silent battles being fought in our post-industrial society that most politicos and unions don't seem to understand or relate to. Economist Michael Hudson explains it this way in my film:

> People have difficulty realizing that the new economic conflict in our society is between creditors and debtors. There's still a tendency of many left-wingers to think in terms of the class war and the wars between employers and employees. But the real economic war, where all the money is being made, is between creditors and debtors because that's the free lunch.

No wonder that financial institutions and real estate companies are now the leading source of political money. Their influence steers politicians away from protecting consumers, as we saw when, and as my film reveals, $151 MILLION was spent on lobbying on the bankruptcy bill that was passed with bipartisan support. So when it comes to money issues that matter, the Democrats are as much a part of the problem as the Republicans.

You just can't see the world or real power through a narrow partisan lens as much as you may want to. I have also been unsuccessful so far in getting unions to show the film, even though I spoke with some prominent leaders who agreed that the issue is important and that their members are hurting. Perhaps their reticence has something to do with revenues they depend on from union credit cards.

Jonathan Tasini explained in his blog that there is a lot of credit card money fueling the labor bureaucracy: "The AFL-CIO pockets $25 million a year from the deal with Households Bank."

How do we get the presidential candidates to start talking about the nearly $3 TRILLION dollars in consumer debt, and the mounting trap that this leads to for so many families? The Common Dreams website just ran a report explaining that thousands of liberal young people can't take time off to get involved in politics because they are working overtime at lousy jobs to pay off their student loans and debts.

And what about those Americans relying on pricey payday lenders and check cashing joints? In the name of economic justice, we must add the demand for debt relief to all of our other concerns. We can't just take America back from the Republicans without also taking it back from the banks, hedge funds, and predatory lenders.

Throughout American history, debt has been a key issue. It was one of the problems that led the colonists to revolt against the British. Main Street has been struggling for liberation from Wall Street for decades with waves of populist movements that won many reforms and a better life for millions. Just as there are business cycles, there are cycles of protest. Why are our political parties submerging this issue?

Conferences in hotels may help promote political focus, but it is in the streets outside the beltway, not in the suites within it, where change has to happen first. Political races matter, but they are not the only road to transforming a society in which economic inequality is deepening.

UPDATE: The organization behind the conference did organize a well-attended screening of *In Debt We Trust* on Capitol Hill. Little came out of it. Congressman John Conyers sponsored a second showing in April 2008.

OCTOBER 29: CALIFORNIA BURNING, WALL STREET CHURNING

Disparities in coverage continued for months even after the media "discovered" the credit crisis story and understood how serious it is. By October of 2007, we finally began getting network news stories about growing income inequalities and debt issues. Yet the gap between the reporting on this crisis and others was very apparent to me when the media went all out to document raging firestorms in California. I wrote about that this way:

TWO DISASTERS SIDE BY SIDE. BOTH INVOLVE A MASSIVE LOSS OF people's homes. One is about California burning, the other about Wall Street churning. The one we saw on TV the most was not necessarily the most serious. In one, the flames of out of control fires, perhaps, in a few instances, the work of firebugs, becomes a spectacle for wall-to-wall "BREAKING NEWS" coverage. There were around-the-clock helicopter shots and constant online webcam footage, as well as a visit by a President feigning concern and throwing money at the problem.

In the other, there are far fewer humanizing feature stories along with a great deal of dry and arcane business-section commentaries. TV crews are not going live to the neighborhoods facing massive foreclosures or investigating the "mortgage bugs" that profited from the far less visible subprime fraud disaster. There are no webcams with time-lapse photography chronicling the decline of neighborhoods as homeowners default on unaffordable loans.

The President is not speaking at photo-ops on Wall Street to denounce the investment banks and hedge-fund financiers responsible for losing billions, plunging the country into a recession, and upsetting the world financial system.

Both stories are dramatic – and both have led to suffering. The forest fires have claimed lives, including those of several "illegal" immigrants, as of Friday. "I imagine we will be finding bodies into next year," Sgt. Mike Radovich of the San Diego Sheriff's Department told the *New York Times*.

In all, 1,800 homes were destroyed in California as of Friday. A half a million acres had been consumed. Those responsible for containing the damage blamed the weather in the short-term and climate change in the long-term, as well as earlier fire-fighting techniques. This disaster is expected to cost $1 billion.

There were reports that some of the relief helicopters had been grounded for bureaucratic reasons and worries that arsonists contributed to the conflagration. Some of the fires appeared to have been set intentionally. Yet intentional actions also drove the targeting of families in a pervasive subprime mortgage fraud that threatens to lead to far more homes lost, not 1,800, but an estimated two and a half million. (The *LA Times* says foreclosures in California are at a record high. The third quarter's total surpasses 24,000, which is a record.) More homes are at risk in the fires that have yet to be contained.

It's hard to predict how many of these people will get sick or die because of psychological disorientation and homelessness. Many of them are poor, while those scarred by the fire lived largely in affluent communities.

Which victims are getting the most positive media attention? That's a no-brainer. It's the suburbanites, not the urbanites, who are the most sympathetic.

Senator Chris Dodd, chairman of the Senate Banking Committee, characterized the subprime crisis as a "50 State Katrina." This disaster has already cost over a trillion dollars – maybe more. Meanwhile, President Bush used Katrina as a partisan political symbol, contrasting California's hands-on Republican governor with the former Democratic governor of Louisiana, whom he blamed for the weak response to that crisis. He declined to discuss questions comparing the federal response to both calamities. Reported the *Toronto Star*:

> There are many factors that separate the chaos and death that swallowed New Orleans in the wake of Hurricane Katrina and the orderly evacuation and relatively minuscule loss of life in this week's wildfires. In politics, image can sometimes trump substance, and that lesson appears to have been at the heart of the response of California Governor Arnold Schwarzenegger, who, in a dizzying schedule of events, has comforted victims, firefighters and the displaced and freed up the state's resources.

Of course most of the media coverage has stayed with the "action" and pathos in the present, showing spectacular flaming forests like some 60's light show, and then the aftermath with families in tears at the burned out shells of what were once their homes.

The coverage, however, asked few questions about who and what's behind this "apocalypse now." Author Mike Davis, who has followed California fires and analyzes them in depth, adds a context that is missing in most of the reporting, writing:

Exactly a decade ago, between Oct. 26 and Nov. 7, firestorms fanned by Santa Anas destroyed more than a thousand homes in Pasadena, Malibu, and Laguna Beach. In the last century, nearly half the great Southern California fires have occurred in October. This time, climate, ecology, and stupid urbanization have conspired to create the ingredients for one of the most perfect firestorms in history. Experts have seen it coming for months.

He dismisses the blame-the-arsonists-news frame in a piece on TomDispatch.com:

This is a specter against which grand inquisitors and wars against terrorism are powerless to protect us. Moreover, many fire scientists dismiss "ignition" – whether natural, accidental, or deliberate – as a relatively trivial factor in their equations. They study wildfire as an inevitable result of the accumulation of fuel mass. Given fuel, "fire happens."

The best preventive measure, of course, is to return to the native-Californian practice of regular, small-scale burning of old brush and chaparral. This is now textbook policy, but the suburbanization of the fire terrain makes it almost impossible to implement it on any adequate scale. Homeowners despise the temporary pollution of "controlled burns" and local officials fear the legal consequences of escaped fires.

The scale of the "suburbanization of the fire terrain" in the last few years was immense. *USA Today* reported that more than 55,000 people moved to the neighborhoods that were affected since 2000. They are living in the epicenter of the fires. They were allowed to settle in the riskiest wildlife areas vulnerable to the types of firestorms we've seen. The real estate industry encouraged this settlement with support from local authorities. They knew the region was fire prone.

So, when you scratch the scorched surface of this newsy inferno you get deeper causes, a lack of planning and monitoring, not to mention inattention by government. Sound familiar?

These same deeper causes led to the runaway subprime scandal that has already caused losses in the TRILLIONS, and the clear complicity of leading banks that are seeking bailouts to cover up (and seek compensation) for their role in crimes that have triggered a global financial meltdown and a developing recession, and perhaps something worse to come. Democrats charge that the Bush administration is not acting on the crisis because of its fanatical free-market ideology.

New York Times columnist Paul Krugman also sees this crisis as a "disaster," noting, "Maybe the subprime disaster will be enough to remind us why financial regulation was introduced in the first place." The *Financial Times* compared it to "the plot of a hundred disaster movies."

Most of the world sees the U.S. response to this second crisis as morally wrong because it bails out the people who caused it. They also denounce U.S. hypocrisy because it ignores the advice that American officials heaped on Asia during its financial crisis.

William Pesek of *Bloomberg News* writes:

Asians were berated for a lack of transparency. In the late 1990s, the U.S. demanded that reserves figures be published and that clear lines be drawn between governments and private sectors. In the US, dubious mortgage products were sold, repackaged and resold with negligible transparency, while ratings companies approved of the process. The government and the Fed just stood by...

None of this is to defend the economic systems that led to the Asian crisis. Yet now the U.S. is at the center of what Nouriel Roubini, chairman of Roubini Global Economics LLC in New York, calls the "first crisis of financial globalization and securitization." And what is the U.S. doing? Playing a role in hypocritically bailing out those who should have known better.

In short, this still-unfolding episode of self-inflicted disaster capitalism takes us not only to the realm of irresponsible financial policies but to other parallels, like the war in Iraq, suggests Lewis Lapham in *Harpers*, who compares the subprime NINJA (No Income, No Jobs, No Assets) LOANS in the U.S. to support for "freedom loving" Sheiks in Iraq, and THE NEUTRON LOAN that removes occupants but leaves the property intact to the massive displacement of people by the tens of thousands in Baghdad. He also notes that THE TEASER LOAN gets people in mortgages at a low rate and quickly escalates like the rising costs of the war, which was "originally priced" at $50 billion and is now estimated at $2 TRILLLION. (A recent study put it at $3 trillion.)

This is a brilliant comparative analysis that shows how the suspension of reality by politicians or bankers has the same result: misery for millions.

So by all means let's be supportive toward the fire victims who have lost their homes in California's "natural" disaster – and those that may in fires that may soon have Texas burning – but we should do so without forgetting the millions of Americans who will soon lose their homes and their economic stability in Wall Street's man-made storm. Unfortunately most Americans and most progressives seem to be in denial about the economic disaster we are facing.

NOVEMBER 5: HUMPTY DUMPTY RIDES THE WAVES

Humpty Dumpty Sat On a Wall
Humpty Dumpty Had a Great Fall
All the King's Horses, All The King's Men
Couldn't Put Humpty Together Again

— Children's Rhyme

BUT THEY'RE TRYING, AREN'T THEY? AFTER THE MARKETS WENT BALLISTIC last summer in the wake of the disclosure of the subprime "infection/contagion," bankers have been trying to fix this pernicious Humpty Dumpty and restore confidence.

Have they ever? Here's the cycle. First there was jaw-boning and tsk-tsking as the captains of finance capital and big bankers finally woke up and warn of the danger, blaming everyone but themselves. Then, the pundits started lecturing, calling for higher standards of transparency.

Finally, the bailouts began.

The Federal Reserve Bank stepped up to the plate and swung a mighty bat by "injecting" billions to calm the volatility. Soon other central bankers, at their behest, were in the game, too, with hundreds of billions of their own from Europe, Japan, Australia, and even China.

The result: Not much. Panic percolated. More lending companies "imploded." (The total was then 179. By April 2008, it was 247.) It seemed certain that over two million families faced foreclosure and inflation was beginning to raise its ugly head. The dollar was dropping and real, well-paying new jobs were not on the horizon.

The next panacea was interest-rate cuts. Surely that would do it. With much fanfare and a push from the press, from Jim Cramer ranting on CNBC to more sober heads wagging approval in the mainstream media, first the bank lending rate was cut and then the interest rate. The cut was 50 basis points, twice what was expected.

Wall Street was ecstatic. The market partied and stocks rallied. The next day, when the hangovers wore off, it dove again.

The subprime menace was still there in the morning. Soon, the banks were forced to review their unbalanced sheets and, one by one, reported billions in write-downs. Billions! What was clear is that the greed had got them too – they were all stuffing themselves at the trough of predatory lending. They were all complicit.

And in fact, as CNN reports, there is more to come from their binge and purge behavior.

As one blogger summed up: "The 'Fat Lady' Has Not Sung Yet."

First estimate I have seen about losses in Q4 from CNN.Money:

Banks are likely to mark down another $10 billion of mortgage assets in the fourth quarter, according to one analyst's estimates. Merrill Lynch and Citigroup are expected to be hit the hardest.

Mayo estimated each bank would write down $4 billion in the fourth quarter. He said Bear Stearns, Morgan Stanley, B of A and Wachovia are also likely to take markdowns. Banks have taken massive hits from risky mortgage securities in the third quarter. Merrill Lynch wrote down $7.9 billion, and Citi took a $2.2 billion markdown due to mortgage-backed securities and credit trading losses.

His conclusion: "The pain from the subprime wipeout isn't likely to abate anytime soon."

UPDATE: The actual writedowns were much more expensive.

Bear in mind, the banks created these problems by lowering their standards and working in collusion with the alchemists at the ratings agencies that turned their junk into gold.

Then, Treasury Secretary Paulson had a revelation: create a private superfund with $200 billion. In the end, three big banks could only come up with $75 billion, but many experts derided it as just PR that cannot cure the crisis. Oops! Knowing this, what did the Fed do? Cut interest rates again last week, supposedly for the last time. And again, there was a one-day rally followed by a major drop.

Nothing changed. In a Detroit paper, Gail Marks Jarvis compared the Fed's action to a "teaspoon of tonic," explaining:

The incubation period for economic remedies and problems is often six to twelve months, and the economy could be sickened by more than tumbling home prices and the potential that house-poor consumers might not spend much.

Bill Fleckenstein of MSNBC went apoplectic, calling the cut an "act of desperation," comparing it to "using an applause meter to run the central bank." He asked:

> Why in the hell was the central bank easing the federal funds rate with (1) the dollar at a new low, (2) oil at $90, (3) gold at $800, (4) virtually every commodity on the planet going wild, and (5) despite government statistics to the contrary, inflation raging?

Ah yes, statistics. Some new jobs figures were trotted out suggesting a 166,000 new job uptick. Sounded good. Nonfarm payroll employment was said to have risen by 166,000 in October, and the unemployment rate was unchanged at 4.7 percent. Huh... employment rises but unemployment doesn't?

But a blog called Predicto dissected the numbers, revealing that the Bureau of Labor Statistics was actually estimating, not reporting:

> Now, just how much of it was created by the CES Birth-Death Model, which statistically supposes jobs created? Try 103,000 for October. A true skeptic would say 166 thousand new jobs, backing out 103 thousand CES Birth/Death Model estimated, leaves a real gain of 63-thousand, but any port in a storm, right? And the "engineers flipping burgers" report, Table A-12, category U-6 stayed steady at 8.4%. Predictably.

> And while the government is telling us on the one hand how good things are, I can't help but notice that Chrysler is slicing one job in three, with another 12,000 about to get axed. I'm not expecting this to show up as a noticeable blip on the Mass Layoffs report, though. Statistical series which have been historically noisy have all quieted down. All coincidental, I'm sure.

Real analysis and understanding on this crucial issue is missing, like the 50 million "Missing Americans" profiled on PBS by Bill Moyers, who described a vast class of Americans who are suffering in our economy but are rarely in the news.

Author Katherine Newman explained to Bill Moyers:

> The missing class are families that are above the poverty line, but well below the middle class. So they earn about $20,000 to $40,000 a year for a family of four. The federal poverty line is $20,000. They have multiple jobs. Both as individuals and in their households. They often have to press their children into the labor market and pool that money so that their households can maintain themselves above the poverty line...They work every hour that exists. And sometimes that means they're not around very much for

their children. Because they can't stay above the poverty line unless they put in many, many hours.

Many of these "missing" were the people targeted by the predatory lenders.

So far, in the markets and for millions, there's no way out. Manipulated information and illusion drives policy at home as in Iraq. We won't see what we think it is not in our interest to see, and we can't report what we don't see.

And the circle of omission and denial is closed.

Chaper 5
WHAT HAPPENS NOW?

DECEMBER 2007: IT IS NOW THE LAST MONTH OF THE YEAR; THE month that the Christmas Carol tells us is "The month that Jesus was born in." The crisis has not abated. So where is this sad story headed?

What's the prognosis?

As the citizen of a country without an attention span, everyone wants someone else to play forecaster and tick off what must be done. And they want it quick and simple even though there are no real quickie responses to a complicated problem. Almost any reassuring soundbite will do. The questions are predicable. Can't they fix this – after all, isn't our economy oh so "resilient?"

And, yes, your government is trying. George Bush doesn't want to leave office with two million families in the streets. He doesn't want a legacy worse than Herbert Hoover's. The defacto loss of the completely mismanaged war in Iraq is a tough enough burden to carry around.

It's probably not helpful to add that the mismanagement of our economy is an outgrowth of the very corporatist policies that will haunt this country for decades to come. Add to this costly wars, obscenely high levels of corruption, and the list of maladies goes on. This crisis, however, is a bit different because it has built in intensity for years without much visibility or attention. It speaks to structural problems in an economy engineered on the quicksand of debt and delusion.

In order for the economy to function, in order for consumption to continue and profits to keep flowing, people have to believe that everything's all right. They want reassurance and remedies modeled after an Alka Seltzer pill. Put one tablet in water. It fizzes. You drink and feel better in minutes.

The truth is confidence is eroding not because "the masses" hate capitalism, but because capitalism is increasingly not working for them. They know that because prices keep rising and good paying jobs are harder to find. They know that because crime is going up in many cities, and it's harder to make ends meet. And some even know that the very concept of the masses has been replaced by highly stratified classes built on growing income inequality. The idea of classes is now fragmented into demographic niches and segments.

The credit card companies are now encouraging us to pay our rent by charging it. They have jacked up their fees and passed rules that just somehow lead to even more late fees and other charges which have doubled and tripled. All of this has been done by fiat.

Some economic wise men believe that the credit card bubble is the next to go in a widely predicted severe recession.

Personally, I don't know what will happen. It is possible that we will bounce back from the precipice somehow. It's been done before. There are whole industries at risk if we don't. There are a large number of wealthy people and institutions that want to get back to the business of making money. They have a strong self-interest in "normalizing" the system.

What's "normal" for them is, of course, why we are in the trouble we are. At the same time, many of the free marketeers argue that all that is needed is a correction of some undefined kind to put the "fundamentals" in line and bounce back. Capitalism has a history of boom and bust cycles and recovers because there is no perceived alternative.

Yet this time around, we are not talking about a small issue or some anomaly. As *Business Week* noted, "What we're observing, in all its bizarreness, is the ancient paradox of what happens when an irresistible force meets an immovable object. The irresistible force in this case is the U.S. economy... The immovable object is a wall of debt that now can't be paid back."

Who knows – perhaps, there will be another war to divert us from even worrying about any impending crash or give us someone "out there" to blame for it – the Chinese, the Arabs, anyone but us. There are plenty of potential enemies to scare us, not to mention environmental crises or a terrorist attack or two. Anything can happen, and usually does.

As I write in early December of 2007, we do know that the Federal Reserve Bank is likely to cut interest rates again and Treasury Secretary Hank Paulson, a former honcho at Goldman Sachs, is proposing a plan to freeze interest rates on adjustable-rate mortgages as one way to keep some homeowners from losing their homes.

Are these measures likely to work? Not based on their track record so far. The Fed has injected billions into the system to create more liquidity, but the crisis is worse than ever. Paulson convinced big banks to start a superfund but that hasn't had much impact yet. (The idea later tanked.)

Many of the first reports about the initiative were positive – there were 282 listed on Google. But one of them actually did offer some analysis by a conservative who – this is rich – compares the supercapitalist Paulson to a communist. Seth Jayson, writing on the financial website Motley Fool, called it "a plan to punish the public," and a reminder that there are always unintended and unspoken consequences of governmental intervention in the affairs of the holy sanctum of the market:

> If the mortgage crisis and housing bubble have taught us one thing, it should be to watch out for the unintended consequences of greed. Unfortunately, our nation's legislators and political appointees haven't learned that lesson. Recent plans for housing and mortgage bailouts generally run from dumb to dumber. Today, The *Wall Street Journal* reported on yet another scheme, reportedly being spearheaded by Treasury Secretary Hank Paulson. It's an idea so naively populist and antimarket that you would think it came from Hugo Chavez, Evo Morales, or Mahmoud Ahmadinejad, if not for its cringe-inducing, Beltway-wonk moniker: the Hope Now Alliance.

Imagine Paulson's reaction to reading that he is, in the eyes of a right-wing critic on a respected website, acting like a Chavezista or Iranian mullah? Could the government have finally realized that only socialism can save capitalism?

You can't make this stuff up.

The author does note that few of the institutions who profited on the subprime mania will likely be punished except by their own companies, despite the damage they've done:

The fancy securities – what I call Wall Street dog food – have become nearly worthless, and the music has stopped, without any chairs for anyone. Ironically, stupid, leveraged bets on these lousy securities have crippled the banks themselves, and CEOs and other execs have been getting the boot at places like Citigroup, Merrill Lynch (NYSE: MER), and Morgan Stanley (NYSE: MS)...

This writer worries that government bailouts send the wrong message. I'm thinking that, instead of a bailout, we need a "jail-out." Hard time, not financial rewards. After all, this is the biggest bank robbery in history – only the banks are the ones doing the robbing. Jesse Jackson agrees with me, but he fears that "we may have to ignore the sinners to save the saints."

At issue here is the concept of "moral hazard." "By rescuing greedy and naive borrowers from their mistakes, our government encourages others to take big, stupid, bankruptcy-inducing risks, secure in the knowledge that the government will bail them out when times get rough," writes Jayson. "That means trillions of dollars in capital will be ill-invested yet again, something that's much less likely to happen when speculators are made to suffer the consequences of their behavior."

NO FREE LUNCHES

Here's another problem. Someone is going to have to foot the bill for this. Banks and associated entities that will, over the short term, finance this homeowner bailout are not going to do it out of the goodness of their hearts. Reportedly, Hope Now Alliance honchos such as Countrywide and Citigroup are, I'm certain, only proposing this because they hope it will be cheaper than having to pay up for their lending sins all at once.

While conservative critics make telling points about hypocrisy and flawed progress, they only subscribe to market bromides and do not offer a program for economic revitalization. They have nothing to say about growing poverty, inequality, and the economic distress of millions for whom they only propose financial education.

The researcher and writer Tamara Drout, who works for a think tank called DEMOS, identifies some structural problems they ignore. She identifies the real challenge in my film *In Debt We Trust*:

We're not going to educate our way out of this problem. Financial education is wonderful and we need to do more of it but, what's driving a lot of the debt in these households is not a lack of budgeting, or a lack of financial savvy, it's an economy that's increasingly stacked against them.

Debt is a symptom of much larger economic and structural issues facing households. One, we've seen a decline in incomes or a stagnation of incomes, particularly in the lower income household range and also for middle income households. At the same time, costs have really skyrocketted: health care, housing costs, the cost of sending a kid to college, and finally, we've gotta look at, public policy and what has happened. And what we see is a real retrenchment in providing a safety net for households.

While this intense debate goes on, trillions of dollars have been lost along with the reputations of many key institutions. Many fear a severe recession, and some see the dangers of a depression. Don't say it can't happen here. It already has, more than once. Are we due for another crash? Never say never!

Employment is stagnant. Lay-offs continue on Wall Street with top female executives especially getting the blame and the axe at some investment banks. Top financial analysts like John Rogers say there is no quick fix and that things may get worse before they get better, if they do.

"We are only in the early innings of a significant market correction led by the finance sector. When financial firms struggle, they have a big effect on the broader economy, from consumer loans to initial offerings to mergers and acquisitions. A real recovery is going to take a while."

Meanwhile, credit has tightened for everyone, including businesses that live on loans, and the rich are blaming the poor while downward economic mobility becomes a pervasive new reality of life. The middle class is shrinking and the rest of us, according to economist Michael Hudson, are turning into serfs tied to our debts in the same way that the feudal lords tied serfs to their land.

Bear in mind that capitalism is what replaced feudalism – or did it?

Former Chase Bank economist Michael Hudson also told me of an irony: the poor, contrary to conventional prejudices, really do pay their bills, which may be another reason why they were targeted.

What happened about fifteen, twenty years ago is that bankers said they made an anthropological discovery, a breakthrough. They found out that the poor are honest. Almost the only people who believe that they should repay their debts are the poor people. And in fact the less money you have the more you believe that the debts should be paid. What this means is that even though the poorer you are, the higher the interest rate you pay, the poorer you are, the greater the likelihood the bank has that you're going to repay the debt.

If the poor are honest, the lenders who took advantage of them are not.

There is a conflict coming, almost an economic civil war. Its not just a worker-driven class war either – and its outcome is far from clear. Says credit expert Robert Manning:

> What we've seen with this kind of financialization of the American economy, where the democratic system and so many democratic institutions have been co-opted and literally bought by the financial service industry, is that we're seeing a big backlash from the American people.

In the years since 2001, when the U.S. was supported by nations throughout the world, there has been a steady decline in respect for the United States and a lack of confidence in its leaders all over the world. Inside the United States, recent polls show 81 percent of the public now saying the country is moving in the wrong direction.

Gary Younge of the *Guardian* has reported on a deeper shift in American attitudes that perhaps he can see more clearly as a foreigner:

> This sense of optimism has been in retreat in almost every sense over the past few years. According to Rasmussen polls, just 21% of Americans believe the country is on the right track, a figure that has fallen by more than a half since the presidential election of 2004. Meanwhile only a third think the country's best days are yet to come, as opposed to 43% who believe they have come and gone – again a steep decline on three years ago. These are not one-offs. In the past 18 months almost every poll that has asked Americans about their country's direction has produced among the most pessimistic responses on record – a more extended period than anyone can remember since Watergate.

And one main reason is that Americans are hurting in their pocket-books as well as their souls. Younge explains:

> Closest to home is the economy. Wages are stagnant, house prices in most areas have stalled or are falling, the dollar is plunging, and the deficit is rising. A Pew survey last week showed that 72% believe the economy is either "only fair" or poor and 76% believe it

will be the same or worse a year from now. Globalization is a major worry.

Thanks to this crisis, and all of the factors cited in this book, the same lack of respect and confidence for the U.S. that we see overseas has come home. The squeeze is on, and to quote the '60s poet, Mr. Bob Zimmerman, "there's a hard rain that's gonna fall."

THE IDES OF MARCH 2008: SAVING WALL STREET FROM ITSELF

WALL STREET HAS MANY FRIENDS. ITS RECURRING SINS AND TRANSGRESSIONS are pervasive but tend to get a free pass because of the way our society worships markets. Somehow the big boys always tend to take care of themselves with bonuses, incentives, and exotic compensation packages.

What about the rest of us? In this dramatic economic downturn, can we be secure about our investments, retirement plans, and even the banks that hold our money?

Don't think that I, you, or all of us won't be affected by the financial disaster. For starters, the "experts" expect a 25% drop in housing value. Beyond that, a fall off in share price can put our 401k retirement packages at risk. Already an economist at the Bank of America says that the loss from subprime write-offs and declines in share value add up to $7.1 TRILLION. That estimate is already dated as I write. That's a lot of money!

I am not a financial advisor. Like most of us, I need advice. But when I read all the economists saying there won't be a depression, I wonder if they are the same ones who said a recession was unlikely until it was undeniable.

What about the banks? How safe are they?

Recently I heard a talk by FDIC Chairman Sheila C. Bair. She spoke to a group of community activists in a Washington Hotel on the morning of Friday March 14, on the day before the Ides of March, the anniversary of the death of Caesar.

Created during the depression, this agency was put in place in response to the bank runs that deepened the Great Depression of the 1930s. Its role was to insure confidence in banks and the financial system. Without it, the economy cannot function. Its chairman is in the confidence business. If that sounds like a con game, it is.

"Don't Worry Be Happy" could be the FDIC's theme song.

Its mission?

The Federal Deposit Insurance Corporation (FDIC) preserves and promotes public confidence in the U.S. financial system by insuring deposits in banks and thrift institutions for at least $100,000; by identifying, monitoring and addressing risks to the deposit insurance funds; and by limiting the effect on the economy and the financial system when a bank or thrift institution fails.

Before being appointed or anointed to run the FDIC, Bair, a Kansas native, had served as an academic, as an aide for one-time Republican presidential candidate Robert Dole, and later held various executive jobs at the New York Stock Exchange. She had come that morning from her mountaintop as the nation's top bank official with a message of reassurance to the "masses." Perhaps it was a mission of pacification. The text and subtext was: "No problem, all is under control."

At the time of her appearance, the industry she was overseeing was not doing too well. Bank profits had plunged 84 percent by the end of 2007, the lowest in 16 years. The banking system itself was under escalating stress as the credit crisis brought consumer lending and even bank to bank lending to a standstill. Last year, there had been a run on England's Northern Rock Bank that forced the Bank of England to step in to guarantee deposits, a move that did not stop customers from queuing outside the bank and withdrawing £4 billion. The bank has since been nationalized.

The panic there – the lines outside the bank – sent shivers down the spines of regulators the world over.

Bair acknowledged part of the problem, namely that regulations had been slipping and had earlier spoken of "weaknesses and holes in our bank regulation ... at the heart of the current mortgage situation." When she was with the Treasury Department, back in 2001, she tried to get the companies making subprime loans to regulate themselves, as the *New York Times* reported:

In 2001, a senior Treasury official, Sheila C. Bair, tried to persuade subprime lenders to adopt a code of "best practices" and to let outside monitors verify their compliance. None of the lenders would agree to the monitors, and many rejected the code itself. Even those who did adopt those practices, Ms. Bair recalled recently, soon let them slip.

In other words, they told her to get stuffed. And she did!

Now, she was face to face with the National Community Reinvestment Coalition, representing millions of Americans facing foreclosure from their homes, 45,000 every month. Most were not in a good mood.

The community groups. dealing with earthquakes of pain in their own neighborhoods, are aware of the connection between what was done to them and what is now happening to some of Wall Street's top firms. They also recognized that the regulators were not regulating. A business publication had reported that a "favorite move" among the titans of finance was a game called "beat the regulator."

The reality was that over the years fewer and fewer financial institutions were even subject to regulation. A "shadow banking system" had emerged with more assets at its disposal than the commercial banks. The regulators knew that but did little about it.

As James Surowiecki noted in the *New Yorker*: "Most money that's borrowed these days no longer comes from commercial banks, which are responsible for less than thirty per cent of all lending. Instead, in one form or another, the loans are packaged and sold as securities. And since investment banks do much of the selling and buying of those securities, they play an ever bigger role in financial markets."

Thus, as the subprime crisis emerged, observers argued that there was little the government could do, which was just fine with all the apostles of deregulation and free market thinking in the government.

Bair was a regulator in a government that rejected regulation— sort of like a fox guarding the proverbial chicken house.

Ever upbeat, as is her function, she noted that she saw a "silver lining" in the crisis because more and more people in the industry now recognized the importance of regulation. She announced her intent to press banks to give homeowners five years at their current mortgage rates to prevent them from being forced out. She later admitted that she had initially favored restructuring the mortgages over 30 years but "had lost that fight."

Her speech lacked all compassion for the suffering of so many, but in some way, you sensed she was actually one of the "good people" but powerless to go up against the power of the White House and its Treasury Department. She is there to defend bank customers; the Administration is more committed to defending the banks.

I asked a question, well actually two. One, how many banks did she think would fail? And did she support the FBI investigation of mortgage fraudsters? Would she call for the prosecution of the white-collar criminals who engineered the subprime scams that defrauded so many borrowers? She was, I think, startled to hear concerns raised that are usually not part of the ever so polite discourse in Washington, where civility is the currency of conversation.

To my first query, she acknowledged that the FDIC has a list of 76 "troubled" banks – but, given her professionally positive outlook, she said she didn't expect any big disruptions. (Two weeks later, *The Wall Street Journal* would report that "The Federal Deposit Insurance Corp plans to hire as many as 138 new workers to address the potential for rising bank failures." Her speech gave no inkling that such a move was in the cards.)

She was positive in her prophecies but also quite wrong. (Gerald Cassidy, an analyst for RBC Capital Markets, told Reuters on April 7 2008, that "we anticipate 150 banks will fail over the next two years." A day earlier, a commercial real estate blog reported: "The Real Estate market has hit the wall, as space occupied by retailers fell for the first time in decades. This suggests some major bank failures are just around the corner."

Later on, on that very same day, we would learn that there was a run on Bear Stearns in New York. It was insolvent and expected to declare bankruptcy the next Monday.

No one in the room listening to Bair had any idea then of the depth of the crisis to come.

To my second query, about criminality, she was silent. That's not her job, she said. Obviously she hadn't heard the slogan I heard relayed on the Amtrak while training down to DC, "If you see something, say something."

The next speaker, whom I unfortunately missed, was none other than Federal Reserve Chairman Ben Bernanke, who recycled some of his proposals for mortgage reforms, going beyond what he had said earlier but hardly as far as the audience wanted. No one could challenge him from the floor and the newspaper reports only focused on his speech without any reference to comments from the housing activists present. It's almost as if the press practices stenography or at least the regurgitation of prepared texts rather than reporting on the events themselves.

So far, this was a pretty typical interaction between citizens and their overlords. No one present had an idea of what Bernanke was really worrying about. His speech, booked months in advance, was not unlike President Bush's appearance in that classroom on the morning of 9/11. Both men carried out routine appearances perhaps to avoid or deny the crisis that was exploding on their front lawn.

Bernanke was no doubt monitoring the impending collapse of Bear Stearns, the country's fith-largest broker and an institution that had been around for eighty-five years. Because within an hour or two, the Fed would make an announcement that would shock the world. It turns out he had been up half of the night before fashioning an unusual bailout, including funding JP Morgan to buy up Bear Stern's toxic debts and lending directly to brokers, a Fed first. Later, interest rates would be cut to 2.25% – not as much as the bankers wanted, but still the fastest change in monetary policy in decades.

"The marvelous edifice of modern finance took years to build," the *Economist* would later comment. "The world had a weekend to save it from collapsing." The situation was that serious, reported the world's top financial magazine. It was compared to a financial "nuclear winter."

Bear Stearns was going down, a failure that could help bring down the financial system itself. Bernanke huddled with the president's special "Plunge Protection team" to come up with new initiatives. One of the key architects of the bailout was a 46-year-old former Treasury Department official under Bill Clinton, who once worked for Kissinger Associates. His name, according to journalist Robert Novak, was Timothy F. Geithner, the president of the New York Federal Reserve Bank.

Financial writer Allen L. Roland explained the fear and the sense of panic that led to the Fed's unusual intervention:

> Wall street is a giant casino and Bear Stearn's demise is just the tip of the iceberg of a potential complete financial meltdown led by the collapse of the greatest crap shoot of them all – Derivatives.

As Andrew Leonard wrote in Salon: " A couple of things to bear in mind while we watch and see what transpires this week. First: Bear Stearns was the canary in the coal mine. That canary is now dead."

"What happened was we figured out the whole scheme wasn't working the right way," George Tsetsekos, dean of the LeBow College of Business at Drexel University, told CNN. "It's an issue of confidence in the marketplace over the ability of institutions to receive back the funds that were lent." Notice his use of the word "scheme."

"Once you see one bank subject to this kind of run, depositors starting worrying maybe the bank across the street may be equally as susceptible," said Lawrence White, an economics professor at New York University to *Money* magazine. "Clearly that's what the Fed is worried about."

If you were a fellow banker on The Street, you realized that your master of the universe days might be over. "Layoff Fear in Stox Shocks" was the headline in the *New York Post*. Prosperity has been displaced by panic.

Eight thousand jobs had already been lost in the financial sector before "the Bear was sold at a ridiculous discount, bought with $30 billion pumped by JP Morgan, who picked up what was left of the firm at $2 a share. (It had been trading a year earlier at $170.) Some 20,000 Bear employees were now threatened with the loss of their jobs. In the end, enough of them squawked and threatened to fight the deal that JP Morgan upped their offer five times over. (It also emerged that JPM's chief Jay Dimon was on the board of the NY Fed, the organization through which the deal was done.)

Some experts believe that JP Morgan actually overpaid for the bank because the shares they bought had no value. The money was used to monetize junk subprime holdings not yet written off; so much for the doctrine of "moral hazard" that holds speculators should not be rewarded for risky investments. In fact, there is evidence not only of unethical practices but of disembling of Enronesque proportions.

A week earlier, Bear Stern's former CEO bought a Manhattan condo for $28 million, no mortgage needed. In December, compromised Wall Streeters walked off with $31 billion in bonuses, just a billion below the record set a year earlier.

CNN would later ask: "How did we get to this point? How did rising foreclosures among subprime borrowers lead to Bear Stearns being scooped up in a fire sale for two bucks a share?"

The answer starts with investment banks: they sold complex securities backed by debt that was a lot riskier than most realized. The realization that the banks had failed to manage this risk sparked widespread concern among investors and other financial firms. Suddenly, investors found they couldn't put a value on much of what the banks were selling. As a result, the lending markets that keep Wall Street humming seized up because people feared they wouldn't get paid back.

What's worse is that no one knows when it will end.

Every week, it seems, another part of the U.S. financial system falters and the federal government has to come up with a new rescue plan. The Federal Reserve Bank's actions have helped soothe the markets in past crises, but the magnitude of the current meltdown may prove unprecedented, experts said. Today's troubles ensnare not only traditional banks, but investment firms, hedge funds, insurance companies, and non-bank lenders.

It is not at all clear that the Fed's monetary policy is up to the task of straightening out the whole economy. Their arsenal of tools are limited and so far the interest rate cuts are being blamed for also spurring inflation, if not stagflation. Rising food and oil prices will put even more pressure on consumers who are already cutting back, writes the economist Max Fraad Wolff:

> Markets have become rate easing and assistance junkies. Ever greater fixes of Fed liquidity candy are required to get markets high(er). Ultimately, we will see coordinated renegotiation of mortgage principle and/or greater government led bailout and buyout. The Fed and the leading market players Fed policy is unquestionably aimed at, are stuck between two competing realities.

> Two swords hang over the heads of interventionist policy and deregulated speculative reality. The leading banks are too big to fail and too big to bail. The problems are too big and politically sensitive to leave to market solutions. Overt and massive interventions create many and serious problems.

So there is no panacea in sight. All the wise men expect more declines, more cases of insolvency spurring instability.

Take a broader view as Michael Bliss did in Canada's *National Post* and you see this issue in a much deeper context:

> The global economic crisis that has generated the collapse of the investment bank Bear Stearns and the wildest gyrations of central bank policy in generations is almost certain to get much worse before it gets better. But even if it does not, we have reached a turning point in recent economic history. We are witnessing a literal discrediting of the financial community without precedent since the Great Depression. We are experiencing a loss of confidence in our capitalist game and those who play it that will have profound, lasting repercussions.

In England, Larry Elliott, the *Guardian*'s economics editor, went further:

Bear Stearns marks the moment when the global financial crisis went critical. It is now clear that no end is in sight to the turmoil, and the reason for that is that the Fed and the U.S. treasury are no closer to solving the underlying problem than they were eight months ago.

He expects a social explosion when homeowners understand the way they were targeted, writing, "It is somewhat surprising that there is not already rioting in the streets, given the gigantic fraud perpetrated by the financial elite at the expense of ordinary Americans."

Fraud is not a word most American journalist use, but the stench of the scheme behind the subprime scam is so strong that even the Justice Department has been forced to look into it. The Attorney General now says he is "gathering evidence to determine if it needs to create a special task force to investigate possible wrongdoing in the mortgage lending agency."

Bush's Attorney General, Michael B. Mukasey, announced this on a Friday – they always announce important news late on Friday so it will be buried in the minimally read Saturday paper. A story about it appeared at the bottom of page C7 in the *New York Times*.

Mukasey is the former judge who refused to call waterboarding a torture technique – he is no doubt "gathering evidence" on that too. He said his department is trying to figure out "Whether there is a larger criminal story to be told here."

Of course there is, but I doubt they want to figure anything out. So far the probes are so narrow that the real operators will be spared. They are looking into mortgage hustlers, not the operators on Wall Street who bought the toxic mortgages, securitized them, sliced and diced them into structured investment vehicles, and then sold them off to unsuspecting buyers overseas.

UPDATE: In May, the Feds announced a broader criminal investigation.

No wonder, grassroots organizations like the Neighborhood Assistance Corporation of America are now mobilizing on the issue. There will be protests. But violence may also occur since many homeowners are already trashing or even burning down their homes when forced to vacate. Some are moving into tent cities. Foreclosed homes are being turned into crack and crime dens.

If you walk through London's Highgate cemetery and wander over to the grave of the late Karl Marx and then listen closely with your ear to the ground, you might hear a repetitive murmur of the phrase "I told you so" in a distinctly German inflected accent.

You might also see the earth moving ever so slightly, as what's left of the bones below turn over in the realization that capitalists, not the proletariat, are the ones bringing down the system.

Fellow blogger Ian Williams, a former disciple of the bearded prophet, is now chanting, "Shareholders of the world unite," in recognition of the way the world is changing. The fall of Bear Stearns and the collapse of confidence in our financial system is a profound turning point. Those "suits on Wall Street" who have not lost their jobs may spend the next decade in courts fending off lawsuits.

Oddly enough, it seems to take a crisis to make economic reform happen, as economic analyst John Martin observes:

> American financial history is a sine curve of excess, crisis and reform. The Crash of 1906 and the Bankers' Panic of 1907 led to the birth of the Federal Reserve System in 1913. The crash of 1929 and related bank failures led to the SEC and FDIC. The S&L meltdowns led to the Office of Thrift Supervision. The Enron and Worldcom bankruptcies led to the Sarbanes-Oxley law of 2002. Now credit laxity has led to the Bankers Panic of 2008.

So what's next? Already a new commodities bubble seems to be emerging. Can the system avert disaster? Will we ever learn the lessons we never seem to learn? Are we screwed – and if so, how badly? Will we ever trust again?

MARCH 27, 2008 INSIDE BEAR STEARNS

My own experience with investment banks has been limited. In 1987, my partner and I had a meeting with a managing director at Solomon Brothers to solicit help in financing our new company. As I mentioned, when we sat, and talked to him, we noticed his eyes were straying to a Quotran machine on his desk as it tracked the daily trades. Something was clearly going wrong.

He didn't say a word but we started hearing loud noises, groans and phrases like "Oh, Shit." emanating from the trading floor below. We soon learned our timing was impeccable. We had come to Wall Street on the day of a crash. Needless to say, we never did any deals.

I didn't know at the time that it was a Solomon trader, Lew Ranieri, who pioneered the creation of mortgage-backed securities. Solomon underwrote the first issue in 1979. As the *New Yorker* later noted, "the market for the securities became bigger than the market for Treasury Bonds." This led to subprime loans. By 2001, 8.6 % of these loans were subprimes. By 2006, that business boomed to 20%.

I later visited Goldman Sachs to interview an executive and filmed the portraits on the wood paneled wall of Robert Rubin, later President Clinton's Treasury Secretary, now with CitiBank, and his fellow executives. The placed projected, or rather, reeked of power?

In my personal life, I was recruited by a broker who worked with Smith Barney to invest in socially responsible companies. I wasn't paying attention when one of those companies – tied to their partner CitiBank – became WorldCom. Before I put a stop to it, I lost $25,000 when that company went down. I had been betrayed and felt stupid. I had no recourse.

In late March 2008 I was at the epicenter of the crisis, the 47 floor midtown headquarters of Bear Stearns that cost about $1.5 billion to build and was finished in 2001. The building had 1.1 million square feet. A real estate website offered these details:

> Clad in granite panels and glass, the tower culminates with a dramatic 70-foot glass crown that illuminates at night. Bear Stearns' trading operations are located in the podium base on levels three through eight. Containing approximately 42,000 square feet, each trading floor accommodates up to 420 traders. When it was built, it won The Emporis award for the best new skyscraper of the year.

New York Magazine had a slightly different take: "This is a building you wouldn't want to get anywhere near at a cocktail party. Dressed nearly head to toe in dour granite, and geometrically proper, it's stiff to the point of pass-out boredom."

No one was bored on the day I visited.

I went in the company of nearly 300 homeowners, including many facing foreclosure. They were organized by NACA (Neighborhood Assistance Corporation of America) and were protesting the bailout. It was a unique way to experience the collision of two cultures, even a clash of civilizations inside a sparse lobby.

To my surprise, there was not a cop in sight as several hundred interracial and feisty members of NACA marched without a permit from St. Bartholomew's Church, past the posh Waldorf Astoria Hotel and down Park Avenue, past the bank's entangled kith and kin at UBS and Deutsche and JP Morgan Chase. With a quick right turn, they walked right in to the unguarded lobby of a company with the appropriate initials BS. Soon they were chanting, "Main Street, Not Wall Street."

There were mothers with children, Latinos, blacks, whites, one of whom was a former professional boxer. All wore yellow t-shirts with a shark on it and the slogan "Stop Loan Sharks." These folks were militant but in a good mood, chanting as they marched around the lobby as traders and executives in nice suits and white shirts looked on with amazement

They were being confronted by the faces of the people they never saw as they bought up their mortgages, sliced and diced them, and then sold them worldwide. They made a fortune on these very people in their glory days but they're over now. Only the Federal Reserve Bank's possibly illegal intervention saved them, at least until the pink slips start flying.

They looked at the folks "in their lobby" as people from another planet – but clearly the members of NACA connected Bear's affluence to their own pain. That's why so many got up at 5 a.m. in Baltimore and Boston and Springfield, MA, to come to New York to speak on behalf of all homeowners on the edge of eviction because of fraudulent *subcrime* scams.

Bruce Marks of NACA said afterwards that many of the employees at Bear Stearns took it personally when their building was invaded, but so do the homeowners. He said that NACA's campaign against predators is just starting and that they will take the fight into the faces of other bankers and even their children so they know what their parents do. He was tough, clearly an adept street fighter because, tactically, he took the enemy by surprise. He used bullhorns against the billionaires.

And, then, when the police did arrive, he and his troops left to fight another day with no arrests, no surrender, and no compromise.

As word spread in the city's newsrooms that Bear Stearns was being occupied, the media turned out in droves. They were all there just as they hadn't been there while this crisis built in intensity.

When I later checked in on Google News, I found the pattern we know so well – reporters downplaying the turnout, omitting the demands, and making the protesters look foolish. Here are some examples:

THE "COVERAGE"

First, Reuters. Notice how they describe the people as "about 60 pro-testers," not homeowners or people facing foreclosure but protesters. Also look at how they describe the Bear Stearns employees – soon to become former employees – but then don't quote any official from the firm.

> NEW YORK (Reuters) – About 60 protesters opposed to the U.S. Federal Reserve's help in bailing out Bear Stearns entered the lobby of the investment bank's Manhattan headquarters on Wednesday, demanding assistance for struggling homeowners.
>
> Demonstrators organized by the Neighborhood Assistance Corporation of America chanted "Help Main Street, not Wall Street" and entered the lobby without an invitation for around half an hour before being escorted out by police.
>
> "There are no provisions for homeowners in this deal. There are people out there struggling who need help," said Detria Austin, an organizer at NACA, an advocacy group for home ownership.
>
> Bear Stearns employees were alternatively amused and perplexed, taking pictures on their cell phones.
>
> "Homeowners, that's more than $1 trillion (in mortgage debt), you're crazy," one man in a suit screamed at a protester on the street.

I guess "one man in a suit" became the stand-in for Bear Stearns. Funny, I was wearing a suit.

THEY REALLY WANTED THEATER TICKETS

Then there was *Dealbreaker*, a Wall Street tabloid. They were even more snide towards the protesters but at least put the number at 200, quite a few more than Reuters. But their second paragraph is as ignorant as it is insensitive, suggesting that the demonstrators "wandered off to do whatever it is demonstrators do after a demonstration. (We're guessing: wait in TKTKS line for Xanadu tickets.)"

They seem to have wandered off? Not really – many came from as far away as Washington and Boston and had to return home. The police had asked them to disperse since they had no parade permits. And so they did. But you wouldn't know it by reading this "insider" account:

> Over 200 protesters from a housing advocacy group made it inside

Bear Stearns corporate offices at 47th and Park Avenue. The protest was organized by the Neighborhood Assistance Corporation of America, which was founded by union activists. (They were the ones in the yellow shirts.) After being ejected from Bear's lobby, they headed over to JP Morgan Chase. And, a few moments ago, they seem to have wandered off to do whatever it is demonstrators do after a demonstration. (We're guessing: wait in TKTKS line for Xanadu tickets.)

NOTE THE WORDS: "WITHOUT AN INVITATION"

Do you need an invitation to enter an office building? Reuters apparently thinks so, and CNBC and the *New York Times* concurred: "Demonstrators organized by the Neighborhood Assistance Corporation of America ... entered the lobby *without an invitation* for about half an hour before being escorted out by police."

YAHOO also ran the Reuters dispatch. MSNBC used the number 200, not 60. (I counted at least 300).

One young woman from CNBC was in front of me collecting "soundbites" and trying to get some NACA protesters outside Bear Stearns to talk to her. "What," she asked, "would you like to tell CNBC?"

They didn't want to say anything more, but she persisted, asking for their names. Two women just turned away, and when they declined to perform for the camera, she turned to me, because I was next to them and asked for my comment as if I had any standing there. I wasn't a NACA member.

So I let her have it with both barrels, rhetorically, that is, expressing my frustrations with the unbalanced media coverage of this crisis. Her cameraman seemed to enjoy what I was saying. I kept speaking quickly and I could see her looking for a pause in my "response" so she could cut me off. I know those techniques, having practiced them in the past. Fortunately, my colleague, the Serbian Director Mira Vukomanovic, was there and started filming them filming me. So what I had to say ended up on You Tube.

CNBC did interview one banker at Bear who said, anonymously of course, that he sympathized with the protest and would probably lose his job and his house. Few at Bear were talking about the issue or the protest – perhaps because they are in shock, crying or, in some cases, sneering.

One young man in the Bear camp was interviewed by the *New York Post*. I have to put this in CAPS lest you miss it. He was identified as a 23 years old.

IT SEEMS KIND OF FUNNY TO PEOPLE UPSTAIRS... IT'S LIKE A BIG JOKE. WE REALLY DON'T KNOW WHAT THEY ARE PROTESTING ABOUT.

Bear's former executive James Cayne was described as a suspender snapping, cigar smoking exec. The *New York Times* wrote in 1993: "James E. Cayne's company biography devotes 10 lines to his achievements at Bear Stearns, 13 lines to his achievements at the bridge table."

Not everyone was enamored with him. From that same profile: "Others were less generous, portraying Mr. Cayne as the Dan Quayle of Bear Stearns, a consummate strategist in his career and his game but sometimes given to saying the wrong thing at the wrong time."

They point to instances like his comments in *M* magazine a few years ago. He was quoted as saying that a woman facing pressure, at the bridge table or the trading floor, would "probably have to go to the ladies' room and dab her eyes."

He is the one doing the "dabbing" these days.

But if he is, he dabbed all the way to the bank, as financial writer Dean Baker noted in comparing him to the "welfare queens" once used as derogatory symbols of people profiting at public expense.

If the welfare queen is dead, then it's time to say, "Long live the welfare king." This person really exists, his name is James E. Cayne, and taxpayers just handed him almost $50 million. Mr. Cayne got this gift when J.P. Morgan renegotiated the terms of its takeover of Bear Stearns. The buying price went up fivefold, fetching Bear Stearn's stockholders $1.2 billion instead of the $236 million in the agreement brokered by the Fed last week....

James E. Cayne did especially well as a result of the taxpayer's generosity because as the former CEO of Bear Stearns, and current chairman, he owned a great deal of the company's stock. To put the taxpayer's gift to Mr. Cayne in some context, this is approximately equal to the amount paid in TANF (Temporary Assistance for Needy Families) to 10,000 working mothers over the course of a year.

What was even more outrageous than Cayne's reward was the lack of outrage that greeted this news, as if it was BAU (Business as Usual) and to be expected. Perhaps it is.

MARCH 29, 2008: FED UP

PRESIDENT BUSH HAD FINALLY HEARD THOSE OF US WHO HAVE BEEN railing for financial reform, and putting Wall Street under what the Jamaicans once called "Heavy Manners," a set of rules and regulations aimed at trying to stabilize the volatile markets and curb avaricious banks who have managed in less than a decade to bring the economy down upon themselves and the rest of us.

Suddenly in the run-up to April Fools day, and in rapid order, the "Lions of Legislation" on the Hill, and the warring candidates on the campaign trail have discovered that the financial system is on the verge of collapse.

"Do something" is the mantra, as a flurry of new "plans" displace old ones, all aimed at fixing "the mess." The *LA Times* reports: "Congressional Democrats are turning up the heat on the White House and Republicans in Congress to respond more aggressively to the mortgage crisis when lawmakers return next week from their spring recess."

In response, despite its obsession with surges and bombing Iraq back to its idea of "normalcy," the White House says it now feels our pain and has decided to act. Well, at least, to let former Goldman Sachs CEO Hank Paulson, now our Treasury Secretary (in the tradition of former Goldman Sachs exec Robert Rubin, who followed the same career path) impose yet another new pacification plan.

Paulson has studied the crisis, studied it deeply, and realized the culpability of the brokers and the banks in engineering the disaster. His solution: kick the ball over to the Federal Reserve Bank. He knows that most Americans – and most of the media – think the Fed is a neutral government agency with a public interest mandate. They think it has the expertise and the power to swoop down and save us from our misery despite the fact that eights months of rate cuts and capital "injections" have failed to stem the contagion of collapse.

The *New York Times* pictures the exercise clinically in positive terms as a police raid, sort of like a SWAT team.

> The Treasury Department will propose on Monday that Congress give the Federal Reserve broad new authority to oversee financial market stability, in effect allowing it to send SWAT teams into any corner of the industry or any institution that might pose a risk to the overall system.

The proposal is part of a sweeping blueprint to overhaul the nation's hodgepodge of financial regulatory agencies, which many experts say failed to recognize rampant excesses in mortgage lending until after they set off what is now the worst financial calamity in decades.

Sorry to disabuse the newspaper of record and anyone who believes this formulation but the Fed is a private agency with no constitutional authority run by bankers for bankers. It is a privately owned central banking system. Bankers sit on its many boards. The banks in turn get to borrow money at rates the Fed sets, and tack on interest and fees for loans. The Fed is there to do their bidding, and save them from themselves. When they run into trouble, they are often bailed out.

Bankers pressed for the Fed's formation in a secretive if not deceptive manner: As one historical account explains:

On Sunday, December 23, 1913, two days before Christmas, while most of Congress was on vacation, President Woodrow Wilson signed the Federal Reserve Act into law. Wilson would later express profound regret over his decision, stating:

I am a most unhappy man. I have unwittingly ruined my country. A great industrial nation is controlled by its system of credit. Our system of credit is concentrated. The growth of the nation, therefore, and all our activities are in the hands of a few men. We have come to be one of the worst ruled, one of the most completely controlled and dominated governments in the civilized world – no longer a government by free opinion, no longer a government by conviction and the vote of the majority, but a government by the opinion and duress of a small group of dominant men.

In fact, in the recent "unprecedented" intervention to save Bear Stearns with monies leant to JP Morgan Chase through the NY Fed, it turned out that the President of JPM, Jamie Dimon, sat on its board. It also appears that it was JP Morgan Chase really that had to be saved because it was so "entangled" with Bear. If you think this was a conflict of interest, think again. Self-interest seems to be their only interest.

Anyone who has looked carefully at the larger plan knows the odds of it working are nil. The *Washington Post* explained that it "could require congressional action stretching over several years and would not help the economy out of its current credit crisis." Adds the *Wall Street Journal*: "If all the changes get made, they would represent a complete reworking of the U.S. regulatory system for finance. Such an outcome would likely take years and would also require major compromises from an increasingly partisan Congress. The proposal, obtained by the *Wall Street Journal*, is likely to trigger messy feuds over turf at a time when confidence is what's needed."

This is one more effort to appear to at least be doing something, as the blog Naked Capitalism explains:

> There is less here than meets the eye, and what is here is guaranteed not to be implemented during the remaining months of the Bush presidency. And that of course is precisely the point of this exercise. Appear to be doing something and dump the mess in the lap of your successor.

> To the details – Remember where we are: we've had years of misguided confidence that investment banks could be left to their own devices, that the wonders of the originate-and-distribute model meant Things Were Different This Time. Specifically, the powers that believed that risks were so widely spread and diversified that the financial system was now much more resistant to systemic shocks. We've seen what a crock that idea was.

It is just possible that Bush's successor – Obama or Clinton – will see through this charade, although Hillary has already proposed a Blue Ribbon type commission with former Fed Chairman Alan Greenspan and others whose policies led to the crisis. (Her campaign manager Maggie Williams was later linked to a defunct mortgage company making subprime loans.)

John McCain has not only admitted he knows nothing about economics, but has advisors whose free market theology seems to be to the right of Paulson and the Fed's Ben Bernanke, who some conservatives fear are already meddling too much in the economy. His key advisor, former Texas Senator Phil Gramm, a Democrat turned Republican, shilled for predatory lenders for years.

Obama also has a subprime link through his Finance Chairman, Penny Pritzker, who ran a Chicago bank that imploded and owes the government and depositors hundreds of millions. Nevertheless, economics writer Robert Kuttner feels Obama's ideas, spelled out in a recent speech, are evolving in a progressive direction:

> The speech also showed real understanding and subtlety in grasping how financial "innovation" had outrun regulation, as well as a historical sense of the abuses of the 1920s repeating themselves. Obama is one of the few mainstream leaders – Barney

Frank is another – calling for capital requirements to be extended to every category of financial institution that creates credit. This is exactly what's needed to prevent the next meltdown, but if it were put to a vote now, it would be rejected by legislators from both parties because they are still in thrall to market fundamentalism and Wall Street. That's where presidential leadership comes in.

The only candidate challenging the Fed directly has been Congressman Ron Paul, who has been more of a maverick than McCain despite the latter's claim on that nickname.

It may be too late to wait until next year for real reform which is why this issue must be taken up aggressively by social change activists, not just partisans and pols. Noriel Roubini and other economists who predicted the meltdown say: "It's time to face the truth – the U.S. economy is no longer merely battling a touch of the flu; it's now in the early stages of a painful and persistent bout of pneumonia."

Can any of the plans, proposals, and polemics we have heard so far make any difference?

APRIL 2, 2008: A FIRST ACCOUNTING

THE BANKS OF SHAME

MOST OF THE REPORTING ON THE CREDIT CRISIS REVOLVES AROUND numbers: how much each bank has "written down," i.e., admitted had been invested into worthless "asset based securities," that is, in monetary terms. There is never any discussion of how so many eminent institutions – major brand names in banking – got swept up in the subprime euphoria or how much they made on the sale and resale of securities that a *New York Times* columnist labeled "malodorous." Others have compared these mortgages to "toxic waste."

Many of these mortgages were misrepresented to buyers or sold as part of a scheme that often involved false appraisals that made the homes appear to be worth more than they were. High fees were also charged by unscrupulous mortgage brokers. If ordinary laws were enforced here, there would be fines, if not jail sentences, handed out for dealing with stolen property. The banks themselves would also be liable to their victims, including home owners and the institutions who bought these securities because they had been highly rated. Law firms the world over are adding subprime departments to initiate and defend the massive litigation they anticipate.

How much money was involved? Here's a breakdown as compiled by the *Wall Street Journal* Data Group on just bank losses as of April 1, 2008. Bear in mind that many banking authorities do not believe that the banks have disclosed all of their losses.

Banks in China and Japan that also traded in these securities are not on this list.

BANK	REPORTED WRITE DOWN IN BILLIONS
UBS	37
MERRILL LYNCH	25.1
CITIGROUP	21.6
AIG	17.2
MORGAN STANLEY	13.1
BANK OF AMERICA	7.7
DEUTSCHE BANK	7.4
ROYAL BANK OF SCOTLAND	6.0
CRÉDIT AGRICOLE	6.0
AMBAC	6.0
SOCIÉTÉ GÉNÉRALE	4.8
BARCLAYS	4.5
CIBC	4.2
FORTIS	4.2
CREDIT SUISSE	4.1.

This of course does not encompass the entire financial impact on these institutions, which includes accounting costs, litigation, and reductions in share prices. More waves of write-downs are expected from these banks and regional institutions. Some think there is at least another $100 BILLION to be disclosed.

Also to be factored in are hundreds of millions, if not billions, "injected" into the system by Central Banks like the U.S. Federal Reserve to save banks and assure liquidity. It has been reported that banks have received $136 billion from government and private sources.

As of late 2006, the Mortgage Lender Implodo-Meter reported that 246 major U.S. lending operations have "imploded. The Ml-implode.com website reported as of April 1 that as of mid 2007 at least 72 hedge funds "at 40 outfits had imploded." All of these numbers will, of course, change.

CHAPTER 6

DEBT AS A GLOBAL ISSUE

THIS CRISIS IS NOW GLOBAL

MY OWN INTEREST IN THE DEBT ISSUE IN AMERICA STEMMED FROM what I knew about how debt was used to make developing countries dependent on former colonial powers. My ideas for a campaign for debt relief in America were inspired by the fight for debt relief in Africa. In the course of promoting *In Debt We Trust*, I traveled to South Africa, Europe, and Australia and wrote about how debt is a global concern.

As I tracked the growing debt crisis, I realized that its impact was international. I have yet to see a complete list of how much money was lost by overseas banks and shareholders who were suckered into investing in what they were told were lucrative "asset-based securities." They, too, were enticed into investing on the basis of false representation, buying up securities that rating agencies had not studied closely and banks had not verified. Central bankers worldwide were forced to put up billions to defend their markets as well.

A website called Vigilant Investor reported on which banks pumped a reported and whopping $460 BILLION in one week into the markets "in order to allow the big players to avoid selling off otherwise healthy assets to cover for heavy losses related to the unfolding housing debacle in the U.S., led over the cliff by subprimes."

Here's their rundown:

Central Bank	Amount
U.S Federal Reserve	$86 billion ($48 + $38 repo's)
European CB	$230 billion
Japan	$100 billion
Australia	$42 billion

Many bankers in Europe were shocked by the lapse in normal lending practices and spoke out about the crisis. About 3.5% of Bank of China securities were affected. The Industrial and Commercial Bank of China admitted holding $1.23 billion in securities based on subprime mortgages. Later, Japanese banks and one in Kazakhstan were embroiled in the scandal.

Will these overseas banks seek to retaliate in some way? Like their American counterparts, they have a self-interest in stabilizing the system, not destroying it. But these developments will not bolster confidence worldwide in U.S financial practices.

The G-8 countries were shocked by the way this crisis continues to deepen. On February 9, 2008, the financial ministers, regulators, and central bankers met in Japan to assess the problem. Reuters reported:

> Financial regulators and central bankers delivered a grim assessment of the credit market upheaval, warning that worse may lie ahead as banks tighten lending and an economic slowdown spreads.

> In an interim report to the Group of Seven finance ministers, the Financial Stability Forum cautioned against a rush to regulate into this vicious cycle of credit write-downs, preferring to allow markets-based systems to operate. But authorities must remain on heightened alert, ready to jump in and impose discipline to the messy re-pricing of credit risk where necessary, it said.

Banks showed their vulnerabilities in many counties as in France, where a young trader was accused of causing a $7 billion loss. Banks were sold in Germany, and in England the liabilities of the Northern Rock Bank were absorbed by the government after a run on the bank. In early February 2008, Larry Elliott, economics editor of the *Guardian* wrote:

> When questioned about their role in causing Britain's debt addiction, the banks throw up their hands in horror. "Wot us?" they

say. "Not our fault, guv: we are simply listening to our customers and giving them what they want."

In reality, we no longer have banks but high-street debt factories. Borrowing is aggressively marketed; there is more profit to be made out of a customer who has an overdraft than one who is in credit. And the notion that debt is socially acceptable, even admirable, is inculcated from an early age, not least through student loans. A much better way to have funded the expansion of higher education would have been through a progressive graduate tax, but that was a public-sector solution, whereas student loans allowed the private sector to cash in.

In America, credit card debt remains a silent and yet ticking time bomb as delinquencies rise and some fear another bubble bursting. Reports the *New York Times*:

In December, revolving debt – an estimated 95 percent from credit cards – reached a record high of $943.5 billion, according to the Federal Reserve. The annual growth rate of this debt increased steadily in 2007, reaching 9.3 percent in the last quarter, up from 5.4 percent in the first quarter.

The amount of debt that is delinquent – in which minimum payments are late but the accounts are still open – also appears to be on the rise. The Federal Reserve found that 4.34 percent of the credit card portfolios of the 100 largest banks that issue cards was delinquent in the third quarter of last year, up from 4.07 percent in the previous quarter. Charge-offs – accounts closed for nonpayment – also grew in that period, and banks expect charge-offs to keep rising in 2008.

So no wonder that bank regulators are now monitoring possible bank collapses feigning a wave of bank closures, a development with clear global implications. Internet journalist Mike Whitney noted:

The FDIC has begun the "death watch" on the many banks which are currently drowning in their own red ink. The problem for the FDIC is that it has never supervised a bank failure which exceeded 175,000 accounts. So the impending financial tsunami is likely to be a crash-course in crisis management. Today some of the larger banks have more than 50 million depositors, which will make the FDIC's job nearly impossible.

Reuters confirmed this forecast using the word "surge," a phrase more common in Iraq war reporting,

Dozens of U.S. banks will fail in the next two years as losses from soured loans mount and regulators crack down on lenders that take too much risk, especially in real estate and construction, an analyst said.

The surge would follow a placid 3-1/2 year period in which just four banks collapsed, all in the last year, RBC Capital Markets analyst Gerard Cassidy said in a Friday interview.

Between 50 and 150 U.S. banks — as many as one in 57 — could fail by early 2010, mostly those with no more than a couple of billion dollars of assets, Cassidy said. That rate of failure would be the highest in at least 15 years, or since the winding down of the savings-and-loan debacle.

Add all this up, recognize the way our global system is interconnected and globalized, and you realize that what happens here will happen elsewhere soon enough. That's why fear is spreading in financial circles worldwide, as economist Max Fraad Wolff describes the volatile global market:

The Hang Seng and Shanghai gyrations have been stomach turning. European and Asian markets have delinked, relinked, delinked and tumbled. The only consistent trend is down, down, down.

Multiple theories have been fed through the meat grinder with the allocations they inspired. Trillions of yuan, U.S dollars, yen and euros in paper wealth have been transformed into fuel for a fear inferno.

This contagion suggests that the idea that various markets in the global economy can somehow be delinked or "decoupled" is not going to happen. We are all in the same boat, and as of this writing, that boat is leaking. Badly.

Conclusion: The economic crisis is global.

VISITING SOUTH AFRICA

DURBAN, SOUTH AFRICA: SOUTH AFRICA HAS BEEN AN EPICENTER of change in the world. With the overthrow of apartheid and the emergence of its new economy, new problems have emerged. Political and racial apartheid may be gone but economic apartheid of a great gap between rich and poor continues to fester with vast disparities in wealth and growing intractable poverty. Debt is emerging as a leading issue in this country as it is throughout the African continent.

Even as Nelson Mandela and his movement overthrew the shackles of a racist system, they found themselves as a matter of first business forced to pay off the debt of the government they replaced. The all-white government had borrowed widely to try to keep the system of racial domination in place, and now its former victims and new victors had to pay off their obligations. What an irony.

Today South Africa is fully integrated into the market system with sprawling suburbs and giant malls. Consumption is a religion here like it is in the United States. Many writers here like Matshilo Motsei write about the need to reintegrate moral values in a capitalist society driven by a "What do I stand to gain?" mentality, as opposed to one that asks, "What's at stake for the country?" She quotes several leaders decrying the "growing consumerist and materialist nature" of the culture, in which the ultimate outcome is "a breakdown of moral values fuelled by greed, corruption and criminal activity."

Sound familiar? I am here to show *In Debt We Trust* at the Durban International Film Festival that features independent productions from 77 countries. It was an honor to have my film here since many films document problems caused BY the United States government, not IN the United States. The first screening was packed and held in a regular movie theater in – of all places – a casino with rows of ATM machines on every wall sucking the money out of the accounts of the endless streams of suckers that come there to get rich. In a way, it is a palace of debt of another kind.

I started the screening by asking the audience if they felt that my film *In Debt We Trust* was relevant there. The audience almost unanimously said it was. Afterwards people raised questions and shared their experiences. The comments came from a Zulu woman who had lived in exile in the United States, a Muslim father concerned about materialism in his kids, and a white activist who stressed the need for education at the primary level.

I came away feeling that we now need to promote the film internationally. I was told about a new consumer protection law and many organizations concerned about the issue that may want to show the film. What I saw was that this is a global issue that is slowly becoming understood as a global problem. The organizers of the Festival did too, writing, "The debt issue is an increasing global problem as more people buy into America's false dreams."

I wonder: is America to blame or is it our globalized and hyper-charged capitalist system controlled by a small number of financial institutions?

SOUTH AFRICA'S DEBT REFORM

As we rail against and expose abusive credit practices, we are often hard put to imagine how this problem can be addressed.

Recently, when I was in South Africa, credit abuses were rife. But as I was leaving, I read about a new National Credit Act that went into effect on July 1, 2007. It came about after years of organizing and struggling by a well-organized coalition of community groups, labor unions, and political activists. In many ways it offers an example of what people can fight for and win. It was part of a campaign for the reform and transformation of the financial sector, which is dominated by four big banks.

While the campaign was not successful in all of its aspects – the banks lobbied hard to force compromises and water down key provisisons – it is a model in some respects of what we in America might adapt in terms of limiting credit abuses. Debt Relief became an issue in Africa, but it is now a relevant demand for economic justice world-wide. It started dealing with the debts run up by governments but must now encompass consumer debt as well. (Most countries in the South have repaid external debts to countries in the North already.) Debt relief has to become a universal demand.

South Africa has come up with new rules to restrain abuses of consumers. Here's what their National Credit Act Covers:

Preventing the reckless lending of credit,

Preventing South Africans from taking credit without being able to afford it,

Monitoring of interest rates for all credit lending,

Protecting customers with the ACT.

No more misleading and deceptive marketing by credit lenders will be allowed. For more information, please go to http://www.nca.org.za or check out the National Credit Act.

As one South African website explains: "The Credit Act is there to prevent people from spending money they don't have. It's there to help the banks manage the massive CREDIT DEBT this country has and it's to stop RECKLESS LENDING of money by the banks. The act

puts banks and other lending sources on the spot with possible consequences for them if they are found to have advanced loans irrespon-
sibly (responsible lending ACT). It's all to do with what's known as
predatory lending practices and global issues."

All of these measures have not solved the problem. On March 30,
2008, Johannesburg's *Star* reported:

> Repossessions up as middle-level earners fall prey to economic
> pressure

> Increasing numbers of cars, household appliances, furniture and
> even homes are being repossessed from middle-income South
> Africans every day. Economists say tighter market conditions, high
> interest rates and a weakening rand are to blame...

> Xolisa Vapi, the head of communications at First National Bank,
> said "There is a lot of stress on consumers due to all the increases.
> Consumers are panicking. They have home loans, vehicle loans,
> credit-card debt and are continuously hit by fuel increases. All of
> this is causing a lot of strain and clients are falling into arrears.
> Therefore more assets are being repossessed. Consumers often
> finance one debt with another. This is dangerous."

Sound familiar?

AN OPEN LETTER TO BONO RE: DEBT RELIEF

THE CAMPAIGN FOR AFRICAN DEBT RELIEF, AND THE TYPE WE NEED
here in America, has benefited from the very vocal advocacy of popular artists, especially Bono, the lead singer of the Irish rock band U2.

When the world's most prominent rock star was named to edit a
special edition of *Vanity Fair*, the glitterati magazine that influences
our national buzz machine and cultural zeitgeist, I wrote to him to
urge that he also publicize the need for debt relief in the United States.
I have worked with him on rock and roll projects, admire his commitment, and hoped that he could connect the concerns of poor people in
the third world with the plight of increasingly poor Americans.

Our first encounter took place many years earlier. It was also South
Africa related but well before Mandela helped free South Africa. It was
at one of the last recording sessions for the anti-apartheid record "Sun
City" that I was helping to produce back in 1985. We were in the base-
ment of a now shuttered famous studio in the Village, the one Jimi

Hendrix once owned. Musician Little Steven Van Zandt invited Bono there to sing on the project. Not only did he agree, but he was inspired to contribute an original song. He created and did a solo rendition of a song called "Silver and Gold," which brilliantly put the apartheid crisis in an economic context, making the connection between all the suffering in that country and its great wealth and exploitation in its mines. He understood then how important it was to challenge financial power. In fact, it was the sanctions campaign, of which Sun City was a part, that helped bring down that racist system.

Bono went on to become a high-profile champion of Africa, as an artist, diplomat, lobbyist, and negotiator. His eloquence, celebrity, and Irish "moxie" enabled him to confront the rich and powerful from a mountain top in Davos to the General Assembly of the UN, from an outhouse in the bush of an impoverished African country to the White House and Congress, not to mention the stage of his sold out concerts and on every TV network. He has pushed, persuaded, cajoled, charmed and maneuvered the likes of Bill Gates, George Bush, and even conservative Senator Jesse Helms, to support debt relief and the fight against AIDS. He is a passionate campaigner. No one can say no to him.

I wrote:

If you want to get Americans to show solidarity with Africa, show some solidarity with them. Lets make the issue of Debt Relief in America part of the global fight for economic independence in our interdependent world.

True, the impoverished former colonies of the Third World have it worse, with many sick and hungry people living in dire poverty, often on $2 a day. But suffering is relative and often causes the same misery, disease, and despair wherever you go. Ask the homeless in America. Read about our own pervasive and growing poverty. You know there is a festering and neglected third world in the innards of every "rich" country.

And don't stop there.

Look at the millions who are trapped in a debt they will never escape from, almost like modern serfs. Read about all the outsourced jobs, the closed auto plants, the wave of foreclosures as the housing bubble bursts, the credit card crunch, the rise in bankruptcies, the students leaving college with an average $40,000 in loans, and the billions in outrageous interest rates and all kinds of fees. This does not just impact the poor but increasingly the middle class and even those who felt it could never affect them.

Predatory lending is not just an African problem. It is global.

The press is predicting, "More pain is on the way" as big banks falter and the scandalous subprime lending sector – recently considered the "hottest" in the industry – implodes. The bankers and economic wise men who have been denying any problem are singing another tune now as the stock market melts down and the underlying problems of consumer and government debt are seen as the threat they are.

A problem of personal security is becoming an issue of national security and global insecurity. In many cases, the same banks, investment houses, and hedge funds are profiting off of the anguish of untold millions in every country.

So Bono, let's tie the issues together for American readers and African "victims" by recognizing our common humanity and the need to find common ground in fighting shared problems.

Linking the growing debt burden of Americans – and the better-known debt problems in Africa – is a start.

We are working on this issue now and need your help. We have created a campaign called AMERICANS FOR DEBT RELIEF NOW (Stopthesqueeze.org) and are promoting a film called *In Debt We Trust* (Indebtwetrust.com) to raise pubic awareness. We are reaching out to give a massive but invisible problem more visibility and a sense of urgency.

In the name of love, Bono, and our shared values and common beliefs, will you help us get the word out on this effort, support us as we support you, and make the issues and promise of global economic justice a reality.

Let me know if you will help!

UPDATE: I received no response from Bono

THE FIRE BELL IN THE NIGHT

NEW YORK, MAY 2, 2008: THOMAS JEFFERSON USED A PHRASE IN A letter that is still ringing all these years later. Here's his thought written centuries ago:

I had for a long time ceased to read the newspapers or pay any attention to public affairs, confident they were in good hands, and content to be a passenger in our bark to the shore from which I am not distant, but this momentous question like A FIREBELL IN THE NIGHT [caps mine], awakened and filled me with terror.

So many of us were content like that in the years leading up to the slow motion crash that rocked our economy in August 2007, and many still remain comatose like that today.

We were, all too many of us, confident we were "in good hands." On May 2, 2007, our President told America's general contractors – so many of whom are out of work today – "we're proving that pro-growth economic policies with fiscal discipline can work. And our budgets are shrinking [sic]. The best way to keep them shrinking is keep the economy growing and be wise about – and setting priorities with your money."

There was a fire bell ringing that very night, and he didn't hear it, that is, if he could ever hear much besides his own voice. (Today he says the economy defies a quick fix!) Wall Street was making money by the ton just a year ago, and our regulators were cheering them on while most of our media was dozing. Credit card debt was up 7.6% – almost $3,000 a person. There were warnings of an impending collapse but few paid them any heed.

A one-time Republican strategist named Kevin Phillips was already ringing that fire bell. He had documented the rise of the Financial-ization of our economy in which a credit and loan complex–using debt as its driver–was dominant, controlling over 20% of GDP. He warned of the consequences, in the hijacking of our future and our economy. Our system had become, he argued, a house of cards. In a new book, *Bad Money: Reckless Finance, Failed Politics and the Global Crisis of American Capitalism*, he documents how those cards started tumbling in painful detail.

This reality should, in Jefferson's words, wake us up and "fill us with terror." (Odd that thought of "terror," written so many years ago. How prophetic!) Perhaps we have been fearing the wrong terror-ists? Yet even now, most of the media would rather debate Reverend Wright's words or TV youth star Miley Cyrus's sexy photo than the calamity in front of us and our world, all thanks to unregulated greed and financial manipulations. That's what gave us the subcrime crisis or in Phillips words, "reckless finance" that brought the market down, sending prices and joblessness up.

You can't really track the mounting problems by watching TV or even reading many of our newspapers which failed to cover the crisis as it was building steam from 2002 to 2006, when it might have been stopped. It is usually only after the fact that we realize that the official response is also making things worse.

On April 30, 2008, the Federal Reserve Bank cut interest rates again down to 2% – the seventh cut since last September. So far, the Fed's actions have not ameliorated the problem. In fact, many on Wall Street believe that the Fed was more the cause than the cure for the crisis.

The *Financial Times* reported that Henry Kaufman, the distinguished Wall Street economist, criticized the Federal Reserve's role in the credit crisis, saying the U.S central bank allowed too much credit expansion over the past 15 years and that this contributed to the market turmoil. "Certainly the Federal Reserve should shoulder a substantial part of this responsibility. . . it allowed the expansion of credit in huge magnitudes," Kaufman said. Earlier in April, he called the crisis a "global calamity."

Now, he is being joined by an insider. A former top Federal Reserve official charges that the Fed's bailout of Bear Stearns will come to be viewed as the "worst policy mistake in a generation."

Reported the *Wall Street Journal*: "Vincent Reinhart, who used to be the Fed's director of monetary affairs and the secretary of its policy making panel, said the event would be compared to 'the great contraction' of the 1930s and 'the great inflation' of the 1970s."

Run that by me again – "the great contraction?" Duh? Does he mean the Great Depression? Then, we had a government that tried to end it. As of this week, only 2,000 homeowners facing the threat of foreclosure have been helped by government programs while as many as three million homeowners face homelessness!

If you read the financial blogs linked on essential websites like Ml-implode.com, you get a much more sobering picture. According to the *RGE Monitor*, we are in the THIRD year of a housing recession.

They report: "We are in the third year of the U.S. housing recession and the bottom does not seem to be in sight yet. Housing starts (and completions) are falling but not yet fast enough to offset the sharper fall in demand (home sales) and therefore to insure a fast absorption of the rising home inventories that keep putting downward pressure on prices."

Do you know what this means? The number of vacant homes

reached a record high of 18.6 million units, which was a 1 million increase in the past 12 months with a record 4.1 million vacant homes for rent, and the rental vacancy rate rising to 10.1%.

One out of 194 U.S households are in foreclosure. Housing prices are falling with expectations in some quarters they will drop a further 20%.

Translation – in a society in which realty is considered reality: this is still an ongoing disaster with worse to come.

Patrick.net reports:

Salaries cannot pay for current house prices. This means house prices must keep falling or salaries must rise much faster. You probably noticed that your salary is not rising much, and that inflation in food, energy, and medical care has been very high. This leaves less money available to pay for housing.

Another website, Minyanville.com, sees not just a subprime crisis but a deepening consumer consumption crisis.

It's important to recognize that with each passing day, as credit is tightened and unemployment grows, more and more asset classes and population groups will be affected. And you need only look at the news from BMW or last week's earnings report from Harley-Davidson and Starbucks to see that consumers can no longer afford their aspirations.

Another site, Denninger.net, sounds angry, a sign of the ugly mood that is starting to go public as the only upturn appears to be a rise in the lack of consumer confidence:

If you're operating under the premise that the losses have been (mostly) recognized and we are now going to see "write ups" somewhere down the road, you're more than wrong. You're delusional.

Are we delusional or just not paying attention? And are we even aware of the link between the housing crisis and the newly emergent international food crisis? In *Asia Times*, Otto Spengler argues: "The global food crisis is a monetary phenomenon, an unintended consequence of America's attempt to inflate its way out of a market failure. There are long-term reasons for food prices to rise, but the unprecedented spike in grain prices during the past year stems from the weakness of the American dollar. Washington's economic misery now threatens to become a geopolitical catastrophe.

So what now? Will the desperation so many people feel go inwards or outwards? Here are two stories on these two tendencies. The first is from AP:

> A man upset over thousands of dollars in fees owed to a condominium association brandished a gun and took two association employees hostage before he was killed by a SWAT team, authorities said. Deputies "were screaming at him to put the gun down, but he didn't seem to be paying attention," said Ross Torman, 30, a resident who watched the standoff from his nearby balcony. "He just put that gun right to his head and that's when they began to shoot."

The Housing Panic blog reaches into history to remind us of an uprising that saw martial law imposed in Iowa in 1933 after "a mob of 150 farmers dragged Circuit Judge Charles C. Bradley from the bench, manhandled the 60-year-old jurist and threatened to lynch him unless he promised not to sign further foreclosure orders."

Don't think never again. If it has come to this — it can come to that.

SUMMER 2008: THE CRISIS BECOMES AN ISSUE

AS THE SUMMER OF 2008 APPROACHED, AS THE SUBPRIME COLLAPSE neared its first anniversary, the economic crisis, initially denied, and then reportedly resolved, was back with a vengeance. In truth, it had never gone away. It had only burrowed deeper. There still was no light at the end of this Big Dig.

By June, it had become clear to one and all that the fixes proposed by the industry and the government — a smattering of new rules, presidential stimulus pronouncements and packages as well as interventions by the Federal Reserve Bank — were not up to the task of fixing or "correcting" what had become a global calamity.

It was also clear also that the condition of our economy had become the primary concern of the American people, and the number one issue in the American election. Debates on economic policy between the candidates had begun but they had yet to touch the fundamental issues.

For one thing, in most of the media and the polls, it was still "AAU" (All About Us), as if what happens in the U.S economy in a globalized world is separate and disconnected to what happens to people "out there."

It was as if our growing deficit, subprime crisis, and dropping dollar only affects the United States. Of course, that's not the case. OPEC has blamed the rising price of oil on speculators, the subprime scandal and the engineered fall of the dollar.

Massive movements protesting U.S trade policy emerged in South Korea, showing that many people "out there" do not want to be controlled by U.S corporate policies. All around the world workers began challenging rising gas prices. AFP reported:

> Auto plants in Spain were paralyzed and Portugal's main airport banned planes from refueling as a third day of strikes by thousands of truckers caused heightened chaos and shortages.

> Truckers in Thailand also threatened to strike while their counterparts in South Korea plan to stop work, as the outrage over soaring fuel prices intensified around the world.

In response, the Saudis, fearful of being demonized, agreed to pump more and charge less. But there was little protest in the U.S. Perhaps because we were too busy watching prices go up on TV, or mesmerized by the NBA basketball finals or on horse races on the track or by politics.

Our political leaders were not encouraging us to act, while the Congress was unable to pass any reforms to stop the bleeding.

Most of the media avoided offering any global perspective. Most Americans didn't know that without loans and investments from China, the Persian Gulf, and various sovereign wealth funds, our economy would have fallen much further, if not collapsed completely.

Many have commented on the United States' lack of energy independence but, we also lack financial independence. We are hotwired into world trade and an interdependent global economy. Why?

So far, planetary issues and global concerns – climate change, global trade, energy, population, war and peace, and growing inequality have been largely rendered non-issues in our highly partisan economic debate. When the G-8 Finance Ministers meeting in Japan warned that surging oil and food prices threatened the world economy, the story was played on page 10 of the *New York Times* under photos of Russian tourists dancing and playing cards. Outside the U.S, the collapse of our housing market is viewed as the cause of the spiraling down of economic growth and the spiraling up of prices.

Speculators are now cashing in. There has been little reference here to what newspapers, like Germany's *Der Spiegel*, are reporting:

After investing in high-tech stocks and real estate loans for years, legions of speculators have now discovered commodities like oil and gas, wheat and rice. Their billions are pushing prices up to astronomical levels – with serious consequences for ordinary people's quality of life and the global economy.

We are mostly hearing about meager stimulus checks, not strategies for sustainability. We are constantly bombarded with polarizing issues, not probes into the interests behind them.

John McCain, the "free marketer," was blasting Barack Obama as a tax and spend liberal. Obama, in turn, derided McCain for pushing tax cuts for the rich.

So far it sounded like just about every presidential race of the last 30 years, featuring the classic Democrat-Republican debate with the former posturing as populists and the latter claiming to stand for individual freedom.

What's missing, of course, is that this verbal duel is taking place in the middle of unending wars and three global calamities – food, fuel and finance – that thus far have not been really popularized or discussed with the voters.

Obama has touched on the housing crisis and the stranglehold that credit cards have over many, as AP reported:

He would bar credit card companies from raising interest rates without the borrower's approval and from applying higher rates retroactively; establish a federal credit card rating system; and bar interest charges on items such as late fees.

This is a needed reform but does not address the consumption addiction that leads us all to pile on more and more debt. Maybe Obama can't see that because, as he told CNBC, "Look. I am a pro-growth, free-market guy. I love the market."

McCain, meanwhile, as politicians tend to do, changed the subject and went after Obama for suggesting that an end to NAFTA could hurt business. There's little concern about what this trade deal has done to American workers.

Blogger Jayne Stahl explained:

Since 2001, the U.S. has lost more than 2 million manufacturing jobs, and nearly 1 million professional, and information service, positions, and NAFTA trade deficits alone have resulted in the loss of hundreds and thousands of jobs.

Nor does it come as breaking news to most of us that real wages have stagnated in the past thirty-odd years, and have actually fallen in the past year. It's the same old song, since the great Depression, of the rich getting richer while the rest of us shine their shoes, but not since the 1920's has the disparity between rich and poor been this great. If things keep up at this rate, the U.S. Treasury may have to declare bankruptcy.

The growing national and consumer debt remains a non issue even as former Comptroller of the Currency, David Walker, warns that Americans also have become "addicted to debt," and the accumulating IOUs "may sink our ship."

Various forms of debt are now counted in quadrillions according to Bloomberg, which noted "the market for derivatives grew at the fastest pace in at least nine years to $516 trillion in the first half of 2007. Credit-default swaps, contracts designed to protect investors against default and used to speculate on credit quality, led the increase, expanding 49 percent to cover a notional $43 trillion of debt in the six months."

Imagine? Quadrillions! Commented Kevin DeMeritt, president of Lear Financial:

Whether you're an astronomer or an economist, that's an awfully big number. In case you need a mega-number refresher course, million is followed by billion which is followed by trillion which is followed by quadrillion (and, okay, quintillion and sextillion follow that). Yes, it takes a thousand trillion to make up one quadrillion, and, sadly, that's where we now find ourselves with the derivative situation.

Wow. So what we have here are really structural problems, not subject to clever slogans or minor adjustments. Tinkering won't help much! Whoever becomes president will inherit a crisis, not a condition. It is the whole system that's out of whack, not just a policy here or there. The debate on the economy has yet to explain this to the American people.

And they better do it quickly because some financial institutions began warning of a crash on the horizon. Said the *Banking Times*:

The Bank for International Settlements (BIS), the organization that fosters cooperation between central banks, has warned that the credit crisis could lead world economies into a crash on a scale not seen since the 1930s.

In its latest quarterly report, the body points out that the Great Depression of the 1930s was not foreseen and that commentators on the financial turmoil, instigated by the U.S sub-prime mortgage crisis, may not have grasped the level of exposure that lies at its heart.

It's time for more of us to start "grasping" the seriousness of the moment. The Royal Bank of Scotland issued a warning on June 17, said London's *Telegraph*, advising clients:

... to brace for a full-fledged crash in global stock and credit markets over the next three months as inflation paralyses the major central banks.

"A very nasty period is soon to be upon us – be prepared," said Bob Janjuah, the bank's credit strategist.

The Financial blogs like Mish's Global Economics Report were arguing that there is more to come, citing a laundry list of worries:

- Bank failures
- A monoline fallout
- $500 billion option ARM crisis coming up
- A rising unemployment rate
- An imploding commercial real estate market
- Rising junk bond defaults
- Rising numbers of foreclosures and bankruptcies
- Rising credit card defaults
- Economic picture worsening

Recently, China was condemned for "marketization without democratization." Yet, how much democratization, accountability, or even transparency is there in our private-sector dominated economic system in which most politicians have little leverage? Unelected financiers, bankers, and Wall Street firms call the shots.

In fact, when China's economic team met with their American counterparts in mid-June, they challenged the pressure they were under to deregulate their markets, pointing to how deregulation allowed the subprime crisis to unfold. As their economy grew and as ours contracted, it seemed clear that the free market fundamentalists had little to offer the Market-Leninists of Beijing.

This is not just a debate over different policies or priorities.

None of our politicians were speaking to the three million families facing foreclosure. Or to the inflation shooting ever upwards along with rising unemployment.

Finally, the legal system began speaking out. In mid-June, Federal prosecutors charged the managers of two Bear Stearns hedge funds that collapsed a year ago with securities fraud. That represented the first criminal case against executives involved with complicated mortgage securities. The *New York Times* said it raised alarms across Wall Street. On the same day, they were indicted, the FBI reported rounding up more than 400 people nationwide in mortgage related scams.

It took nearly a year, but my focus on the criminal nature of this problem — the "subcrime dimension" was being vindicated. And no one was being spared. Some judges in California began trying and jailing homeowners who walked away from their mortgages as their equity dropped beneath their obligations. Across the country, homes were loosing value as housing values dropped and foreclosures mounted.

William Tabb saw an implosion coming to the whole system of financialization and wrote about it in *Z Magazine*:

> Within a year Bear Stearns had collapsed and the Federal Reserve, which had previously declined to regulate investment banks, hedge funds, or private equity groups, needed to bail out the whole shadow banking system out or the effects could be catastrophic. The Fed's belief that one such failure could spread across the entire financial system meant that it was ready to pump money in huge amounts to prop up the system whose problem was not illiquidity, but insolvency. Investors had bought overpriced assets and, if the market was allowed to work and prices fall to realistic levels, much of the financial industry would collapse. Because they had allowed this to happen by not regulating the industry, taxpayers would be forced to save the high rollers.

> The consequences for any one sector of finance is rarely independent and protected from the consequences of trouble in other financial markets.

More banks were still writing off subprime loans and there reports in mid-June that the Lehman Brothers investment bank was about to be sold. Wall Street banks reported a 50 percent decline in profits.

Despite all of these developments, mainstream media was still trying to pump up confidence. The *Washington Post* ran a story arguing that the public is just uninformed:

So far, the economy is holding up better than it did during the last two recessions in 1990 and 2001. Employers haven't shed as many jobs, the unemployment rate is still relatively low, and gross domestic product has kept rising. Things are nowhere near as bad as they were in the Great Depression, or even during the severe recession of 1982-83. The last time consumers were this miserable, in May 1980, the jobless rate was 7.5 percent and inflation was 14.4 percent. Now those numbers are 5.5 percent and 4.2 percent respectively.

This paradox has created a unique challenge for those guiding the economy, who worry that Americans' pessimistic views will become a self-fulfilling prophecy. Two-thirds of the economy is consumer spending. So if people's negative outlook leads them to cut their spending, a steeper downturn could happen.

Of course, the meteoric rise in gas, food, and other expenses does tend to produce negativity but the "positivity" of the article glosses over growing inequality, the collapse of much of the middle class, and the weakening of unions.

Perhaps its not surprising that a newspaper that could only see good coming out of the war in Iraq would use the same rose-tinted glasses in its approach to the economy.

Their approach, also clear in other feature stories on the origins of the crisis, stretched to achieve journalistic "balance" by offering "the best possible light" and then adding a big BUT:

Seen in the best possible light, the housing bubble that began inflating in the mid-1990s was "a great national experiment," as one prominent economist put it – a way to harness the inventiveness of the capitalist system to give low-income families, minorities and immigrants a chance to own their homes. But it also is a classic story of boom, excess and bust, of homeowners, speculators and Wall Street dealmakers happy to ride the wave of easy money even though many knew a crash was inevitable.

The subtext here is that what happened was a case of unintended consequences – good intentions gone awry. This is a classic story all right, but not in the way it is intended. It is a classic case of the journalism of rationalization, a part of a perpetual search for the silver lining in every disaster. The question now, as the screw turns, as the news goes from bad to worse, as the soft-soaping and the white washing does little to change the national mood, is when will the American people realize how badly they have been had and turn on the plunderers?

FANNIE MAE: WHAT DO YOU HAVE TO SAY?

JULY 13, 2008: AT THE BOSTON GLOBE, THE CHALLENGE AFTER THE prior week's panic over the fall in the stock price of America's leading mortgage agencies, Freddie Mac and Fannie Mae, was about how to find a reassuring silver lining in a highly destructive financial storm.

"WHEN WILL IT STOP?" That was the large type headline in the Sunday Business section followed by this subhead: "The good news: Many analysts agree the current downturn will not topple into a full fledged depression, And the fed is taking unprecedented actions to prevent one." The only bad news was "there is no way to stop the shockwaves." How the goal posts have shifted! For months, as I have documented in grueling detail, mainstream outlets denied that a recession was imminent. They avoided the "D" word. Now they were talking about preventing a depression. Suddenly, comparisons with the 1930s are in vogue but always with the view of denying they exist.

The emphasis was on confidence building and reassurance. Arguably we have just heard the worst financial news in months with a major bank failing and the institutions with trillions of dollars in mortgages – the centerpiece of the housing market, threatening to collapse – even after the Treasury Secretary Henry Paulson personally advised investors that the government support companies Fannie Mae and Freddie Mac were still strong. The market heard the reassurance and rejected it with stock prices in both of these institutions dropping to new lows. Understand the scale of this problem. These two companies own or guarantee half of America's $12 TRILLION mortgage market. If the government has to pick up this debt, it will double the national debt. Investors in the companies own $5.2 TRILLION of the debt securities backed by Fannie and Freddie. No one was quite sure why their stock prices collapsed. Everyone in the financial world admitted there was a panic. One analyst called it a "blaze."(For me, use of this word conjured up memories of the fire that engulfed Wall Street in its earliest days.) Ironically while the insiders spoke of the blaze, most of the media focused on wildfires in California. They could be seen; this one could not, except to those in the know.

THE RESPONSE

On Sunday, a day before the market opens, the Fed announced that there is plenty of money available if the two mortgage backstops needed it. The Federal Reserve and the U.S. Treasury announced steps

Sunday to shore up the mortgage giants Fannie Mae and Freddie Mac, whose shares have plunged, as losses from their mortgage holdings threatened their financial survival. The Fed said it authorized its New York authority to lend to the two companies, "should such lending prove necessary." If the companies did borrow directly from the Fed, they would pay 2.25 percent – the same rate given to commercial banks and big Wall Street firms. The Treasury Department announced that the Bush administration will ask Congress for authority to prop up Fannie Mae and Freddie Mac.

Problem solved? Not so fast.

Contrast the Fed's heady intervention and the *Boston Globe*'s sunny disposition with a report from the Trends Research Institute, a small think tank, published the same day:

> The "Panic of '08" that we had predicted is "ON." Only the blind can't see it, the deaf don't hear it and those in denial won't admit it. America's economy has taken a direct hit. The nation's financial superstructure is collapsing. Those waiting for the "official word" and hesitate to take survival measures will go down with the sinking ship of state.

> The Economic 9/11 that we had warned would "topple corporate giants" and "crush the man on the street" hit on Friday. While an economic terror strike was long in the making and the devastation long predicted, the financial markets melted down and panic hit the Street on the news that the nation's two largest mortgage finance companies, Freddie Mac and Fannie Mae, were on the brink of failing.

Even as the Federal Reserve Bank rushed in for one of its now expected multi-billion dollar rescue – what many saw as a temporary fix – there was fear that we may be at some tipping point. Are we, perhaps, "tipping" beyond that point of no return?

LOSS OF FAITH IN FREE MARKET RELIGION

Also falling with the stock market and public confidence was faith in some widely held tenets of economic ideology, as E.J Dionne explained in the *Washington Post*:

> The biggest political story of 2008 is getting little coverage. It involves the collapse of assumptions that have dominated our economic debate for three decades.

> Since the Reagan years, free-market clichés have passed for

sophisticated economic analysis. But in the current crisis, these ideas are falling, one by one, as even conservatives recognize that capitalism is ailing.

"We are in a worldwide crisis now because of excessive deregulation," Rep. Barney Frank, D-Mass., the chairman of the House Financial Services Committee, said in an interview.

He notes that in 1999 when Congress replaced the New Deal-era Glass-Steagall Act with a looser set of banking rules, "we let investment banks get into a much wider range of activities without regulation." This helped create the subprime mortgage mess and the cascading calamity in banking.

As oil prices climbed and foreclosures mounted — up 56% in June — it seemed as if the whole system was unraveling. Tom Petruno of the *Los Angeles Times* cataloged the "fraying of faith":

In Wall Street's version of a bank run, investors drove shares of Fannie Mae and Freddie Mac to 17-year lows, signaling a gnawing lack of faith in the companies' ability to survive rising mortgage defaults without government help.

Later in the day, regulators took over IndyMac Bank of Pasadena, saying the $32-billion lender had collapsed under the weight of bad home loans and withdrawals by spooked depositors. It was the second-largest bank failure in U.S. history. Soon, there were depositors lined up outside the branches seeing to withdraw their money. A front page photo of this spectacle undoubtedly sent shivers into high places in Washington and Wall Street

"This is a flare-up in the financial forest fire that is far beyond anything we've seen before," said Christopher Low, chief economist at investment firm FTN Financial in New York.

And it is triggering worries that would have been unthinkable even a year ago — including that the U.S. Treasury's debt might lose its AAA credit grade because of heavy blows to the nation's fiscal health from the housing mess.

Just four months ago, many on Wall Street believed they had seen the worst of the credit crisis rooted in the housing market's woes.

For *New York Times* columnist Gretchen Morgenson who has been trying to blow the whistle on financial irresponsibility for years, these latest developments were predictable and depressing:

It's dispiriting indeed to watch the United States financial system, supposedly the envy of the world, being taken to its knees. But that's the show we're watching, brought to you by somnambulant regulators, greedy bank executives and incompetent corporate directors.

This wasn't the way the "ownership society" was supposed to work. Investors weren't supposed to watch their financial stocks plummet more than 70 percent in less than a year. And taxpayers weren't supposed to be left holding defaulted mortgages and abandoned homes while executives who presided over balance sheet implosions walked away with millions.

Over the course of this 18-month financial crisis, we have lurched from land mine to land mine.

Once again those who feared the worse were validated more than those expected the best.

DECEITFUL SOCIALISM

One irony is that to some critics, the truth was that for all the talk of a free market, institutions like Freddy and Fannie were actually examples of government control, a form of socialism or state capitalism gone wrong. That was the take of the financial writer Wilhem Butler:

> There are many forms of socialism. The version practiced in the U.S is the most deceitful one I know. An honest, courageous socialist government would say: this is a worthwhile social purpose (financing home ownership, helping my friends on Wall Street); therefore I am going to subsidize it; and here are the additional taxes (or cuts in other public spending) to finance it.

> Instead the dishonest, spineless socialist policy makers in successive Democratic and Republican administrations have systematically tried to hide both the subsidies and size and distribution of the incremental fiscal burden associated with the provision of these subsidies, behind an endless array of opaque arrangements and institutions. Off-balance-sheet vehicles and off-budget financing were the bread and butter of the U.S federal government long before they became popular in Wall Street and the City of London.

> The abuse of the Fed as a quasi-fiscal agent of the federal government in the rescue of Bear Stearns is without precedent, and quite possibly without legal justification.

This all burst in to the surface on another Black Friday, July 11, when world financial markets began quaking because of the threats to two government-linked companies with five TRILLION dollars in mortgages.

A year ago, the Dow was about to hit 14,000; this past week it dropped below 11,000. Panic, volatility, and fear can no longer be contained. On talk radio, conservative callers still mostly lambast irresponsible borrowers, but more and more recognize that this crisis is systemic and non-partisan in origins.

CARLY IS CONCERNED

Even John McCain's ex-CEO, economic advisor Carly Fiorina, who of course doesn't want to blame anyone or name anyone, says "there was a situation where there was greed on Wall Street, there was a lack of transparency around a new set of financial instruments... there were a whole new set of financial players who were less regulated than banks, and all that together created a situation, which now is rippling through the economy."

"The situation" – that's a rather vague way of putting it.

PHIL GRAMM'S COMPLICITY

As it turns out, one of McCain's closest advisors, former senator and subprime lobbyist Phil Gramm who criticized Americans for "whining" and showing signs of "mental depression," played a direct role in planting the seeds of the subprime "situation" that started the ball free-falling downhill and gathering more than mere moss. Appearing on *Democracy Now* with Amy Goodman, journalist David Corn explained that it involved

> ... a sly backroom legislative maneuver mounted by Phil Gramm, who was Republican chairman of the Senate Banking Committee in the '90s...

> It was the week that the Supreme Court was giving the election to George W. Bush. As often happens in Washington, Congress had yet to pass most of the appropriation measures that are needed to before that Congress coming to a close, and so they were lumping together, you know, six, seven different appropriation bills into one mega bill, working all hours of the day

> And in the midst of all that chaos, Senator Phil Gramm slipped into this must-pass spending bill a 268-page bill, the Commodity Futures Modernization Act...a portion of the bill deregulated these

financial instruments called "swaps...The problem is that these swaps, thanks to Phil Gramm's bill, are totally, totally unregulated, and the swap market is something like now about four times the size of Wall Street, in terms of securities that are regulated. And it really turned a lot of the economy into a secret casino, all this action going back and forth, people betting on bets.

And how this related to the subprime crisis is, about this same time, you know, securities firms started bundling all these bad or risky mortgages and securitizing them, and then they would sell these securities or buy them and then buy swaps or sell swaps to cover the possible loss. So it really enabled a lot of firms to go hog wild on the subprime stuff.

The subprime "stuff" has now led to a massive rise in foreclosures and a fall in profits as investment banks are forced to write off billions in bad investments. That, in turn, destroyed credit markets and confidence in Wall Street. Even after interest rates were cut seven times by the Fed, little improvement was registered, except the rise in joblessness and inflation.

And that is what is behind, at least in part, the current fall of mortgage giants Fannie Mae and Freddie Mac. Add in the Bush policies of lowering the value of the dollar, and you've got higher oil prices. Add in speculators and short sellers and a total lack of effective regulation, and you get the possibility of a system collapse.

The Administration that led us into war overseas by raising fear of nukes has stood by while our economic wellbeing was being nuked.

HOW LONG WILL IT LAST?

The truth is that this crisis will not be turned around anytime soon. As economist Joshua Rosner puts it: "People say we're in the final innings of the credit crisis. We're in the late innings of the first game, and this is the World Series." The hedge fund Bridgewater Associates, said the London *Telegraph*, "has issued an apocalyptic warning to clients that bank losses from the worldwide credit crisis may reach $1,600bn (£800bn), four times official estimates and enough to pose a grave risk to the financial system."

Banks are already failing. Just this past week, IndyMac Bank's assets were seized by federal regulators. The bank is considered the largest regulated thrift to fail and the second largest financial institution to close in U.S. history. This is the fifth bank to fail this year. More will follow, as Diane Francis explained in Canada's *National Post*:

> This week's Indymac [failure]... marks the opening of Part Two of the credit crunch. Smart money says many members of the U.S. financial sector will be defeated by their own foolishness and, therefore, the wise would be ill-advised to invest in banks or other financial institution stocks anywhere for a while. This is not the beginning of the end, but the end of the beginning. So stay tuned for more bank failures in the U.S., thanks to the lack of regulatory oversight, massive frauds and lack of restrictions on the cowboy mortgage market.

Reuters found an expert with some numbers: "More than 300 banks could fail in the next three years," said RBC Capital Markets analyst Gerard Cassidy, who had in February estimated no more than 150.

The *Washington Post* reported: "It appeared to mark a new phase in the U.S. financial crisis, with fears of a contagion effect that could yet weigh more heavily on the global economy. With world capital markets interconnected as never before – financial problems at U.S. banks are affecting pension funds in Japan as well as depositors in California – a mounting sense that America's financial crisis is still far from touching bottom is adding to global troubles, including rising overall inflation and soaring energy prices."

The Naked Capitalism site connects the fall in the markets to the credit crisis and puts this thought more lyrically: "What accelerates and amplifies the downwave in stock markets is the state of our brave and newly inter-connected world where all investors are effectively neurons firing in a vast collective brain. And the global investment brain has suffered a stroke, an ischemic shock triggered by a sudden catastrophic lack of confidence mixed with heady deleveraging."

Merrill Lynch warned that the United States could face a foreign "financing crisis" within months as the full consequences of the Fannie Mae and Freddie Mac mortgage debacle spread through the world. The *Chicago Tribune* reported "Prices of bank shares plunged widely and, in one case, trading of National City Corp. stock was halted temporarily on a day when fallout from the mortgage meltdown continued to infect local financial institutions."

To downplay all of this and make it less worrying, Fed Chairman Bernanke told Congress that the economy was "facing numerous difficulties." The SEC put a thirty day freeze on "naked short-selling" to stop traders from rumor mongering and undermining institutions that the government is trying to stabilize. No sooner did the government "act" than analysts said the new rules would have no effect. On the right, the government was attacked for "stealth nationalization." Other pundits said that the institutions had already been nationalized. No one pointed out that the Federal Reserve Bank is not really a government run or accountable agency. Like the federal mortgage agencies, it operates in its own netherworld. Sebastian Mallaby of the Council on Foreign Relations said it has a "murky public/private status" that he described as "odious."

President Bush reiterated his belief that the economy is sound. His comments were largely ignored as new reports surfaced of mounting inflation driven by this crisis and oil prices.

SOME CAUSES TO CONSIDER?

How did all this happen?

1. **Warnings were ignored.** One example: Bruce Marks, the CEO of NACA, the Neighborhood Assistance Corporation of America (Naca.com), which is leading the fight for affordable home ownership and opposing foreclosures, testified before Congress in 2000 warning of the consequences of Fannie And Freddy getting into subprime lending. His concerns were noted and forgotten.

In several cities, community groups protested against Fannie Mae's role in financing predatory lending. These major firms had clearly became part of the problem, not the solution. Each also had a foundation funding projects in the Congressional districts of supportive Congressman buying political influence with grants to Jesse Jackson among others. In 2004 Fannie Mae's chief executive had been forced out because of a $6.3 billion accounting scandal. Former CEO Franklin Raines blamed the Bush Administration for his problems.

There was a form of amnesia inside big banks as well in connection with the securitization of mortgages. Revealed Gillian Tett in the *Financial Times*:

A few years ago, Ron denBraber, an outspoken Dutch mathematics geek, was working in the risk department at Royal Bank of Scotland when he became alarmed about the models being used to price collateralized debt obligations.

Most notably, he concluded that the so-called Gaussian Copula approach then in use at RBS (and many other banks) significantly underplayed risks attached to the most senior pieces of debt, creating a danger of future, large losses. So he duly tried to raise the alarm. But, as he tells the tale, he faced hostility. "I started saying things gently - in banks you don't use the word 'error', but the problem is that in banks . . . people just don't want to listen to bad news," Mr. denBraber recalls.

2. The Fed under Alan Greenspan encouraged the securitization of mortgages calling it "financial innovation." Today, he rails out at the crooks and criminals who cashed in on an industry he boostered.

3. The Wall Street firms ignored worries raised by their own risk managers and ploughed resources into the slimy waters of a shadowy underground banking system. They made a fortune — until they didn't. Some were bailed out like Bear Stearns via JP Morgan; others were taken over in various ways or encouraged to merge with stronger institutions.

Earlier this year, the FBI called many of their practices criminal and have already indicted hundreds in the mortgage business with only a few symbolic busts, so far, of truly fat cats. Nevertheless, much of the subprime "dream" now stands exposed as a subcrime scheme.

New rules by the Federal Reserve Bank seem too little and too late. As CNN reported,

"Had these rules been in place, many of these things wouldn't have happened," said Ken Wade, chief executive of NeighborWorks America, a national community revitalization group chartered by Congress whose board is made up of bank regulators. The late Edward Gramlich, a former Fed governor who served as chairman of NeighborWorks' board, pushed unsuccessfully to rein in the mortgage industry.

Now the Fed wants more power and seems to want to push the SEC aside, which is the only regulatory body that did regulate in the pre-Bush era.

The *Minyanville* financial blog insists this will be a disaster:

The Federal Reserve has mismanaged America's money supply. They have sucked vast wealth away from the middle class to support rich institutions which they call "the system." Why would we give vast new powers to the berries that run the Fed when they have proven they don't know what they are doing?

As for Congress, AP reports: "Final passage of a package has been delayed for close to two months due to substantive disagreements as well as countless procedural delays.

On Thursday, Senator Dodd lamented how long it has taken to move the bill through. "Candidly, we can't wait any longer." He cited the latest foreclosure data, showing 250,000 new foreclosure filings in June, up 53% from a year earlier.

"A lot of us hoped the market would take care of all of this and there would be light at the end of the tunnel," Dodd said. "[But now] the only light at the end of the tunnel is a train coming."

That train is headed for a train wreck. The *Wall Street Journal* insists the new bill will not help most homeowners in need: "Lawmakers can say they've 'done something' about the crisis. The only problem is the bill won't work. Contractual and incentive problems in securitized mortgages will defeat the legislation's attempt to provide a significant amount of relief."

IMPACT ON FAMILIES

At the same time, the focus on the loss of property slowly began to shift to more stories about the human costs of growing homelessness. Reports OneWorld.net:

The United States' current record-breaking rates of mortgage foreclosure will directly affect 2 million children this year and next, according to a recent report from First Focus, a bipartisan child advocacy organization.

"Our homeless education liaisons are noticing increases in the number of students who are homeless, not just in high-poverty families but also those who have typically been middle class and facing this for the first time," says Patricia Popp, state coordinator for homeless education in Virginia.

Apparently the financial crisis has had another impact too; in "a twist of irony — considering money issues can often drive a wedge in a relationship — today's shaky economy is stabilizing marriages. For example, in South Florida's Miami-Dade County, where real estate values have dropped 20 percent, almost congruently, divorce filings from January to May of 2008 are down 18 percent from the same period in '07.

So we are back to minus square one. Fannie and Freddy may be too big to fail but Washington taking on their trillion dollar obligations could double our already unsustainable national debt. This disaster already impacts the global economy. The losses are at 80 percent.

WHO ARE THE REAL LOSERS

Canada's Global Research website offered an assessment not to be found in any mainstream media outlet. It reminds us of the role of debt burden as a key cause of the crisis.

> What is really taking place, however, is that the producing economy of working men and women is being crushed by the overall debt burden on households, businesses, and governments that could reach $70 trillion by 2010. The financial system, including mortgage giants Fannie Mae and Freddie Mac, is bankrupt, as the debts it is based on cannot be repaid.

> This is because the producing economy of people who work for a living simply can no longer generate enough purchasing power for people either to pay their debts or allow them to purchase what is being sold in the marketplace. In turn it is the debt burden and the loss of societal purchasing power that are crashing the stock market. Thus the collapse of the financial economy has started to destroy the producing economy as well.

> It's a "perfect storm," the result of a 200-year-old financial system where money is largely created by bank lending and where since 1980 our industry and jobs have been increasingly outsourced abroad to cheap labor markets. Thus domestic incomes have stagnated while the nation's GDP has not been able to keep up with the exponential growth of debt.

> While the mainstream media are blind, deaf, and dumb as to the causes, the victims within the middle and working classes are seeing their livelihoods ruined, jobs taken away, pensions eroded, homes foreclosed on, and are being saddled with ever-increasing debt and forced to work under more and more stress due to rising burdens of taxation, gas and food price inflation, and bureaucratic rules and regulations. The only places a more-or-less normal life may still be possible will be the wealthiest imperial centers like Washington, New York, Houston, Chicago, or San Francisco.

ROLE OF THE MEDIA

As the crisis exploded, University of Berkeley Economist Brad DeLong was asked to appear on the BBC's News Night program to explain the new "situation." DeLong prepared key points and rushed off to the studio only to find that BBC, like so many U.S media outlets that also discussed the issue, showcased it as a debate with hopes turning it into a hot button issue. When the discussion began he found himself being challenged not by an expert on the issue but a partisan political operative.

He was incensed to be up against Grover Norquist, known as the strategist of far right wing lobbyists in Washington. He wrote about this all too typical "media moment" on his blog:

"I FIND THAT I AM ON WITH GROVER-FRACKING-NORQUIST!! I FIND THAT I AM ON WITH GROVER-FRACKING-NORQUIST!!! WHO HAS THREE POINTS HE WANTS TO MAKE:

* Barack Obama wants to take your money by raising your taxes and pay it to the Communist Chinese.

* Oil prices are high today and the economy is in a near recession because of Nancy Pelosi: before Nancy Pelosi became speaker economic growth was fine – and she is responsible for high oil prices too.

* Economic growth is stalling because congress has not extended the Bush tax cuts. Congress needs to extend the Bush tax cuts, and if it does then that will fix the economy, and if it doesn't then the economy cannot recover.

I am not paid enough to deal with this lying bullshit. I am not paid enough to deal with Grover Norquist and his willful stream of defecation into the global information pool.

It is as Paul Krugman says somewhere: Grover Norquist's M.O. – George W. Bush's M.O. – the entire Republican Party's M.O. these days is (a) find a problem (i.e., financial crisis and threatening recession), (b) find something you want to do for other reasons unrelated to the problem (i.e., extend the Bush tax cuts), (c) claim without explanation that (b) will solve (a), and so (d) profit – because Peter Cardwell of BBC/Newsnight is too busy being the objective journalist referee of the yelling match to do his proper job."

DEEP CAPTURE?

Throughout this investigation, I have frequently indicted the media's failure. As I was completing the project, I was turned on to a website called www.deepcapture.com that argues that many financial journalists are in the pay of hedge funds and financial institutions.

Patrick Byrne, CEO of Overstock.com, founded Deep Capture to

168

challenge institutions he and his team claims are "captured" by the system. He praises several investigations in provocative terms arguing that there is a "circle of corruption," involving:

> Wall Street banks, shady offshore financiers, and suspiciously compliant reporters at the *Wall Street Journal, Fortune*, CNBC, and the *New York Times*. If you ever wonder how reporters react when a journalist investigates them (answer: like white-collar crooks they dodge interviews, lie, and hide behind lawyers), or if financial corruption interests you, then this is for you. It makes Grisham read like a book of bedtime stories, and exposes a scandal that may make Enron look like an afternoon tea."

This work deserves an examination.

A FED FOR HEADS

This approach is all too common At least one newspaper carried a rather unusual proposal. Peter Kennedy wrote on Oregon's SalemNews.com:

> The mortgage market has crashed; gone to pot. The *NY Times* reports Freddie Mac & Fannie Mae stocks are crashing; who knows where they will be next Monday after the Fed buys-bails them out.

> The dollar & stock market are falling; oil hit a new record high of $147 per barrel. Climate change and world food shortage and the wars continue. As a modest proposal, I suggest that Freddie Mac, Fannie Mae, the FED, McBush needs some marijuana to help them adjust their Eco-economic attitude. Perhaps a Joint Session of Congress would help.

Yes, it had come to that. At least his cynicism was laced with humor aimed at....er...transcending the "situation." And as for the week ahead, Reuters reached into children's stories to make its prognosis:

> With the Goldilocks economy long gone, investors this week will wrestle again with the three bears of financial markets – banking woes, slow-to-stagnant economic growth and rising inflation.

Right now, the bears have it.

CHAPTER 7

LAST WORDS

AFTERWORD 1: IS THIS STORY BEING TOLD?

MANY THINK SO, BUT AS READERS OF THIS BOOK HOPEFULLY HAVE LEARNED by now the story has not been told well. Many of my media colleagues don't necessarily agree, and continue with reactive reporting that avoids deeper questions and structural realities. Unfortunately the daily reports and human interest features don't connect dots that need to be connected.

That's why I was pleased when Greg Mitchell, editor of *Editor & Publisher,* the newspaper industry's trade magazine agreed to take an article from me about flawed financial reporting. Clearly, he recognized the issue was legitimate and wanted to share a critical view with his colleagues.

For five years, Greg had waged a one-man editorial crusade for better Iraq war reporting in his publication and had just published a collection of his columns in a book called *So Wrong for So Long.* Publishers had told him in 2005 that a book wasn't needed because the war would soon end and his critique would be seen as passé. His book came out on the war's fifth anniversary in which retrospectives for the most part ignored the poor performance by the press.

As the author myself of a film (*WMD: Weapons of Mass Deception*) and two books on miscoverage of the war (*Embedded*, Prometheus, and *When News Lies*, SelectBooks), I shared his frustration with an industry that is defensive about criticism and slow to review or reform coverage patterns, and he could recognize mine, including the difficulties I have had in getting my film seen – a cable TV channel turning it down on the very day that Congressman John Conyers, the chairman of the House Judiciary Committee invited me to show it to Congress – and the rejection of this manuscript by a large number of publishers.

(March 27, 2008) – "It is somewhat surprising," Larry Elliott, economics editor of London's *Guardian* observed recently, "that there is not already rioting in the streets, given the gigantic fraud perpetrated by the financial elite at the expense of ordinary Americans." If such a fraud was taking place, and if Wall Street's financial crisis, according to the usually staid *Economist*, was on the edge of "disaster" with a "financial nuclear winter" waiting in the wings, why were American news consumers among the last to know?

On the fifth anniversary of the war in Iraq, our press was papered with retrospectives that dealt with every aspect of the conflict except its own performance. At the same time, another and, arguably, more serious crisis had been underway longer and covered even more poorly.

The *New York Times* finally got around to examining war reporting as a business, not journalism, story on March 24 (below the fold), well after the unhappy anniversary. As a prime excuse for the fall-off in coverage, the story cited a study suggesting a "decline in public interest," as if that was not influenced by the lack of the issue's visibility. Other factors were the expense and danger of covering Iraq.

Those excuses cannot justify the fact that most of the reporting on Wall Street's woes started only *after* the market meltdown in August 2007, and not as this crisis built in intensity since 2001 when a housing bubble was engineered to replace the failed dot.com bubble. The financial world is not in Baghdad, not risky or expensive to cover. In fact, most media outlets have correspondents on the scene every day.

(I would add that the public has not at all been disinterested in the subject: all polls show that the economy's decline tops the list of issues that worry the public. You would think that alone would lead newspapers to do more and better reporting!)

Was the press just not paying attention as hundreds of billions of dollars were swept into exotic structure investment vehicles over years, and then sliced and diced into CDO's and so-called asset based securities? A *New York Times* columnist even admitted that experts and advocates first warned them in 2001 that predatory lending practices were devastating poor neighborhoods, but the issue was not covered in any depth for five years. This has resulted in nearly three million families facing foreclosure and the rest of us losing share and home values.

A day before its "analysis" of the fall off in war coverage, the *Times* business section devoted a staggering 2,905 words to explaining the mortgage crisis. This opus followed a similar spread in the *Washington Post* by two weeks. Both stories explained that the downfall was sparked by the use of overly complex securities designed not to be widely understood. Noted the *Times* story: "It is the private trading of complex instruments that lurk in the financial shadows that worries regulators and Wall Street and that have created stresses in the broader economy. Economic downturns and panics have occurred before, of course. Few, however, have posed such a serious threat to the entire financial system that regulators have responded as if they were confronting a potential epidemic."

Most of the coverage has been relegated to not widely read business sections that focus on the ups and downs of the markets and the way the collapse of these arrangements have affected the fortunes of CEOs and business enterprises, not citizens, consumers and most of all homeowners, many of whom are, or will be, losing their homes.

Dean Starkman, who studied the spotty "business" coverage in detail for the *Columbia Journalism Review*, concluded: "Today, as the credit crisis unravels, the business press can be fairly blamed for inattentiveness to the growing strains on middle-income borrowers. Maybe that's why so many middle-income people don't read it."

There is more to this very sad failure. Many newspapers and TV outlets were complicit. They accepted and made tons of money carrying slick and often deceptive advertising for shady mortgage lenders and credit card companies that encouraged readers and viewers to accept more debt. Some major newspaper are tied into local real estate syndicates and get kickbacks from sales tied to their extensive advertising of homes for sale.

Was there a conflict of interest perceived in taking these ads – which were important sources of revenue in a soft ad market – and producing watchdog journalism warning of the dangers of buying into subprime loans and other injurious products?

Is the press too imbued with our government's mission of inspiring consumer confidence? Is that, in turn, connected to using the news pages to benefit advertisers? Think of all those local TV reports "live at the mall" at Christmas time, cheerleading for more shopping? At the time, it appeared as if everyone was buying everything. It was only later, well after the fact, that we learned that it was the worst Christmas season in five years.

What's worse is that the coverage may have missed the truly criminal aspects of this crisis, the issue so far being raised mostly overseas. This will be fought out in courtrooms worldwide when those who purchased worthless mortgages sue the companies who sold them knowing their true value. Why are the RICO laws not being used to prosecute a scam involving so many "entangled" companies? There is no shortage of data on this fraudulent and discriminatory scheme.

Already the FBI is investigating 14 mortgage companies. Attorney General Michael Mukasey, who never figured out that waterboarding is torture, now says his department is trying to figure out whether there is a larger criminal story.

Don't hold your breath for him to figure it out. Where is our mighty media that devoted so many acres of print to investigating Eliot Spitzer's victimless hypocrisy in looking into a far deeper failure that affects all of us and the future of our society?

Will we wait for the first credit-inspired riots to recognize the size and scale of this catastrophe or only read about it in the British press?

I had no response from the influntial readers of *Editor & Publisher*.

AFTER WORD 2: CAN YOU CHALLENGE THE FINANCIAL NEWS NARRATIVE?

I WOULD LIKE TO THINK YOU CAN. THIS BOOK, AND MY DEBT FILM are attempts to do that. But without access to the airwaves, it's impossible to have much of an impact on the debate that this book calls for.

Earlier, I described an interview I gave to a CNBC reporter outside a protest at Bear Stearns. Actually, it was more like a rant, and it felt good to speak to their camera with some of the arguments I've made in this book. I told her that I believed that CNBC would never run the interview. Footage by an independent filmmaker of my being interviewed was later posted on YouTube and picked up my many Internet sites.

Several people who saw it wrote to me praising my perspective. But then, I learned that a CNBC program, *Power Lunch* actually ran an excerpt of my rap, no doubt to show how open they are. A critic of predatory lending who I admire was being interviewed on the same show. He was startled to see me and told me later that he disagreed because he felt that the channel had been covering all sides of the issue.

I later asked myself if I was wrong about CNBC – where I once worked as a freelance producer. Was I wrong to knock CNBC with my argument that in programming for an elite audience, it tilts toward the pain of CEOs more than the people who are most squeezed by economic policies? The folks there obviously feel they are objective. When they ran a snippet of my challenge, they wanted to show how critics were welcome. It is true that they have had critics of predatory lending on the air regularly.

The channel's CEO noted last December in a memo to employees that they "own" the subprime issue because of the coverage they have given it. Admittedly, I am not a regular viewer but when I worked there came away with the distinct feeling that their approach to business news precluded too much criticism of business. Bear in mind also that crises and controversies draw viewers. Viewing is said to be up 21% over last year. Perhaps I inadvertently made a small contribution to reinforcing its fearless self-image.

Fortune recently did a revealing piece for their corporate cousin CNN about their GE-NBC owned competitors: (I was certainly right to speak of their elite audience.)

> The network has a lock on the wealthiest audience in television. The typical CNBC viewer has a net worth of $2.7 million, with an average income of $156,000, according to Monroe Mendelsohn Research. Measuring only viewers watching from home, Nielsen puts the CNBC viewer's income at $73,000, compared with an average cable viewer's income of $48,000.

Their CEO is quite adept at packaging the product and holding off the new Fox Business Channel, which only tends to draw ten thousand viewers to CNBC's average of 310,000 a day.

The channel is run by broadcast veteran Mark Hoffman who, says *Fortune*,

> ... has added edge and emotion to a network that was heavily criticized in the run-up to the tech bust for its rah-rah business take on the news...

Hoffman, who came up with a four-part mantra for the channel – fast, accurate, actionable, unbiased – began his CNBC tenure wandering the newsroom floor, checking in with reporters directly. Hoffman describes CNBC's formula for 'investotainment' this way: "We're always looking for qualitative combat on the air. Most of these conversations live somewhere between fear on one end and greed on the other. One person wants to unload something, and another person wants to pick it up."

I love this language – "qualitative combat." It also pays off as *Fortune* explains: "Profits have increased 36% to \$333 million since Hoffman joined, according to media research firm SNL Kagan, making CNBC the second most profitable of NBCU's 13 cable channels, after USA Network."

CNBC is also combatitive with its own guests, reports *Fortune*:

CNBC maintains with few exceptions a policy that no interviewee can appear on another network before a CNBC appearance. And bookers are not above sending guests the occasional threatening e-mail.

It has to be noted also that CNBC profited from ads by the Wall Street players behind the very crisis it reports on and now they may have a problem: "The largest subset of CNBC's advertisers is financial services companies, many of which have been hit by the credit crunch, adds *Fortune*. A few years earlier in 2002, the *New York Times* reported on how criticism of CNBC led to change. The *Times* quoted Executive Vice President Bruno Cohen, the executive then running the show.

He and other CNBC executives said those who accuse the network of going soft on analysts and chief executives are not being fair. "Anybody who says that is not a regular viewer of CNBC," said Pamela Thomas-Graham, the CNBC president. "During the bull market, David Faber started calling analysts penguins to indicate how they were moving like a group of lemmings. It was a very skeptical view.

Ron Insana, a CNBC anchor, said critics were blaming the messenger. "We didn't invent the game," he said. "We covered it." Still, executives of CNBC said the network had altered its style of coverage for the new environment. "People are getting much more dimensional coverage than they did before from CNBC," Mr. Cohen said.

A year later, the *Columbia Journalism Review* asked a veteran financial reporter, Ray Brady, to assess CNBC's approach. He spoke of its history.

Critics claim that CNBC's on-screen personalities led the charge into the speculative stocks of the 1990s, stocks that eventually imploded. There are professional questions, as well, about the network's cheerleading coverage of Wall Streeters who were extolling stocks that those same analysts were privately calling "crap." The Merrill Lynch analyst Henry Blodget, for one example, had been a frequent guest on CNBC. His Internet stocks all came crashing down, and eventually it was learned that he'd been recommending stocks on-air that he privately called "junk." (But Blodget came full circle: Mark Haines led Squawk one recent morning with the news that Blodget had been banned for life from Wall Street.) Alan Abelson, the respected financial columnist of *Barron's*, comes down hard on the channel. "CNBC," he says bluntly, "was a product of the stock-market mania. They contributed to it, and they ate off it."

And so, in the end, it seems to be a mixed message—some strong coverage mixed in with lots of upbeat confidence building and exploitation. More radical critics rarely get on the air to offer a counter-narrative of financial developments even as some critical soundbites are welcomed to stir controversy and build ratings.

In the end, of course, I feel I was right about CNBC's mission and orientation. I had tried to interest them in running my film on debt. They don't take independent work I was told. They said it was "too heavy." I then watched what they did produce – a documentary on the business of Extreme Sports. Clearly, even though they are owned by a company first known for manufacturing light bulbs, they are not in the illumination business.

It's still more about heat than light. "Investotainment" is an insightful phrase, but, for me, CNBC is still part of the problem, not the solution.

AFTERWORD 3: FACTION VS FICTION
– MISTAKES THE MEDIA MAKE

"My plan reduces the national debt, and fast. So fast, in fact, that economists worry that we're going to run out of debt to retire."
– President George W. Bush, Radio address, Feb. 24, 2001

MARK TWAIN ONE OF AMERICA'S LEGENDARY WRITERS WAS A GREAT crusader as well as an acute observer of the American era he helped define. He once asked: "Why shouldn't truth be stranger than fiction? Fiction, after all, has to make sense." (His novella, *The Man Who Corrupted Hadleyburg*, was written while he was in Europe on the run from creditors.)

Fast forward a century or more as business and political leaders alike try to make sense of a relatively sudden and unexpected market meltdown in the summer of 2007, the escalating collapse of the housing bubble and credit markets, the write down of billions of dollars in losses by the biggest names in world banking, and the possible displacement of more than three and half million families through foreclosures.

On the "solutions" side, this volatility and free fall led to the feverish interest rare cuts by the Federal Reserve Bank and earlier billion dollar capital injections. When that all but failed, the government led by an alarmed Treasury Department orchestrated the speedy passage of an emergency $168 billion "Stimulus program" that most experts do not expect will, or can, revive a plunging economy experiencing its worst decline in 60 years. (It didn't.)

In fact, according to a personal finance blog and contrary to most news reports that had the government sending out checks, the plan is based on an advance tax refund rebate tied to 2007 tax returns. In the past "refunds like this were banked by wealthy tax owners and are expected to pay off debts by poorer people – not be spent of the most part on consumer goods which is what the plan envisions. This is another example of perceptions not matching up to reality, the way factual language gets turned into fiction, almost a fairy tale believed by most Americans.

Financial advisor Liz Pulliam Weston of MSN dispelled any thoughts that this is government help. "To produce this cash, Congress created a one-time tax credit to reduce taxable income for most taxpayers this year." Remember, this is your money you're getting back, and the rebate checks are basically an advance on your 2009 refund. When similar rebates were sent out in 2001," said tax expert Mark Luscombe, "a lot of people were upset to see their (next) refund reduced." It is expected that the next Congress will increase taxes.

Mark Twain would have seen through this sleight of hand.

Ultimately perhaps Twain's insight will lead to great novels that will capture the underlying culture that allowed so many financial manipulations and so much greed, avarice, and irrationality in this era in the way that great writers of economic upheaval in America like Upton Sinclair, John Dos Passos, or Jack London handled theirs. It seems to have always been true, as a friend who watched his multiethnic city of Sarajevo implode into a Bosnian bloody genocidal war years ago confided to me, "only fiction has to be plausible. Real life has no such constraint."

As a journalist with perhaps less fictional imagination than I need, I can only try to probe deeply into some of the forces that took our economy down in such an unexpected way at a time when our national leaders were looking elsewhere and thought they saw the only threat to our country coming from terrorists hiding in caves in far away lands.

They — and I include among them, representatives of both parties, and most of our mass media — ignored cries for help from victims of predatory lenders dating back into the 1990s, and, then, for years warnings from David Walker, the Comptroller of our Currency and head of the Government Accounting Office (GAO) that our growing debt burden could lead to a sudden collapse threatening our national security. He had been labeled "Dr. Gloom" for his sobering prognostications. In February, 2008, he stepped down from government, frustrated by his inability to promote changes.

Walker was ahead of the curve. Most journalists and pundits were way behind. It was only after the fact, in a continuing round of postmortems that business publications and economists began to try to explain the underlying problem, though still not reflect, on their failure to detect it. While most in the popular press give what amounts to a disaster a short handlabel, "the subprime crisis," turning "subprime" into the top new word of 2007, the role played by debt has yet to be given its due in all the fingerpointing and search for causation.

The National Association of Business Economists understood that and warned: "The combined threat of subprime loan defaults and excessive indebtedness has supplanted terrorism and the Middle East as the biggest short-term threat to the U.S. economy."

Despite a degree from the London School of Economics and a period spent investigating the S&L crisis years back for ABC News, I have neither the formal background or the scholarly tools to fully analyze these far more serious problems in the history of business cycles, or the legacy of economic corruption.

And yet these issues were always fascinating to me. A year before his death, I tried to make a film about the great American Keynesian economist John Kenneth Galbraith, who I met when I was a Nieman Fellow in Journalism at Harvard. I was privileged to spend time with him, and study his work, but could never convince any foundations or Public Television programs of his importance. His book on the reasons for the Depression of the 1930s made a deep impression on me. I remembered that he had written about the relationship of financial crime to Wall Street in his book *The Great Crash-1929* (1961).

His words about what happened then seem almost prophetic now: "The fact was that American enterprise in the twenties had opened its hospitable arms to an exceptional number of promoters, grafters, swindlers, imposters, and frauds. This, in the long history of such activities, was a kind of flood tide of corporate larceny."

Perhaps that's why I was not totally surprised when many of the brightest minds and slickest operators in the investment banks and hedge funds allowed themselves to invest so much in securities that would later prove to have no value and rock the global financial system with a cost of trillions with, at this writing, no end in sight?

Is this a case of the first law of karma − "what goes around comes around?" Is it the result of a virus of market fever and psychology that turned usually prudent financiers into irresponsible buccaneers who suspended all the rules of "due diligence" because of the vast amounts of money to be made?

How did the "contagion" spread so quickly without containment throughout our globalized economy, "infecting" bank after bank in country after country impacting on the state pension system in Florida as well as a small Norwegian town on the Arctic Circle?

Where were the regulators, concerned politicians or executives with fiduciary responsibilities? Why did leading ratings agencies certify worthless paper as "asset-backed?" How could this have gone on for years before this Ponzi scheme was detected and dismantled?

We are not talking about a fixed state lottery in Albania here, but a system of finance on Wall Street and virtually all the wall streets of the world.

It was not until the last week of January in 2008 that America's top law enforcement official Robert Mueller, the director of the Federal Bureau of Investigation, confirmed that part of the problem is criminal and "substantial."

The "agency" he said, is "committed to investigating and prosecuting companies involved in mortgage fraud and other violations in connection with home loans made to risky borrowers."

Mueller told the Associated Press that

... probes were being conducted across the country, including in Hawaii, where he stopped on his way back from a trip through Asia.

"There is not a state that does not have some investigation," he told reporters at the FBI office in Honolulu. "It is a substantial problem but we've been through problems like this in the past.

Fourteen unnamed companies were identified as part of what seems to be a white collar crime wave, bigger than Enron, WorldCom, or the other high-profile, corporate, criminal investigations of our time. This makes the S&L scandal pale in comparison because so many more individuals and institutions are impacted globally.

We may have to wait years for all the facts to emerge on this front, but it does seem that the announced focus of this "investigation" seems only on mortgage brokers, the players lowest down on the scandal's food chain.

UPDATE: On May 5, it was reported that a broader criminal investigation had ben launched.

Already more than two hundred of these companies have imploded or gone belly up. In some cases, records have been destroyed and mortgages sliced and diced into so many pieces that it is hard to even know who owns certain properties that have been sold or resold worldwide. They have been packaged, bundled, and turned into structured investment vehicles (SIV's) or Collateralized Debt Obligations (CDOs). Many homeowners pay bills to mortgage servicer companies, not the real owners of their homes and properties.

There is clearly a bigger web of interrelationships here, argues financial analyst Mike Whitney, who writes with outrage and puts the problem in a nutshell: "The financial system has been handed over to scam-artists and fraudsters who've created a multi-trillion dollar inverted pyramid of shaky, hyper-inflated, subprime slop that they've sold around the world with the tacit support of the ratings agencies and the U.S political establishment."

Even some of the banks that bought into these deals don't have adequate documentation especially on what were called "No doc Loans" knowingly given to people who lacked the ability to pay them back.

At the end of the fourth quarter, *Bloomberg News* "reported the world's biggest banks and brokerages have disclosed more than $120 billion of write downs and credit losses since June." The financial news agency suggests that this was "the worst quarter for banks since the Depression."

It is clear that this story is not over. Banks are more vulnerable than ever. As of late July, seven have failed and over 200, maybe more, are at risk. Many have sold off divisions, closed branches, and sought financing from sovereign wealth funds overseas. There are still more defaults to come worldwide on questionable mortgages and corporate and unsecuritized loans. Many experts agree that there will be a further slowdown in this sector with more restructurings and downsizing to come.

Most of these losses came out in dribs and drabs and many observers believe that they have yet to disclose all their losses. Central Banks have "injected" more than $900 billion in funding to stabilize the system. Add in the costs to foreclosures to lenders and falling property values to homeowners and you have a catastrophe that is then compounded by vast deficit spending on wars and debt payments.

The consequences of these policies and practices were recognized at the World Economic Forum in Davos in January 2008 where the usual upbeat forecasts were replaced by pessimism, even dread. Economist Nouriel Roubini's RGE Monitor summed it up this way:

...uncertainty about the outlook of the troubled global economy and the risks to financial markets took center stage– and the growth outlook was recently downgraded by IMF and investment banks. Fears of global recession are mounting as some of the major non-U.S. economies – notably Japan, the UK, Spain, Italy and Singapore – are facing growing economic weakness in the wake of the economic downturn and the financial crisis emanating from the U.S. Hopes for economic and financial decoupling from the U.S. have been replaced by alarm on systemic risk and financial contagion and concerns about a global economic slowdown. And while the U.S. fiscal policy machine is already moving, high level officials are already calling for global government intervention.

Fears of recession and of a serious financial systemic risk in the U.S. are exacerbated by the trouble in the monoline insurers and fact that the world's largest bond insurer – MBIA – just posted its biggest-quarterly loss ever.

Many experts fear that the worst is still to come.

In fact, banks had yet to disclose all their losses as the *International Herald Tribune* confirmed:

Kenneth Rogoff, an economics professor at Harvard University and former chief economist of the International Monetary Fund, said write-offs related to the subprime problem were just the beginning. With losses from commercial real estate defaults, unpaid credit card bills, auto loans, corporate debt and other items added in, the grand total might exceed $1 trillion.

"We haven't by any means seen everything," Rogoff said. "If it were just the subprime debt, it wouldn't be so bad. We're just entering the recession, so the defaults are just beginning." Rogoff recently co-wrote a paper comparing the current banking troubles to five of the biggest financial crises of the 20th century, including Japan's "lost decade," which began in 1992. He found that the current U.S. housing-fed crisis was following a strikingly similar pattern.

He was not alone. Even his figure is low, according to Andrew Abraham, who reported on a study released by the Bank of America. Its findings are truly stunning but not widely reported, except by AFP:

"Bank of America delivered a report highlighting the current losses of the "Credit Crisis". According to the report the meltdown in the U.S subprime real estate market has led to a global loss of $7.7 trillion dollars in stock market value since October. The crisis, which has spread beyond U.S shores to banks and other sectors worldwide, is "one of the most vicious in financial history," according to Bank of America chief market strategist Joseph Quinlan. In his report, Quiglan states that the losses are worse than any in the past few decades, including Wall Street's Black Monday of 1987, the 1999 Brazilian real currency crisis and the collapse of hedge fund Long Term Capital Management (LTCM) in 1998. Quinlan quantifies the current credit crisis by determining the world market capitalization is currently down 14.7 percent three months after a peak in late October. He has compared this with similar loss three months later of 13.2 per cent after the LTCM crisis, 9.8 per cent for Black Monday and 6.1 per cent for the Brazil crisis. The losses were greater than those suffered after the September 11, 2001, terror attacks, the Asian financial crisis starting in 1997, Argentina's default on its debt in 2001, and the 1994 Mexican peso crisis.

How do you insulate the global economy from a crisis of this magnitude? Unfortunately, this question was not even being raised at the time this was written, perhaps because some business journalists believe its best to ignore bad news.

The problems that the banks face pale in significance to what the American people are confronting. Despite this crisis, consumers are loading themselves up with more and more debt. Consumer debt nearly doubled between 1996 and 2006. As debt climbs, so do defaults. Well after this trend was advanced, the *Washington Post* explained:

> Behind the rising defaults is a tale of two Americas. Those with good credit will almost certainly see lower rates on cars and credit cards as the Fed continues to cut rates this year. But those with bad credit are facing rising rates and being forced to put more money down on cars. Some may not be able to get a credit card or auto loan as banks, spooked by the mortgage mess, have been reassessing the risk of making loans.

> "It's going to be much more difficult for those people who are already in credit distress than it is for those of us who are fortunate and have full-time jobs," said Tony Cherin, a finance professor at San Diego State University.

The *Post*, like all media outlets continue to carry deceptive ads for lenders.

HOW DO YOU DEFINE A RECESSION?

News about the economy is increasingly filled with references to a possible recession. We keep reading about government measures to "stave" it off. While the term is bandied about constantly, few media outlets explain what a recession actually is, or that there is a debate in economic circles about when is near or here.

A report in the *Oakland Tribune* taught me to be suspicious whenever I read about a recession. While this debate continues, it's "reader beware" – and take care to try to understand that economic terms can mean different things to different people. As I write the U.S. government denies we are in a recession while economists at top investment banks confirm that we are.

> The truth is, nobody knows. The responsibility for declaring the stages of the business cycle is informally held by that most dreaded of concepts – a committee of economists. The Business Cycle Dating Committee of the National Bureau of Economic Research uses several economic indicators, including personal income, unemployment, industrial production and sales and manufacturing volume, to determine the health of the economy. It's not true that they declare a recession if economic growth is

negative for two quarters in a row. If it were that simple, we wouldn't need a committee.

If you want to know about the state of the economy in real time, you can't rely on the NBER.

If the NBER did the D.C. weather forecast, here's how it would work. The bureau would gather precipitation data from every neighborhood, then interview residents to make sure the data are accurate. After much deliberation, it would tell us whether it had rained last month.

Same with recessions: The NBER's pronouncements historically come long after recessions have begun, a whopping seven months on average. By the time the bureau announced the recession of 1991, it already had ended.

WHAT'S NEXT?

So what started as get rich quick schemes in many of American's most depressed neighborhoods has led to depressing scenarios that many fear could have even graver consequences. Already Financier George Soros is speaking about the certainty of a global recession "or worse." Clearly this is a systemic crisis, and not easily isolatable. "All crises in the past entailed some form of easy credit, financial innovation, contagion. Credit standards, lending monitoring incentives, and policy response are key," he noted.

Writers are even invoking the worries of top conservative economists like Ludwig von Misses, who said: "There is no means of avoiding the final collapse of a boom brought on by credit expansion. The question is only whether the crisis should come sooner as a result of a voluntary abandonment of further credit expansion, or later as a final and total catastrophe of the currency system involved."

"TOTAL CATASTROPHE?"

It is important to understand these scary relationships even if you are not a doom and gloomer or conspiracy theorist, which I am not. Within two months, the fact that there was a recession was widely accepted. Others began speaking openly of what was next – a depression. London's *Independent* reported this under the headline: "The 2008 Depression":

We knew things were bad on Wall Street, but on Main Street it may be worse. Startling official statistics show that as a new economic recession stalks the United States, a record number of Americans will shortly be depending on food stamps just to feed themselves and their families.

Somehow, the foreign press was far more alarmed than many U.S media outlets. Another *Independent* story spoke of "the end of capitalism as we know it:"

The Western world is in an economic crisis similar in scale to the oil shock of 1973. What we are seeing is nothing less than the unravelling of neo-liberalism − the dominant economic and ideological model of the last 30 years.

My own investigation is still in progress but takes a broader view tracking the rise of a credit and debt complex bigger than the better known military-industrial complex as part of the financialization of American society. It looks at how deregulation is tied to free market ideology and how self-interested players often conspired to get around what laws there are.

I have been investigating this issue since 2005 when I began to produce and direct a feature documentary called *In Debt We Trust*. Since its release, I have been writing about the issues in daily blogs, and in articles published on a wide range of websites.

While I am not a full-time financial journalist, I know that most missed the story for a variety of reasons. I have known quite a few business writers well and was told early on about herding instincts on Wall Street, where rumors of quick hits or losses move markets into panicky transactions. Perhaps that's why there is so much volatility that is later glossed over with vague references to market psychology. Reactions to unexpected news, prejudices, and perceptions often shape decisions as much or more than thoughtful analysis.

When John Gittelsohn, a journalist at the *Orange County Register,* wrote what I thought was an exemplary story about how local lenders and Wall Street firms got together, detailing the operations of 43 companies that later laid off 7,200 workers, I wrote to him to ask why more stories like his don't appear.

He wrote back explaining the difficulties of covering such a complex story and making it interesting to readers. He added these points:

• Hard to find the bad guys. We wrote lots of stories over the past 10 or so years about individual companies facing lawsuits, SEC and FTC investigations. Our archives had lots of stuff about the

Jedinaks and Chisick at Guardian and First Alliance. The *LA Times* did a great series in 2005 about Ameriquest's predatory lending. But these seemed like isolated cases more than a regulatory or industry-wide problem. There were two sides to the equation: the lenders and the borrowers. Telling the story of the borrowers was even tougher, because the people often seemed either stupid or greedy. In the most sympathetic cases, debt was a story about health care costs.

• Media's lack of resources and depth. I covered politics before I joined our paper's business desk in late 2005 and didn't get put onto the subprime story until spring 2007. The piece you saw was a sort of year-end look back. We wrote dozens of stories about the collapse unfolding in our front yard. We poured a lot of resources onto the story after it exploded, but we did a bad job of predicting it. Anyone with a sense of history knows real estate is cyclical. Unfortunately, not many journalists have a sense of history.

• Other news stories had more interest: Iraq, dot-com bust, media consolidation, stock backdating, Britney & Paris.

• Few newspapers – or other media – are eager to do investigations of businesses, because they can threaten you with lawsuits – however meritless. It's easier to go after government malfeasance. Business sections have a tendency to be very rah-rah chamber of commerce. I think the threat of a lawsuit is a lot more persuasive than someone threatening to pull an ad.

According to this senior journalist, these are the institutional factors, financial pressures, and threats leading to a lack of crusading journalism. But there are also frequent sloppiness and inaccuracies.

A blog on what's called "behavioral finance" reports:

The Wall Street Journal surveyed top economists semi-annually, to get forecasts on what bonds were going to do over the next 6 months. The data go back to 1982.

The experts (intelligent people all, to be sure), were wrong in the predictions of the direction bond yields 66% of the time. That is to say, when asked 6 months from now will the yield on a 10 Year Treasury be A) Higher or B) Lower... they got it right 1 out of 3 times.

Do you realize how bad that is? The unfortunate truth is that employing a black-tailed marmoset to throw darts at a board marked "higher" and "lower" would be a better predictor! The fact is, human beings are notoriously lousy predictors of future market events. A study by George Wolford and associates at Dartmouth College found that even rats and pigeons out-perform humans in short-term market prediction. (No word on marmosets).

Bubbles are rarely foreseen, as investors scramble into opportunities delivering high returns. The housing sector has always been a centerpiece of economic activity. The question now: Is its collapse a harbinger of worst to come? True or not, self-interest and money-making are the real drivers in the world of finance and the world most people try to survive in. Finance is also the real driver in the world of politics.

It's hard to believe that as the house of cards comes tumbling down, there seems to be a trifecta of failure. The government is unwilling to act decisively. The Congress prevaricates. And the media, with its tilt towards upbeat "free market" boosterism, has mainly kept this terrible tale of woe and threat to our futures hidden from the public at the very time when exposure might have stopped these practices before they became too deep and/or expensive to "fix."

In early April, the *New York Times* carried a poll reporting that an unprecedented 81% of the American people felt the country was moving in the wrong direction. The first reader to comment on the report wrote: "81% may think the nation is going in the wrong direction, but if you care about the future of America and its citizenry, 100% of us are screwed."

What he didn't know is that our media joined our regulators and government in contributing to the screwing of the American people.

Now you know.

A POETIC LAMENT: BUSINESS NEWS

I was in the market for a new market
And found one

Only the aisles
Were called Tranches
and there were no
Breakfast foods with Special K
only credit derivatives
with fewer calories of culpability

There was a sale on Cubed CDO's
in the financial instrument section
where the meats used to be
And where I waited for an in-store speculator to slice
an asset bubble of exotic SIVs (structured investment vehicles)
How Tasty – AAA+ they were, along with
A Steaming Equity sandwich
Which you could value and price
Which is always so nice

Oh yum, and then I was advised to avoid the
pool of risky loans of RMBS's (Residential
Mortgage Backed Securities) in the back
And instead taste a subprime treat
In front of the Regulatory Oversight counter
Right next to the list of fat tail events where
The bonds and the funds and the deviation events
Avoided defaults and delinquencies
And made us all rich on other people's money.

May we bless The Big Ben at the Fed?
And praise the Gods of CNBC
For Jim Cramer's mad and mighty mouth
And then cut the discount rate together before we
Charge it or swipe it at the register with
our collateralized debt obligations

So we can securitize our way home
Before we find it gone
Cause the foreclosure boys got there
Before we could
Contain the
Contagion

Don't panic or get manic
The Economy is Strong
Our President says
And Says Again and Again
Until he believes It

And remember:
Leverage is everything

Danny Schechter
December 2007

ADDENDUM: RESOURCES ON THE ISSUES

1. LEARN MORE

Hopefully, readers will seek out other information on this crisis. I have found several websites helpful for tracking the stories that don't make it into the mainstream media:

1. Monitoring the mortgage business – www.Ml-Implode.com. See all the blogs listed on the site

2. Contrarian Economic Analysis – www.itulip.com, www.UN-debt.net

3. Credit and Debt Squeeze Blog – www.stopthesweeze.org

4. Daily News Stories – www.carolynbaker.net

2. INFORM YOUR CAMPUS OR COMMUNITY

HOST A SCREENING of *In Debt We Trust* and hold a discussion before or after the screening to raise awareness

CONTACT YOUR REPRESENTATIVE by visiting The Debt Hits Hard website and the Campaign for College Affordability website.

CONTACT THE MEDIA and demand a better coverage of the Debt Crisis. Tell them about your situation and experience, tell them about *In Debt We Trust* and ask them to improve coverage of the debt issue in the U.S and write about the issues raised in this book with more depth and dimension.

3. TELL YOUR FRIENDS AND YOUR EMAIL LISTS ABOUT THIS INITIATIVE – HELP US BRING THIS CAMPAIGN TO OTHERS.

4. NEED A FAIRLY PRICED MORTGAGE – VISIT NACA.COM

5. CONTRIBUTE TO THE CAUSE.

Send your tax-deductible contribution to support not for profit educational work on this issue.

Americans for Debt Relief Now, The Global Center 575 8th Avenue, New York, New York 10018

(Checks can be made to the Global Center. Mark for "Debt Relief Outreach.")

Subscribe to the *Stop The Squeeze Newsletter* at www.InDebtWeTrust.org for regular updates on credit and debt issue.

Visit www.CreditCardNation.com for a wealth of resources on credit card issues

6. FIGHTING FOR RESPONSIBLE LENDING PRACTICES

AFFI (Affil.org) is a coalition of organizations pressing for responsible lending practices. More media attention has been focused on abuses than what can be done about them. Here are their ideas. Others can be found on Robert Manning's excellent *Credit Card Nation* website.

PRINCIPLES OF FAIRNESS IN LENDING

Our goal is simple – to establish fair credit policies and practices.

Lending is necessary in our society and can be helpful in building and preserving community and individual assets. Our laws, however, allow lenders to encourage and profit enormously from personal debt. Discrimination and the selling of unaffordable and abusive loans is rampant. Practices that used to be called 'loan-sharking' are now legal. Borrower protections cannot be left to the lenders. We propose these six components of fair lending against which all credit practices and products must be tested – across the life of the loan and its collection.

AFFIL'S SIX PRINCIPLES OF FAIRNESS IN LENDING

RESPONSIBILITY: Lenders must gauge ability to repay and offer borrowers the most affordable and well-suited products for which they qualify. Lenders should demonstrate commitment to the building of personal assets.

JUSTICE: All participants in the making, collecting, holding and buying of debt have a duty to deal fairly with the borrower. It is unjust to prey upon anyone, particularly on those who are vulnerable due to age, health, language, education or other socioeconomic circumstances. It is unjust to charge exorbitant interest rates and fees, to change terms once agreed, and to deny anyone their day in court.

EQUALITY: We all must have equal access to appropriate and fair products and services regardless of race, gender, language, national origin, physical/mental well being, education, lifestyle or socioeconomic status. All discriminatory lending practices must be abolished.

INFORMATION: We require full disclosure of all costs, fees, loan terms, penalties and collection practices in language that is clearly understood by the borrower. Although information is a necessary component to a fair marketplace, it is not a substitute for fair terms, fair treatment and effective regulation.

ACCOUNTABILITY: Lenders must track and report their lending activity. Only with comprehensive reporting can we ensure that the marketplace is free from illegal and unethical practices and that consumers are safe to shop for credit products without risk of being overcharged or directed to inappropriate loans.

THE AUTHOR

Danny Schechter: News Dissector/
Investigative Journalist/Producer/Director

DANNY SCHECHTER IS A TELEVISION PRODUCER AND INDEPENDENT filmmaker who writes and speaks about media issues. He is the executive editor and blogger-in-chief of Mediachannel.org, the world's largest online media issues network.

Schechter is co-founder and executive producer of Globalvision, a New York-based television and film production company now in its 20th year, where he co-produced 156 editions of the award-winning series "South Africa Now" and "Rights & Wrongs: Human Rights Television." In 1998, a human rights special, "Globalization and Human Rights" was co-produced with Rory O'Connor and shown nationally on PBS.

A Cornell University graduate, he received his Master's degree from The London School of Economics, and an honorary doctorate from Fitchburg College. He was a Nieman Fellow in Journalism at Harvard, where he also taught in 1969. After college, he was a full-time civil rights worker and then communications director of the Northern Student Movement; he worked as a community organizer in a Saul Alinsky-style War on Poverty program, and, moving from the streets to the suites, served as an assistant to the mayor of Detroit in 1966 on a Ford Foundation grant.

He has won two National News Emmy awards for his TV work with ABC News "20/20" (and two nominations); two regional Emmys, a National Headliner award, and the Society for Professional Journalists award for an investigative documentary. Amnesty International honored him for his human rights television work. In 2005 he received the George Orwell Award.

Schechter's professional journalism career began in 1970, when he was named news director, principal newscaster, and "News Dissector" at WBCN-FM in Boston, where he was hailed as a radio innovator and won many industry honors, including two Major Armstrong Awards. His television producing career was launched with the syndicated "Joe Oteri Show," which won the New England Emmy and a NATPE IRIS award in 1979. In 1980, he created and produced the nation's first live late-night entertainment-oriented TV show, "Five All Night, Live All Night" at WCVB in Boston.

Schechter left Boston to join the staff at CNN as a producer based in Atlanta. He then moved to ABC as a producer for "20/20," where during his eight years he won two National News Emmys. Schechter has reported from 51 countries and lectured at many schools and universities. He was an adjunct professor at the Graduate School of Journalism at Columbia University. Schechter's writing has appeared in leading newspapers and magazines including the *The Nation*, *Newsday*, *Boston Globe*, *Columbia Journalism Review*, *Media Studies Journal*, *Detroit Free Press*, *Village Voice*, *Tikkun*, *Z*, and many other newspapers, magazines and websites.

OTHER WORKS BY THE AUTHOR

BOOKS

Squeezed: America As The Bubble Bursts (ColdType, 2007)

When News Lies: Media Complicity and the Iraq War (SelectBooks, 2006)

The Death of Media (and The Fight for Democracy) (Melville House, 2005)

Embedded: Weapons of Mass Deception: How the Media Failed to Cover the War on Iraq (Prometheus Books, 2003; ColdType.net – ebook version, August 2003)

Media Wars: News at a Time of Terror (Roman & Littlefield, 2003)

News Dissector: Passions, Pieces and Polemics (Akashic Books, 2001; ebook version – electronpress.com, 2001)

Hail to the Thief: How the Media "Stole" the 2000 Election, Ed. with Roland Schatz. (Inovatio Books, Bonn, Germany, 2000; electronpress.com – ebook edition, 2000)

Falun Gong's Challenge to China (Akashic Books, 1999, 2000)

The More You Watch, the Less You Know (Seven Stories Press, 1997, revised 1999)

FILMS AND TV DOCUMENTARIES

Viva Madiba: A Hero For All Seasons (Nelson Mandela at 90) (2008, Videovision) Contributing Director

Recount Democracy (2008, Pathfinder Films)

Boob Tube (2008, Pathfinder Films)

A Work In Progress: Putting the Me Back in Media (2007)

The Journalist and The Jihadi: The Murder of Daniel Pearl (2007, HBO) Consulting Producer

In Debt We Trust (2006)

Weapons of Mass Deception (2004)

We are Family (2002)

Counting On Democracy (2002)

Falun Gong's Challenge to China (2000)

Nkosi: Saving Africa's AIDS Orphans (2000)

A Hero for All: Nelson Mandela's Farewell (1999)

Globalization and Human Rights (1997, PBS) co-director

Sowing Seeds/Reaping Peace: The World of Seeds of Peace (1996)

Prisoners of Hope: Robben Island Reunion (1995, co-directed by Barbara Kopple)

Countdown to Freedom: Ten Days that Changed South Africa (1994), narrated by James Earl Jones and Alfre Woodard

Sarajevo Ground Zero (1993)

The Living Canvas (1992), narrated by Billy Dee Williams

Beyond JFK: The Question of Conspiracy (1992, co-directed with Barbara Kopple)

Give Peace a Chance (1991)

Mandela in America (1990)

Mandela: Free At Last 1990

The Making of Sun City (1987)

Student Power (1968)

TV SERIES

South Africa Now (Executive Producer) 1988–91

Rights & Wrongs (co-produced with Rory O'Connor; anchored by Charlayne Hunter-Gault) 1993–1997

TV PROGRAMS

The Tina Brown Show, Editorial Producer (CNBC), 2002

The Last Word, Broadcast Producer (ABC) 1986

20/20, Producer (ABC News) 1981–1988

Sandi Freeman Show, Producer (CNN) 1980

Five All Night, Live All Night, Producer (WVCB-Boston) 1980

The Joe Oteri Show, Producer (WLVI, Boston) 1979

The Ten O'Clock News, Reporter (WGBH, Boston) 1978

For continuing coverage and updating on the issues discussed in this book, visit Danny Schechter's News Dissector blog on Mediachannel.org (http://www.newsdissector.org/blog)

For more on Danny Schechter's work, see
www.newsdissector.org/dissectorville

Plunder book Website: http://www.newsdissector.com/Plunder

This book has been produced in collaboration with Tony Sutton, editor of ColdType.net

Download the *ColdType Reader* emag free each month from
http://www.coldtype.net

Feedback welcome: dissector@mediachannel.org

A CRISIS OF BIBLICAL PROPORTIONS

"I'm not talking New Testament biblical, I'm talking Old Testament hellfire and brimstone. This is the worst credit crisis we've ever seen."

– Mitch Stapley, Fifth Third Bank Executive,
May 16, 2008

Printed in the United States
205598BV00001B/472-531/P

9 781605 203157